*f*P

Also by Allen St. John

THE MAD DOG 100
The Greatest Sports Arguments of All Time
(by Christopher Russo with Allen St. John)

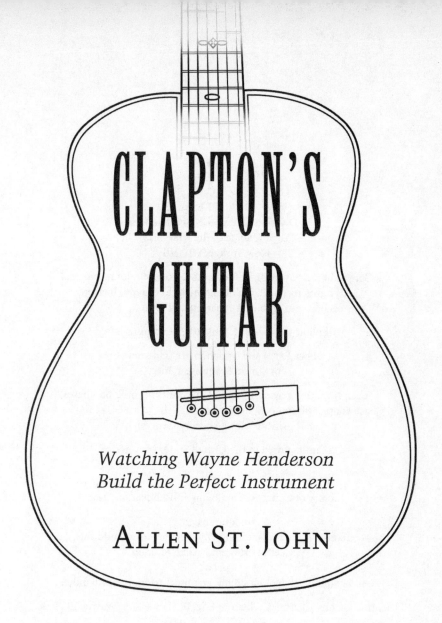

CLAPTON'S GUITAR

*Watching Wayne Henderson
Build the Perfect Instrument*

ALLEN ST. JOHN

FREE PRESS

NEW YORK   LONDON   TORONTO   SYDNEY

FREE PRESS
A Division of Simon & Schuster, Inc.
1230 Avenue of the Americas
New York, NY 10020

FREE PRESS and colophon are trademarks
of Simon & Schuster, Inc.

For information regarding special discounts for bulk purchases,
please contact Simon & Schuster Special Sales at 1-800-456-6798 or
business@simonandschuster.com

Manufactured in the United States of America

1   3   5   7   9   10   8   6   4   2

Library of Congress Cataloging-in-Publication Data

St. John, Allen.
Clapton's guitar : watching Wayne Henderson build the
perfect instrument / Allen St. John.
p. cm.
Discography: p.   Includes bibliographical references and index.

1. Guitar—Construction I. Clapton, Eric. II. Henderson, Wayne. III. Title.
ML1015.G9S69 2005
787.87'192'3—dc22   200505729

ISBN-13: 978-0-7432-6635-2
ISBN-10:   0-7432-6635-8

To Sally, Ethan, and Emma, the music in my life.

CONTENTS

The guitar is a wonderful instrument which is understood by few.

—FRANZ SCHUBERT

That little round hole and that bit of wood, that's the truth.

—KEITH RICHARDS

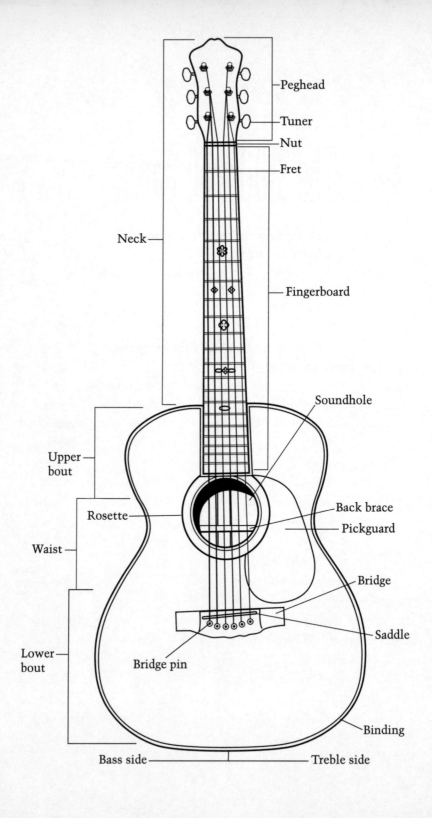

Peghead

Tuner

Nut

Fret

Neck

Fingerboard

Soundhole

Upper bout

Rosette

Back brace

Pickguard

Waist

Bridge

Lower bout

Bridge pin

Saddle

Binding

Bass side

Treble side

CHAPTER ONE

The $100,000 Guitar

I THINK IT'S *GREAT*," said Eric Clapton as he looked first at
his host, and then at the magical instrument on his lap.
"Especially on the top strings. It's easy to bend. It's got a good
ringing quality."

And so begins the legend of Clapton's guitar. The scene was a
recording studio in New York City in 1994. Tim Duffy, a recording engineer by trade, was showing Clapton his facility, hoping
he'd sign on to cut an album there. And while the legendary performer was suitably impressed by the audiophile-quality recording gear, what captured his imagination was Duffy's own
acoustic guitar.

"It's flat," Clapton continued. "It's incredibly flat."

"The tone?" Duffy asked, somewhat puzzled.

"The fingerboard," Clapton replied. "Or is that in my imagination?"

Clapton noodled a bit, playing some of the sweet and soulful
blues riffs that had earned him Grammys, gold records, and even
gold-plated guitars.

"It's lovely," he said. "I've never heard anything about this
guy before."

The guy was Wayne Henderson, and it's no surprise that
even Eric Clapton, one of the world's certifiable guitar freaks,
didn't know anything about him. Henderson lives in rural

Rugby, Virginia, population 7, where until recently he split his time between building extraordinary guitars and delivering the mail to his neighbors. He has built maybe three hundred guitars over the last thirty-five years, as many as the popular C.F. Martin factory in Nazareth, Pennsylvania, can finish in a busy afternoon. But in just a few short moments with this guitar, Clapton had discovered one thing. Wayne C. Henderson might just be the greatest guitar builder who ever lived. A Stradivari in glue-stained blue jeans.

"You want one?" said Duffy, sealing one deal, perhaps in the service of sealing another.

"Yeah I'd *love* to get one."

"What size?"

"The same as this."

That's the first story about that guitar. Here's the next one.

A few weeks later, a man entered Duffy's studio and approached our engineer.

"I want to buy your guitar," he said.

"Well, it's not for sale."

"This is the guitar that Eric Clapton really liked, right? Well my daughter is a big Eric Clapton fan, and I want to buy it for her."

"It's not for sale."

"Yes, it is."

Duffy explained how special this guitar is, and how long he waited for it. He'd taken it to Africa when he was eighteen.

"I've been on camels with it. I've been on dhow boats with it. I've dated girls with it," he said. "I've been everywhere with this guitar."

The man listened patiently, and when the ranting subsided, he extracted a checkbook from his pocket and scribbled. "Is this enough?"

Duffy squinted. The check was made out in the amount of $100,000.

"Is this some kind of a joke?"

"Would you prefer cash? I'll go to the bank if you want."

The money wouldn't go to buy the engineer a Mercedes. Duffy, you see, wears another hat as well. He is the head of the Music Maker Relief Foundation, an organization that's devoted to providing the basics for indigent blues musicians. When he went out to do field recordings of great players like Guitar Gabriel and Etta Baker, he was shocked to see the choices forced upon them by their financial situation: food or diabetes medicine; rent or a winter coat; eyeglasses or bus fare to the optometrist. So he started the Music Maker Foundation as a way to give a little something back to these remarkable, but unknown, musicians. A six-figure check would buy a lot of groceries. That's what Duffy was thinking.

What he said was, "Let me think about it." Wayne Henderson guitars are one to a customer. If he builds you one, you can pretty much forget about getting a second. So the engineer called Wayne himself and told him the story.

"That could solve a lot of problems for me," Duffy said sheepishly.

"It's your guitar," replied the ever-practical Henderson with a laugh. "If you want to throw it out the window it's okay by me."

So stashed in a dusty cubbyhole in Wayne Henderson's workshop is a Xerox copy of the $100,000 check Duffy got in payment for one of Henderson's guitars..

"I still miss that guitar every day," said Duffy ten years later. "I wish I still had it."

IN ADDITION TO MAKING superb instruments, Wayne Henderson is a gifted guitar player, or as he refers to himself, "a pretty good picker."

The first time I met Wayne Henderson, in the winter of 2001, he was holding court in his own modest way in the Haft Auditorium at New York's Fashion Institute of Technology, greeting friends who had come to marvel at his playing and to remind him gently about the guitar that he had promised to build them. Henderson, fifty seven when I met him, is a bantamweight with a full salt-and-pepper beard, a reddish complexion, a slightly wary smile, and an omnipresent baseball cap. He is also that rarest of commodities, a man who is a virtuoso in two separate yet related fields: Paganini and Guarneri rolled into one.

As he demonstrated onstage an hour earlier, Wayne Henderson is a guitar player's guitar player. He doesn't have the name recognition of, say, the bluegrass legend Doc Watson. But when it comes to the sheer ability to send a torrent of notes tumbling from the soundhole of an acoustic guitar, and yet make it seem like no big deal, Henderson has few peers. But on this night, he was the token guitar player, playing boom-chuck backup behind a collection of fiddle players from all over America. This is roughly the equivalent of having Curt Schilling pitch batting practice. Despite his limited role, which he happily accepted, a good chunk of the audience showed up just to see him play a tune or two. He didn't disappoint. To open the show, Henderson started with a few jokes about his hometown—"it's so small we have to take turns being the mayor, the preacher, and the town drunk"—and a slightly off-color story about the old lady and the elephant:

"With only seven people not too much happens in Rugby, but one time a circus was coming through town on their way to the big city . . . Mouth of Wilson. But they got to going a little too fast around one of the turns on the mountain road and they broke a wheel off one of those big old circus wagons. It turned over on the side of the bank, and spilled out all kinds of circus animals. We had lions, tigers, giraffes, zebras, things like that running around. And that stirred up an awful lot of excitement because we were used to rabbits and squirrels and possum. Old Farmer Jones who lives down the holler was pretty disappointed. He had found the hippopotamus and put it in his hog lot. He thought he was going to have bacon for the next ten years.

"But the strangest thing was that they lost the elephant.

They could not find a thing as big as an elephant. They searched high and low. And someone gave word to the sheriff's department that they had seen it near this old lady's farm. And since she didn't have a phone, the sheriff himself went out there to check on it and asked her if she had seen the elephant.

"Turns out that she didn't know what one was. She didn't have a television and she had never even seen a picture of an elephant in a book. So he tried to describe what it was and asked her if she had seen it.

" 'Why, yes, I did,' she told the sheriff. 'Just this morning, there was a big old animal like that around here. And you know what? That thing was in my garden pulling up every one of my cabbages with its tail.'

"The sheriff scratched his head and asks, 'Pulling up cabbages with its tail? What in the world was he doing with them?'

"And the old lady said, 'You wouldn't believe it if I told you.' "

The New York audience roared. Wayne delivered the punch line with the same kind of knowing these-are-my-people wink you get from Woody Allen or Richard Pryor, and that's what made this joke worthy of Letterman instead of *Hee Haw*.

When the audience settled back down, Henderson demonstrated timing of a different sort. He picked up his guitar and ripped through "Lime Rock," a fiddle tune so intricate and complex that Yo-Yo Ma, who recorded it on the cello with Edgar Meyer and Mark O'Connor, has marveled at its difficulty. But Henderson sashayed through this fingerbuster with a casual flair that left both his fans and his fellow musicians slack-jawed.

The only question among musicians is whether Henderson builds guitars better than he plays them. Each Henderson guitar has been built by hand, one at a time, made to order, from start to finish by the man himself. When you order a Henderson guitar, you can be sure that it's been built by Wayne Columbus Henderson. He charges an almost ridiculously modest $1,500 for one of his guitars—other builders charge ten times as much—or he might barter for something like a new interior for his 1957 Thunderbird.

Wayne uses exotic materials on some of his guitars, all-but-extinct Brazilian rosewood for the sides, indigenous Appalachian red spruce for the tops, piano-black ebony for the bridge and the fingerboard, and abalone and mother-of-pearl for the jeweled inlays around the edges.

But the magic in these guitars comes not from the ingredients, but from the chef. Wayne's personal guitar is built from plain, unfigured mahogany, and to the untrained eye, this battered instrument looks like something that would command $25 at a garage sale.

Pick it up, or better yet hear Wayne play it, and you will appreciate the difference. Every note seems to explode out of the soundhole, with a volume that's almost shocking, yet each note is still sweet and smooth. In guitar parlance, it's a cannon.

What makes his guitars so good? Perhaps it's that other builders must rely on the feedback of other players to fine-tune their instruments, but Wayne can put a guitar through its paces as well as anyone on earth. He is his own test pilot. Or maybe some people simply have the gift of being able to make a piece of wood sing, and Wayne Henderson is one of them.

How do you make a guitar? "Well you just get a pile of really nice wood and a sharp whittling knife," I heard Wayne tell one of the fiddlers backstage. "Then you just carve away everything that isn't a guitar." Revealing his Appalachian roots, he emphasizes the first syllable of *guitar*, so that it rhymes with *sitar*. It sounded, at first, like more of Henderson's typical self-effacement. Then I talked to John Greven, himself a legendary luthier who has built guitars for George Harrison and Mary Chapin Carpenter and who had worked with Henderson in the repair department of world-famous Gruhn Guitars in Nashville. "Wayne is the only guy I ever saw who could build a guitar with a penknife," Greven said with a laugh. "He had this little four-inch knife and he'd carve braces and linings, whatever. We said,

'Wayne, we've got all these tools over here, use whatever you want', and he said, 'Shucks, I don't know how to use all that stuff,' and he just went back to using the penknife."

In January of 2001, a few weeks before Wayne's New York gig, I decided to commemorate my fortieth birthday with a Wayne Henderson guitar. A couple of years earlier, I had seen a feature story about Wayne in *Acoustic Guitar* magazine. That story mentioned in passing that Henderson had built guitars for several famous players, and that Eric Clapton was on Wayne's waiting list, but that didn't sway me. What got my attention were the curvaceous lines of his signature peghead. If form followed function—and it usually does in the guitar world—this would indeed be a special instrument. And a guitar seemed like the right thing to commemorate this kind of a milestone birthday. A guitar, an acoustic guitar, is a living thing, almost. And commissioning a guitar is an act of hope. Guitars age like violins, and with even a modicum of care, this guitar would last a hundred years. My Wayne Henderson guitar would outlive both its builder and me.

So on my birthday, I called Wayne.

"I'm a big fan of your music, and I love your guitars," I stammered.

"Well, thank you kindly," he replied.

We talked a little bit about his forthcoming gig in New York, before I cut to the chase. I want a guitar. A twelve-fret 000, pretty much like the one he's playing on the cover of his latest album, *Les Pik.*

"Could you send me a letter telling me what you want?"

No problem.

"There's a little bit of a wait."

That's okay.

"I'm retiring from the post office this summer, so I expect I'll be able to build a few more guitars and not keep people waiting quite so long."

Great.

"And you're gonna have to remind me a little."

Sure.

And thus began the first little overlap of Wayne's World and mine.

THE ERIC CLAPTON STORY has become a bit of a rural legend in the hills around Rugby, Virginia. On that night in New York City, one of Wayne's fans—a guy named Bob—told me this tale, about the time that Eric Clapton—or more precisely, one of Eric Clapton's people—called Wayne and had an I'd-like-you-to-build-me-a-guitar conversation similar to mine.

As Bob tells it, Wayne agreed in principle—he's an agreeable sort—but he insisted on talking to Clapton himself to iron out some of the details. Clapton, who will only reluctantly talk to journalists, will talk to Wayne Henderson.

There was a catch. "I'm pretty particular about who works on my guitars," Henderson explained to Clapton, no doubt, with a slight twinkle in his eye. "I'm sure you've got some good guitar builders over there in England, but I want to do the setup work myself so I know the guitar plays right."

"All right," replied the man who inspired the saying "Clapton Is God."

"So you'll have to come here to pick it up."

"That's not a problem," Clapton hedged, "but traveling can sometimes be a bit difficult what with the crowds and all."

"Aw heck," said Henderson, "I didn't even know who you were till last year. And there's only six other people in Rugby and none of 'em even like your kind of music."

Silence on the other end of the transatlantic call.

"I suppose that we could walk down Main Street buck naked and I reckon nobody'd care."

Thus Eric Clapton joined The List. It's a great story. But Wayne insists it never happened.

———

LIKE MANY GUITAR BUILDERS, Wayne Henderson has a waiting list. But unlike most builders, it's not on paper, a computer, or a dry-erase board. I came to realize, as I spent time with Wayne, that The List is in his head. There are fewer than three hundred Wayne Henderson guitars in existence and behind each one is a tale of patience and perseverance on the part of the buyer. If getting a Henderson guitar is a guitar picker's idea of heaven, then it's only fitting that it's preceded by an indeterminate period in purgatory. Wayne Henderson doesn't build guitars so much as bestow them.

Just after he told me the probably apocryphal story about the Clapton phone call, I asked Bob what kind of guitar Wayne was building for him.

A twelve-fret dreadnought.

How long have you been waiting?

"Almost ten years," he answered.

Bob had visited Wayne's workshop, which was built with the money from a National Heritage Fellowship grant he'd received from Hillary Clinton at the White House in 1996. Bob had seen the wood—a lovely set of café-au-lait-colored rosewood that Wayne set aside for his guitar. And yet he still waited. Why? Bob had a theory. Bob is the only man on earth to own two guitars built by John Arnold, a guitar builder in Tennessee, whose reputation approaches Wayne's own, and whose output is even smaller. "Wayne doesn't think I need another guitar," said Bob wistfully.

A youngish woman with long dark hair approached Wayne after the show. She gushed about his playing. She asked about Helen White, Wayne's longtime girlfriend and musical partner, a multitalented fiddle player, rhythm guitarist, vocalist, and songwriter in her own right. She said nothing about the petite, easy-to-play double-ought-sized guitar she's been waiting for.

Wayne smiled the smile you smile at the repo man.

"You know I've got a real nice piece of wood picked out for you," Wayne said.

He's not big on making small guitars. She'd been waiting for twelve years.

Those who've had to wait are not merely those with too many people (Clapton), too many guitars (Bob), or an order that doesn't inspire the chef (the young woman). Grammy winner Gillian Welch, who'd been a friend of Wayne's since before she was famous, had to wait seven years for her guitar. Joe Wilson, who booked Henderson on this show and put together the Masters of the Steel String Guitar tour that took him to Carnegie Hall, only got his when he started sending Wayne a mock-threatening postcard every day.

But there are ways to jump The List. Roy Curry did it by winning the guitar contest at the annual Wayne C. Henderson Music Festival ("Third Saturday in June, rain or shine"). Terry Barnes did it by being a pain in the ass, pestering Wayne with weekly postcards, phone calls, and the occasional drop-in visit.

And Bob Wright—another Bob—did it by merely being at the right place at the right time. Much to my misfortune. After the show at Haft, Wayne handed off the guitar he'd been playing— number 243, if you're keeping score—to Wright, a bluegrass guitarist from Staten Island. It almost didn't happen that way.

Wright's guitar wasn't so much a guitar as it was part of an elaborate scheme. When Henderson found out about the New York gig (his second; the first was at Carnegie Hall)—he hatched a plan. He'd make a guitar for one of his customers in New York. He'd bring the guitar up, play it at the show, deliver it to its new owner, and go home empty-handed with a few bucks in his wallet. Two birds, one stone.

So he got busy, building one of his contest guitars—a simple but elegant mahogany dreadnought—for Wright, who had placed his order less than two years before. The first part of the plot went off as planned. Wayne completed the guitar the night before his flight. He made it through three connecting flights without the fragile instrument going missing or getting mauled by some brutish baggage handler.

There was a flaw in Wayne's plan.

"I still haven't heard from the guy I built this one for," he said to me at lunch, a few hours before the show. He had lost Bob's phone number, so he sent him a letter. No reply. And this clearly had been bothering him.

So between lunch at a Korean restaurant and rehearsal, Wayne invited me up to his room to check out the guitar. He plucked 243 out of the case, tuned it up, and handed it to me. It was deceptively light, always a good sign in instruments.

I strummed an open G chord. It was bright and rich.

Then I strummed another one. I couldn't believe my ears. It was twice as loud as the one I strummed a second ago. The tone was now Einstein bright and Rockefeller rich.

I strummed another chord. Louder still.

This guitar, so new that it thought it still was a tree, was coming to life in my hands. I hacked my way through a remedial version of Doc Watson's "Deep River Blues," delighted and yet slightly disconcerted by the way the guitar continued to blossom from verse to verse, even chord to chord, like a blooming daffodil enhanced by time-lapse photography.

I put it back in the case.

"I guess if he doesn't show up, you've got yourself a guitar," Henderson joked to me.

"I guess so," I joked back.

"He's not joking," assured the other Bob, as Wayne drifted out of earshot. "He's not going to take that guitar back to Rugby with him."

The Mick Jagger in me craved the instant gratification that this happenstance would afford. See guitar. Play guitar. Buy guitar.

But the Cotton Mather in me craved the wait. I wanted a guitar built my way, to my own specs. If the wait stretched into the next decade, so be it. Besides, cutting the line just didn't seem right. But up to showtime, there was no buyer for W. C. Henderson number 243. It looked like I might have myself a guitar.

After the show, I eased my way to the front of the stage. There greeting Wayne was a big guy, with a blond beard and wild hair, wearing a flannel shirt and jeans. Wayne handed him the guitar.

Holding, no, clutching his new prize with two hands around the neck, Wright was wearing the frazzled but happy look of a man who had almost hung up on Ed McMahon.

Turns out that Wright had been on tour in New Orleans, and had only gotten back to his home in Staten Island a couple of hours ago. He was sorting through his pile of mail when he found the note from Wayne . . . "in New York on February 8" . . . Looks at the calendar. That's today . . . "at eight o'clock" . . . Looks at his watch. That's now. Kisses his wife hello and goodbye at the same time, grabs a wad of cash from his guitar fund—$900 he had stashed in a drawer for just such an emergency—and heads off to a Manhattan-bound ferry.

"Nice guitar," I said.

"Thanks," he replied, still beaming. I could see that Wayne had sketched out at least part of the day's drama for him. "And I'm sorry."

Thus I moved back onto The List. Somewhere behind Eric Clapton. Or not.

CHAPTER TWO

Ella's Little Brother

L ET ME TELL YOU about my other guitar. A while back I read a *New Yorker* story that left an impression. It was about the writer Muriel Spark, the author of *The Prime of Miss Jean Brodie*, who made a habit of buying herself a little gift to commemorate the publication of each book. This anecdote struck a chord with me because a) I like gifts, even from myself, and b) the gift in the story was a previously owned diamond watch from Cartier that she wore every day—until she discovered that it was an heirloom worth many thousands of dollars. But that's a different story.

I had just published my first real, bona fide, advance-and-royalty-deal book and I wanted to have a tangible reminder, something that I could point to besides a statement from the mortgage company. However, I wasn't a fine watch kind of guy.

No, I wanted a guitar. A good acoustic guitar. A Martin or something, perhaps? I had been fascinated with guitars my whole life, from the red bass that Danny Bonaduce didn't play on *The Partridge Family* to Bruce Springsteen's Fender Esquire, a reasonable facsimile of which sat in my office, bought with one of my first paychecks. I played guitar a little, not very much and not very well, but enough that a guitar would be more than a wall ornament.

I told my wife, Sally.

"Are you buying this guitar to play, or just to have?" she asked, as indulgently as possible.

That gauntlet thrown down, I did a little research and settled on a Martin 000-28, purchased at Matt Umanov's, a shop in Greenwich Village frequented by Bob Dylan among others, on the afternoon of the first game of the 1998 World Series. The guitar was beautiful. The price was right. But with guitars, as with Bordeaux, vintage is everything. My Martin was built in the 1970s. The rumor is that these guitars were inconsistent in quality because many of the workers were on drugs. ("Hey, dude, hand me some frets.") The less romantic likelihood is that the beancounters at Martin realized that the company's lifetime warranty on an object as inherently fragile as an acoustic guitar was costing them money.

The alternative: build the guitars as sturdily as possible. Guitars from this era—as highly polished as a coffee table and just as heavy—more closely resemble furniture than musical instruments. This cut down on the warranty claims, and killed the sound. But most of the folks strumming John Denver songs didn't care. A few aficionados, however, like Stephen Stills of Crosby Stills Nash & Young, and Clarence White of The Byrds fame, began seeking out the company's older, better instruments made thirty and forty years earlier. These pioneers of vintage guitar geekdom disagreed as to what made these guitars great. Was it their gossamer-light construction? The good old wood? Forty years of playing and aging? Whatever the reason, the period from the beginning of the Depression to the start of World War II became known as the Golden Age of the Acoustic Guitar. The good word, and sometimes an actual instrument, was passed from player to player, from rock star to rock star. (Stills reportedly gave Eric Clapton a vintage Martin 000). This, of course, added to the mystique of the instruments. Decades before *Antiques Roadshow*, guitars that had once been dismissed as shabby old guitars gradually became respected as great-sounding instruments and eventually evolved into all-but-priceless vintage antiques.

So I soon came to realize that my mid-1970s Martin was a good guitar, but not a great one. Time to sell. It turns out that Eric Clapton owned a guitar much like my '74 Martin, and was also looking to get rid of it too. On June 24, 1999, he auctioned off more than one hundred of his guitars at Christie's, the New York auction house that normally deals with Vermeers and Pollocks. The proceeds were going to the Crossroads Centre in Antigua, a drug rehab center that Clapton helped to support. According to the auction catalogue, Clapton said that his 1974 Martin 000–28 "means a great deal to me." Further speculation is that this is the guitar upon which "Wonderful Tonight" was written. The bidding started at $5,000. It ended at $170,000.

Suitably emboldened, I put my *All in the Family*-era Martin in the classifieds of a guitar bulletin board—Christie's wasn't interested—made a joking reference to the Clapton auction, and set the price at $1,650 plus shipping, $150 more than I paid. Within twenty-four hours, I got my price, from a lawyer in Arkansas.

Why did I sell it? Because the weekend before, I had bought Ella, a 1929 Martin 00-28, a guitar with a voice as big and sweet and agile as Ella Fitzgerald's. This tiny guitar with the giant tone was made at the very beginning of the company's Golden Age. My acquisition of Ella started with a search on eBay, trying to get an idea of what my 1974 guitar might be worth. Then I spied Ella. It was a striking guitar, even in the blurry digital photos posted on the auction site. It had the elegant proportioned body and slotted headstock of a classical guitar. It also had that most attractive attribute of all—the bidding had not yet topped $1,000.

As I would learn as the time ticked away until the auction's end, this particular model occupied an interesting place in the history of C.F. Martin & Co. Martin has been the preeminent builder of acoustic guitars since the early nineteenth century. Mark Twain owned a Martin, as did Carl Sandburg. By the end of the 1920s, Martin was just beginning to put steel strings on its guitars after a long period of resisting this change. So this guitar was one of the first to be braced for the additional tension—a set of steel strings can exert a wood-ripping tension of 200 pounds on a guitar top, while a set of classical strings made of gut or nylon only pulls 140. The lightly built steel-braced twelve-fret guitars from the late 1920s are considered by many the best-sounding instruments that Martin, or any other guitar maker, ever made. All my Internet guitar friends told me to go for it.

And so I bid. And I bid and I bid and I bid. The price inched up. In its way, the bidding was as furious as that at Christie's, even if the amount was considerably smaller. At 2:29 on Wednesday, I "won" the auction, but didn't meet the reserve price. A flurry of e-mails ensued between me and the seller, Heavenbound1. We agreed to talk on the phone.

Here was the deal. Mr. Heavenbound—a minister from Pennsylvania—had a side deal to sell the guitar to a collector in Japan if it didn't meet its eBay reserve of $2,500. I offered him $2,600. I emphasized the hassle he'd face packing the guitar and getting it through customs. He hemmed. He hawed. I could feel the guitar slipping away.

"I'd hate to send this guitar over there to Japan after Pearl Harbor and all," he said out of the blue.

Did I want to lecture him about geopolitics? Sure. "Um, yeah. A good old guitar like this should stay right here in the U.S. of A. Right close to where it was built with good old American hard work." He believed me.

I learned that the guitar had no case, and shipping it through the mail would be like stuffing a Fabergé egg in a FedEx envelope and hoping for the best. The Rev lived near Altoona, Pennsylvania. I lived in Montclair, New Jersey. I got out a map, found a town where we could meet halfway, and arranged a meeting at a local pizza parlor, Saturday, two o'clock.

I arrived on time. I ordered a slice. I looked at my watch. I ordered a soda. I looked at my watch. I ordered another slice.

"I'm waiting for someone," I told the waitress, without her asking.

I could see the questions on their faces. Who was I meeting, and why? Was this a drug deal? An armed robbery? An exchange of government secrets?

I walked outside. No luck. No Reverend.

I nibbled at another slice and pretended he wasn't an hour late. Ninety minutes late. Almost two hours late. I tried to forget that I had left my wife and my two-year-old son at the Crayola factory—which closed at five—in Easton, a good forty-five minutes away. Just as I was walking outside for the last time, assuming I'd been stood up and the 00-28 was on its way to Japan, an overstuffed Subaru station wagon pulled up.

"You Allen? I'm the Reverend" said a trim man in a black suit, as he extended his hand. "I'm sorry I'm late but they were doing construction on Route 80."

He introduced me to his friend, a stout man with only small stumps where the fingers on his right hand had been. The Reverend pulled something from the back of the wagon, swaddled in a blanket like a foundling, and we walked back into the restaurant. As I unwrapped the guitar, my waitress seemed relieved that the transaction in question involved a guitar and not NORAD launch codes or a couple of kilos from Colombia.

I hoped that the guitar had been played twice by its original owner—once on VJ Day, once on the Bicentennial Fourth of July—wearing a Pashmina robe and surgical gloves. No such luck. There was a really ugly repair on the Brazilian rosewood side of the guitar, partially concealed with black Magic Marker. The top was worn away to raw wood. Pickwear, in guitarspeak, or perhaps the previous owner had fingernails like a Kodiak bear. And the bridge? It was there. But the bone saddle upon which the strings should rest was missing. In its place were six tiny pieces of guitar string positioned carefully to keep the steel strings off the ebony bridge, an unconventional arrangement to say the least. The slotted headstock had a curious round hole drilled just off center.

On the other hand, the guitar was as light as a balsa wood glider, more like a heavy idea than a light object. You could see the saw marks from the giant blade that had long ago sliced an ancient Brazilian rosewood trunk like a giant cheese log. And if guitars needed hard playing to develop their tone, this one had seen plenty of that.

Here's the story, as best I could divine it. This guitar had been hanging in some Pennsylvania Dutch farmer's barn for most of the century, hence the hole. The farmer, or perhaps his heirs, happily sold the guitar to a local antique shop for slightly above garage sale price. And the Reverend, or perhaps his one-handed cohort, had the foresight to rescue it from the antique shop for a few more bucks.

Now any sensible person would have taken one look at this orphaned guitar and run away. I was prepared to act like a sensible person.

Then I played it. It chimed like a thousand church bells.

"This guitar could heal the lame, wake the dead, negotiate peace in the Middle East," I wrote to my Internet friends later that night. "This is Excalibur, Roy Hobbs's Wonderboy. The tone is as smooth as a used Mercedes dealer and as funky as Rick James before rehab. I have seen the Truth and it has an Adirondack spruce top." It was a writer's hyperbole, but not by much.

This combination of ugly exterior concealing this kind of transcendent inner beauty appealed to me. It looked like hell, but it sounded—the good Reverend notwithstanding—like heaven. On another level, this guitar was the Charlie Brown Christmas tree. It needed a good home. It needed me.

As I was picking a little tune, vacillating between doing the smart thing or doing the right thing, I heard a voice from behind the pizza counter.

"Play a little more," said the man behind in lightly accented English. "That's a beautiful guitar." He was right. I handed over the money.

THEN OF COURSE, Ella had to be put back to some semblance of her prior glory. The man to do that, I had been assured, was T.

J. Thompson. Forty-something, with the angular build of a tennis pro and a quiet but intense bedside manner, he didn't work fast, he didn't work cheap, but he did things right.

Thompson had repaired a guitar for Eric Clapton and had been chosen to do the repairs on Buddy Holly's priceless Gibson J200 before it went on display at the Buddy Holly Center. Regluing the bridge and replacing a few pieces of binding were straight out of Luthiery 101, but it got Thompson his fifteen minutes of fame in a guitar magazine.

"The easiest job I've done in years, and this is what people notice," he said with the slightest trace of annoyance. "At least I had something to show my father."

Thompson's tiny repair shop is located in one of the few quasi-industrial buildings in otherwise tony West Concord, Massachusetts. Park in the back, climb up the metal stairs, make your way past the organic cloth wholesaler and the kids' furniture factory and you're there. Wedged in one corner is a band saw, in another is a spray booth. In the middle is Thompson's work table, riddled with ancient guitar parts.

A visit to T. J. Thompson's shop isn't for the squeamish. At a certain level, guitars are like laws and sausages: the less you know about how they're made, the better. This whole room is littered with disembodied parts: a 1934 D-28 neck here, an OM-18 body there, a delicate pyramid bridge somewhere else. In this sad state, these valuable guitars reminded me of injured athletes sitting on the sidelines in their expensive suits, all potential energy with no outlet.

But like a modern-day Dr. Frankenstein, Thompson brings these carcasses back to life. He showed me a Martin 000-45 from the early 1930s. It's a close cousin to my guitar—a little bigger but similar in shape—but it had clearly lived a different life. It had only the lightest patina to indicate its advanced age. It was a high-end instrument, with intricate abalone inlays on every edge. That detailing made the guitar worth close to $100,000.

It also made this guitar T. J. Thompson's problem du jour.

"How would you go about replacing the kerfing on this guitar?" he asks rhetorically.

The kerfing is a strip of wood sliced almost all the way through at quarter-inch intervals—think about a cross between dentil molding and a comb. It's snaked around the top and bottom edges of the sides and glued on before the guitar is assembled. The top and back are then glued to the kerfing. It's hardly a stretch to say that this four-ounce strip of wood holds a guitar together. On this guitar, the kerfing was failing, and it was Thompson's job to figure out how to replace the kerfing without disrupting the original inlay that gave this guitar its value.

I shrugged. He sighed. He didn't have an answer either. Yet.

What makes Thompson one of the best is that he's a perfectionist. In one corner of his shop, I saw a small shelf piled with small pieces of maple, each a bridge plate waiting to be born. Each of these pieces was piled carefully, categorized in a way that only Thompson would understand. Each piece of wood, I would come to understand, is as individual as a fingerprint. He had picked up each piece, flexed it to determine its stiffness, tapped it and listened to get a sense of its tone, then graded it. He was like the master pastry chef in pursuit of the perfect pomegranate. He would replace only a handful of bridge plates in a year, and yet he had a selection of hundreds on hand. This was a lifetime's stash.

It was in a repair shop like this that Wayne Henderson honed his craft. At Gruhn Guitars, across from the Grand Ole Opry in Nashville, thirty years ago, Wayne was charged with taking wonderful old instruments apart and bringing them back to life. In the process he discovered what made them tick. Thompson too builds exceptional instruments. When he gets around to it. When I told him I knew someone who owned one of his guitars, he registered genuine surprise. Thompson is so much in demand as a repairman that he simply doesn't have time to build them anymore.

Thompson turned his attention to Ella like an orthopedist examining a ruptured ligament. He would need to replace the bridge, fiddle with the frets, remove the neck, and adjust its angle—three-quarters of a century of continuous tension had raised the strings too far above the fingerboard. He looked at the funky side repair with a certain admiration. It's hardly how he would have done it himself, but at the moment it was structurally sound—sounder than the 000-45 with the six-figure price tag.

"I'd just leave it alone," he advised.

"Is it going to affect the tone?" I wondered.

"You could patch that with papier-mâché and you wouldn't hear a difference."

He noted that the important parts—the Adirondack spruce top, the bridge plate, and, by and large, the Brazilian rosewood back and sides—were intact.

"After the work is done, this guitar will sound 20 percent better," he pronounced. My heart leapt.

"This isn't a big job," he added, no doubt still thinking about the decaying 000-45. "I'll have it done between two and five months."

You can't rush genius. Two months passed, five months. Eight months. Then a year. "Soon," T. J. Thompson told me over the phone. "Soon." It was more than a year before Ella came back home restored perfectly.

But this wasn't wasted time. In its absence, I began to understand the luthier's place in the world, in my world. I called the Martin guitar factory, and from the serial number (and the miracle of German-inspired recordkeeping), they were able to inform me that my guitar was completed on May 3, 1929.

I entered my own personal wayback machine and wondered about the day that some guitar player whose name is lost to history went into a store, forked over $110, and took this guitar home. The world was different—F. Scott Fitzgerald was the John Grisham of the day, Sigmund Freud was the Dr. Phil, a Stutz Bearcat was a status symbol—and about to change in ways that no one would believe. The stock market crash was only months away. Lying in wait as the Jazz Age wound down were the Great

Depression and another world war. Hiroshima. Dallas. Memphis. Vietnam. This guitar had lived through it all.

And it was in this reverie that the idea of commissioning my own guitar was hatched. I was now Ella's custodian, and it was a job I took seriously. That's why I took her to Thompson to restore her to her former glory. This guitar was a connection to the past, to times I had never seen and people I would never meet.

What Ella needed was a younger brother. Ella's little brother, an heirloom-in-waiting soon to be built by Wayne Henderson, would be my connection to the future. Sure, I would have a hand in its creation, from spec'ing the woods to writing the check, to breaking it in. But to think of it as nothing more than my new guitar was missing the point. A Henderson is a lifetime guitar to be sure, but the cold reality is that its lifetime would likely be longer than mine.

As the twenty-first century stretched toward the twenty-second, Ella's Baby Brother would meet people I would never meet, go places I would never go, see things I would never see. Someday, I imagined, some stranger will pick up Wayne Henderson 353—or whatever its number would turn out be—and casually strum a G chord. And as the sound slowly decayed, that Man of the Future might enter his own wayback machine and wonder for a moment about the guy who played it for the first time and what the world was like at the crack of the millennium. I liked that idea, and I knew Wayne would too.

CHAPTER THREE

Wayne's World

Y OU CAN MEET YOURSELF going backwards." That's the
way guitar picker Roy Curry describes the road to Wayne
Henderson's guitar shop. Route 58, in southwest Virginia, near
the North Carolina border, probably started life as a primordial
deer path, the quickest route between some clear, cold stream
and a patch of particularly succulent vegetation. It's paved now,
and has been dubbed the Crooked Road, Virginia's heritage music
trail, but the deer haven't adapted. Herb Key, the bassist in
Wayne's band, has hit seven of them with various motor vehicles
in the last decade.

Rugby, Virginia, exists on the outskirts of twenty-first-
century America. It's about ten miles down the road from Mouth
of Wilson, and almost twenty from Independence, a town of a
couple thousand where you can chow down at Aunt Bea's Barbecue Express, a small fast-food chain, still cashing in on the eternal popularity of *The Andy Griffith Show*. Another fifteen miles
toward the Interstate and you reach Galax, the home of some of
America's best traditional fiddlers. I assumed I'd find guys sitting
on the porch with banjos, guitars, and an upright bass, picking
"Whiskey Before Breakfast." And while those gatherings still
take place off the beaten path, what I found on Route 58 was a
Burger King, a McDonald's, a Blockbuster, a cineplex, a bowling
alley, and a giant new Lowe's, built by the owner of the smaller,

old Lowe's to keep Home Depot away. Except for the odd gun shop, this part of Galax could be suburban New Jersey.

But protected in part by this preternaturally twisty road, Rugby remains unspoiled. Before my trip, a guitar buddy briefed me. "It could be seventy-five years ago," he said. "There aren't any tourist traps. Hell, there aren't any tourists." I like a two-lane road loaded with switchbacks as much as the next guy, but as I drove to Wayne's shop, my adrenaline rush was tempered by a tinge of carsickness. Even the Virginia Department of Highways seemed to have a sense of humor around here. One sign announced a 55 mph speed limit. Not fifty yards down the road came a left-hand hairpin turn that's steep, blind, and unmarked. Only Jeff Gordon wannabes—and tourists—push the speed limit around here.

Turn left onto Tucker Road, and the dense hardwood forest gives way to a narrow pastoral valley dotted with tiny baby firs. On the right I noticed a little forest of telephone poles. For forty-nine weeks out of the year, they just stand there, forming a kind of timbered Stonehenge. When it's time for the Christmas tree harvest, these poles support dozens of high-watt work lights for the serious business of trimming and bagging trees. While most people want to preserve the illusion that their *Tannenbaum* came from somewhere in the Great White North, odds are that it came from well south of the Mason-Dixon line, perhaps from the hillside just outside Wayne Henderson's workshop. But in another irony of modern life, it's the Christmas tree farmers who are keeping out the Super Wal-Mart.

Henderson's workshop is a modest one-story brick structure, just across the driveway from his modest brick house. Sandy, the old yellow hound dog chained up outside, hardly noticed me as I entered the little anteroom. On one side rested an ancient soda pop machine—45 cents buys you a can of Mountain Dew, Dr. Pepper, Cheerwine, or Chocolate Cow, but no Coke or Pepsi—on the other lay a dusty pile of guitar cases waiting to be filled.

The door to the shop proper was closed, so I knocked. "C'mon in," shouted Wayne, and I could tell from the reaction that the door's closed not to keep strangers out but to keep the air-conditioning in.

"Howdy," he said. "Nice to see you."

I explained that I just wanted to stop in and say hi before I headed back to New York—I had come down for the ninth annual Wayne C. Henderson Music Festival—but I quickly learned that no excuses are necessary to stop by at the guitar shop. Wayne, his brother, Max, Gerald Anderson, the mandolin maker who shares this workspace, Wayne's best customer, Gabby Bumgarner and Gabby's dog, a small nine-year-old short-haired mixed-breed named Bandit, are perched on stools in a loose semicircle, conducting an informal debriefing about the festival, which took place the previous Saturday. The conversation bounced back and forth between the guitar competition— "He sure could pick the *guit*-tar," they said about Roy Curry, the lucky winner of a brand-new Henderson—to how best to get rid of the garbage from the after-party at Wayne's house.

"Do you still have the Dumpster over there?" Wayne asked Max, who lives just a few miles south over the North Carolina border.

The shop is a pleasant space, maybe thirty feet by twenty, with six windows and an abundance of natural light. A giant worktable topped with rock maple tongue-and-groove floorboards salvaged from a bowling alley is the room's centerpiece, while the perimeter is lined with power tools. It is also, to put it politely, a wreck. In one corner, thousands of dollars worth of valuable tonewoods are piled haphazardly next to an overworked air conditioner clogged with sawdust. The band saw is crammed uncomfortably next to the belt sander. Coiled air hoses dangle ominously from the ceiling like neon yellow pythons. That large central table is piled with more guitar wood, boxes of Wayne's CDs, the odd newspaper, and a couple of guitar bodies in different stages of completion. On the far wall is a collection of cubbyholes, each overstuffed with paperwork from would-be Henderson owners.

"I think your letter's in there," Wayne said optimistically.

Right next to Eric Clapton's, I thought to myself. I would find out later that my letter was only a couple of cubbies down from a snapshot of Clapton playing Tim Duffy's Henderson guitar.

The walls are adorned with bumper stickers, concert posters, and postcards from guitar customers. Right above the phone, written on the wall itself, is an IOU for a free haircut. A copy of my latest book, which I had sent along to Wayne only a week before my arrival, was sitting on the long workbench, the neon orange cover already covered by a quarter-inch of sawdust.

I had been assured that the shop had never been neater. Before the festival, several local women volunteered to come out and tidy up for the party.

"I ain't gonna find nothing for a week," Henderson said with a grumble. He didn't seem overly concerned. Indeed, later in the afternoon he discovered that one of the partygoers—or one of the cleaners—had somehow or other jammed a towel into the thickness sander, rendering it, well, broken, then folded another towel on top very neatly to conceal the problem. Wayne didn't utter so much as a cross word.

"I reckon it takes a lot to get under my skin," he said softly.

Max was about to leave with the garbage, so I wandered out around the side of Wayne's brick house ready to lend a hand. On the sunporch stood a row of industrial-strength trash bags filled to the brim with Styrofoam plates and two-day-old potato salad. They were left inside so as not to attract the attention of the local fauna, which can range from nosy raccoons to curious black bears. We held our noses and dumped the bags into the back of Max's old Ford pickup, which had likely been on duty since the Kennedy administration.

No sooner had we returned to the shop than Wayne's daughter, Elizabeth, an eighteen-year-old clad in a bright red New York Athletic Club T-shirt, bounced into the room.

"Daddy, do you know anyone who can change my oil?"

A bright and sophisticated freshman-to-be at North Carolina State with her father's piercing blue eyes and inquisitive gaze, she clearly had one foot out the door. She was here for a visit for the festival, but she lived with Wayne's ex-wife near Roanoke. Wayne lived alone in the brick house across the driveway from the shop. His mother, Sylvie, now past 90, had moved into a nursing home after she broke her leg in a fall. Wayne's girlfriend, Helen White, had her own house on a hilltop down the road. Their state of domesticity was such that one Christmas Wayne built her a fiddle and another he paid for a new septic tank.

"I'll think of you every time I use it," Helen said.

Waiting for her answer, Elizabeth absentmindedly rolled a tiny red Hot Wheels Thunderbird that one of Wayne's customers had no doubt sent along. Wayne's single indulgence—a real '57 T-Bird—had just been painted the same color.

"That'd just be a big mess," Wayne said. "Why don't you just go down to the filling station in Independence?"

"Can you come with me?"

"It's just a couple miles down the road."

"Can't you at least call them?"

Wayne picked up the phone, the deal was done, and Elizabeth disappeared. "That boyfriend of hers was out here the other day," said Wayne, as the door slammed. "I didn't like him much at first." Wayne paused for a beat, as if he were waiting for his mandolin player to catch up, and added, "Then I saw how big he was."

This was the elaborate setup to one of Wayne's venerable jokes. In comedy, as in music, timing is everything, and Wayne's got it in spades. "This cowboy pulls into a town in the Wild West, and he ties his horse outside. When he gets back from the general store, he sees that someone has painted his horse pink. Now that's about the worst thing you can do to a cowboy, paint his horse pink, so he's fit to be tied.

"He rushes into the saloon, busts right through the swinging doors, and hollers, 'Who's the low-down, no-good, lily-livered varmint who painted my horse pink?'

"Over at the poker table, the biggest meanest hombre stands up reeeeeal slow. He must be six foot six and close to three hundred pounds.

" 'I reckon that would be me,' he tells the cowboy matter-of-factly.

" 'Well, sir,' said the cowboy, 'I just wanted to tell you that I think she's dry and ready for a second coat.'"

Bada boom. Belly laughs all around.

And speaking of second coats, Wayne ambled over to his workbench reluctantly and announced, "Maybe I'll do some inlay work." Which is a little bit like Michelangelo walking toward the Sistine Chapel and telling his neighbors, "Gotta go paint the ceiling today."

Wayne's project today: finish the fingerboard extension on Gabby's twelve-fret Brazilian rosewood dreadnought. It looked simple—attaching three two-inch pieces of abalone trim to the body of the guitar—but it wasn't. The challenge was to get this piece of trim to fit around the perimeter of the neck without gaps or overlaps. Wayne was clearly not relishing the prospect. This particular operation, I soon discovered, was just about the most exacting, labor-intensive part of building a guitar. Just about every other step in building a guitar has a fudge factor, but not this one.

Wayne's prep work consisted of slicing a sheet of abalone shell that was a little bigger than a business card into eighth-inch strips, his fingers dancing only millimeters from the band saw blade. Then he took some paper-thin strips of wood—called purfling—and carefully built a tiny frame for the pearl by gluing strips to the side, forming a pinstripe by alternating black layers with off-white. Then he took the neck of the guitar off the workbench and oh-so-carefully fit it into the dovetail joint on the body. He whittled a pencil to a razor point with the tiny penknife he'd use throughout the operation, and scribed around the perimeter of the dark ebony onto the paper-white spruce top.

This was clearly a measure-twice, cut-once job, because a single slip with the minitature router and this lovely guitar body built of endangered Brazilian rosewood and fine Appalachian red spruce would become a pile of bejeweled kindling.

On the other hand, Wayne Henderson works best on deadline, and today he had two. In the morning, he'd be leaving for Washington where he was participating in the Smithsonian's Folklife Festival. And it was Gabby's birthday today—sixty-one candles on a three-alarm-fire of a cake.

A giant man with a red face and a white beard, a prodigious belly and an easy laugh, Gabby would be a first-call Santa Claus at Macy's. Dressed in a tight white T-shirt and cutoff denim overalls and a Maltby's Gun Shop feed cap, Gabby is as much a fixture at Wayne's shop as the table saw. He and Bandit, a small black and gray terrier mix with no tail, drive two hundred miles round-trip to Rugby every Monday and Wednesday, just to sit around and watch some or another guitar being built. After years of waiting— he couldn't quite remember how long he'd been making this trip—his guitar was finally nearing completion. Gabby's also a bit of an instigator. As Wayne was fitting a couple of tiny strips of wooden purfling to the abalone, Gabby started in with Bandit.

"Gimme some sugar," he exhorted the napping canine.

Bandit jumped up as if he were poked with a cattle prod. The doddering dog didn't quite have the strength to jump up into Gabby's lap and give his master a slobbering doggie kiss, so he circled around the floor maniacally, howling and growling as if possessed. Wayne looked up at Gabby, furrowing his brow beneath his reading glasses as if to say, (a) I do my best work when it's quiet, and (b) This is your guitar I'm working on.

Gabby's earned his slot on The List with more than perfect attendance. Last year, he said sadly, he lost a 1939 D-28—a rare pre-war guitar known to collectors as a herringbone for its delicate top trim—and an even more valuable Gibson Mastertone banjo when his truck caught on fire. Understanding his rep as a guy who's told a tall tale or two in his day, he pulled the charred remains of the mahogany guitar neck from underneath a work-bench, as if to say "Here's proof." The metal frets were melted, but the old-style C.F. Martin logo was visible beneath a thin layer of carbon.

"I almost cried when I saw what happened to that guitar," he said.

That next week, when Gabby showed up, Wayne had pulled a piece of obscenely beautiful Brazilian rosewood from his personal stash. Brick-red in color, deeply veined with black spidery lines, this plank was cut seventy years ago, from a tree that was maybe four hundred years old. Once-in-a-lifetime wood. "This be okay for your guitar, Gabby?" Wayne asked.

"When Wayne showed me that wood, I did cry," Gabby said, half-laughing.

There's another knock at the door. Eyes roll. "C'mon in," Gabby shouted as Wayne continued to tweak the inlay. It's a hus-band-and-wife team. He's tall but stooped, with a close-cropped beard and glasses, while she has a salt-and-pepper perm and an easy smile. They've brought an old unstrung Gibson for Wayne's neck man, Herb Key, to repair. Or at least that's the excuse. "Um, I was wondering about," the man stammered, "talking to you about, well, about building me an instrument." He never used the word guitar. It was always *instrument*.

"Well, first you've got to figure out what it is you want," Wayne said without even looking up from Gabby's guitar. "And there's a little bit of a wait." This was one of a half-dozen new orders Wayne would take this weekend, and he was similarly pleasant and noncommittal about each one. On the one hand, Wayne's too nice to so much as hang up on a telemarketer, but on the other hand, he hardly needed to drum up business.

The tall guy shifted around uncomfortably, but his wife took up the conversation, doting on the dog lying inert again on the floor, waxing poetic about the scenery around the shop.

"Can we just take some of this back to Charlotte?" she won-dered.

The guests were sucking up to Wayne. Wayne was impervious, but Gabby rose to the occasion. He had a fresh audience, and he was taking advantage of it.

"I like this place so much, I told my son I want to have my ashes scattered here," Gabby explained. "Half between my mammy and my pappy, the other half up on the hill here."

Wayne smiled. Partially because he's heard it before, partially because he seems happy with the compromise—at least he won't have Gabby's ashes in the shop itself, clogging up the air conditioner and sticking to freshly lacquered guitar bodies.

"That's okay by me, but I think the John Deere would have a time with what's left of you," Wayne said with a laugh.

"I've had three heart attacks, open heart surgery, colon cancer, and diabetes," Gabby intoned solemnly, as the visitors prepared to leave. "And that's nothing compared to waiting for a Henderson guitar," he bellowed, laughing the laugh of a man who knew that his wait—for a guitar—was drawing to an end.

OUT ON THE BIG workbench rested a neckless guitar body, but unlike the other unfinished ones on the bench, this one had seen better days. There were big patches of raw wood where the pickguard and bridge had been removed, shall we say, nonprofessionally. The lacquer had yellowed to a lovely amber patina, the surface of the lacquer finish featuring the sort of delicate crazing that you might find on a Ming vase. The brand on the neck block revealed that it's Wayne Henderson number 7. This guitar was built when Wayne was still a teenager, just graduated from high school and delivering mail, but you couldn't tell by the workmanship. To the untrained eye, it could pass for a seventy-year-old Martin. Oh, and one more thing: There was a bullet hole through the Brazilian rosewood back.

While Wayne waited for a piece of inlay to dry, I asked him about old number 7.

"Well, just after my grandpappy died, I'd go over to my

grandma's house and stay over while she got used to being alone in the house and, of course, I brought my guitar.

"One day, Hunter the local moonshiner came over, and he brought a friend of his with him. We didn't much like the looks of him. Hunter was okay, but this other guy was the kind of feller who'd go to his family reunion looking to pick up women.

"He says, 'I hear you built a guitar.'

" 'Yessir.'

"He asked to see it, and I figured it was smart to be polite to a guy like that, so I showed him the guitar. He sat down on the couch and he picked for a while. He was a pretty good picker.

" 'How much do you want for it?' "

"I was looking to get rid of him, so I said, 'Oh, I guess, I couldn't take less than five hundred dollars.' That was an awful lot of money in them days—the story takes place in the late 1960s—so I figured that would scare him off."

"He played it for a couple more minutes and then they left, and I figured that was the end of that.

"The next day, Hunter and his friend come back, and the guy pulls a wad of cash out his shirt pocket and peels off five one-hundred-dollar bills." Wayne paused for a second as if to emphasize the gravity of the situation. "That was more money than I'd ever seen or heard tell of."

If one moment can change the course of a man's life, this was it. He had his seed money and he had his incentive. From then on Wayne C. Henderson added a slash to his self-description: mailman/guitar builder.

"I said to my grandma, 'If I can make that kind of money, well I know what I'm going to do from now on.'" He sank the $500 into wood and supplies, and that was the beginning for the Wayne C. Henderson Guitar Company. It was also the beginning of the end of old number 7.

"I'd see that guitar around now and again, at festivals and such," Wayne continued. "Someone was always beating on it pretty hard, leaving it out in the rain and the like. Now of course this feller and his friends were the kind who liked to play around with guns." Another pause. "So I figure that one day, one of them said to the other, 'Hey, bet you can't shoot the guitar through the hole.' Guess they figured if they shot it through the hole it wouldn't hurt it none."

"Maybe they didn't like the song he was playing," said Gabby, who's clearly heard this story before.

"Well, I don't see no blood around the hole," Wayne snapped back.

As to the guitar's current condition, there's a piece of three-quarter-inch oak flooring holding the top together, more or less. Wayne could, of course, just rip the top off, patch the Brazilian back, and build an exquisite new guitar. But this guitar is part of his creation myth, and perhaps one day he will do his best to restore it to its former glory. "I guess I'll just try to make it playable." And probably a little more than that.

Wayne is not only a master guitar builder, he is a master repairman as well. Back when he was working at the repair shop at Gruhn Guitars back in the 1970s, a holy grail guitar—a 1939 Martin D-45—came into the shop with a huge problem. Someone had shaved down the neck to turn it into a four-string tenor guitar. The other technicians in the shop hatched an elaborate plan for salvaging the old neck that involved laminating strips of mahogany onto the pencil neck, and shimming the fretboard out with ebony.

"How about I just make you a new neck?" Wayne asked the shop's owner, George Gruhn. Gruhn reluctantly agreed, willing to let Wayne waste a little time and wood on the project.

Inside of a week, Henderson had fashioned a replacement neck so perfect that no one in the shop could believe their eyes. That guitar was later sold to Stephen Stills and when the rock star brought that guitar to the Martin factory to play show-and-tell, the late Mike Longworth, the company historian and the man who literally wrote the book on vintage guitars, eyeballed it like a Westminster judge assessing a prize shih tzu.

"Nice guitar," he told Stills. "I think the neck might be refinished."

Stills just grinned.

AT WAYNE'S MUSIC festival a few days earlier, I spent some time hanging out with a guy named Bruce, a large, jolly white-haired man from Knoxville, Tennessee, who could have been Gabby's city cousin. We got to swapping stories about his guitars and he told me about his Henderson. By his own count, he's bought, sold, and traded over seven thousand guitars, but the koa twelve-fret Henderson's the one he's hung on to. While he was in the neighborhood, he dropped off a small pile of Brazilian rosewood at Wayne's shop, as part of a complex trade for a guitar Wayne was building for him.

"I've known Wayne a long time," he advised. "And if I were you, I'd get my name on one of those pieces of wood." And indeed, while I sat and watched Wayne finesse a miter on the inlay with a tiny penknife and a patch of sandpaper, the phone rang. It was Bruce. After a few pleasantries, I realized the conversation had turned to me—"He's sitting right here," Wayne said, and he was clearly not talking about Gabby. While he was calling to iron out the details of the trade, Bruce took the opportunity to put in a good word for "the guy from up North who wrote the book." Bruce had become my guitar matchmaker.

With the door open this wide, I had no choice but to walk through. "So is that Brazilian over there spoken for?" I asked Wayne, when he was done cutting.

"Nope, no, it ain't," he said. "Let's go over and take a look."

Wayne and I shuffled through the two-foot-long boards like they were giant tarot cards. One piece was a deep red color and had straight spidery grain, much like the old-school wood on Gabby's guitar.

"I think that's too small," Wayne said as he held up the template of a guitar back.

A half-inch shy at most.

Then Wayne stopped at a piece with remarkably swirly grain, a virtual Rorschach test: *The state of Kentucky . . . Anthony Hopkins in profile . . . a cloud,* I thought as I looked at the almost psychedelic grain pattern.

I got the sense that Wayne was subtly testing me. The wood was beautiful. But this piece had also clearly been slab-cut from a stump, the kind of wood that most old-school luthiers would reject as being too weak and crack-prone for proper guitar building. If this were the Martin factory in the 1930s, when Brazilian rosewood was plentiful, this particular board would have ended up in the woodstove. This was the sort of wood chosen by people who care more about how a guitar looks than how it sounds. I sighed and moved on to another piece.

The grain on the next one was much straighter—the color reminded me a bit of the back and sides on Ella, my old Martin—but even in this rough-sawn form it had a flamey, almost shimmery figure.

"What about this one?" I asked.

"Oh that's a *nice* piece of fiddleback," Wayne enthused, a nod to the flamed maple used on the back of fine violins. He took the two matching pieces, laid them side by side like the pages of a book, and traced the outline of a guitar on it. Bingo.

"Write your name on 'er," Wayne said, handing me the same pencil he'd used to mark up Gabby's guitar. While I proudly snapped a couple of digital pictures of the Brazilian—the image of the raw wood almost immediately became the wallpaper on my laptop—Wayne finished up the inlay.

It was exquisite, a little piece of art deco jewelry. The perfectly mitered abalone gleamed seamlessly against its intricate black and white frame, setting off the top like a string of pearls against alabaster skin. Not accounting for a couple of phone calls, it had taken Wayne a total of five hours to finish, using mostly a sharp knife, a little sandpaper, some Titebond glue, and a lot of patience. Wayne was pleased with a job well done, and Gabby was beside himself.

"When people see that they're gonna think I've got some pictures of Wayne in a compromising position," he bellowed.

In celebration, Wayne and Gabby and I headed over to Ona's—the nearest restaurant, five miles back toward Mouth of Wilson—for a dinner of barbecue sandwiches and sweet tea.

Afterward, as I was ready to hop in the car, Gabby handed me an axelike implement. It was both elegant—the subtly curved handle had a Shaker-like grace—and purposeful—one could see Freddy Krueger brandishing it in some as-yet-unmade *Nightmare on Elm Street* sequel.

"You know what that's for?" Gabby asked.

I shrugged.

"That there's a foot add," Wayne explained. It was a tool used by the settlers to build log cabins, to smooth and notch the ends, so that two-hundred-year-old oaks would fit together as precisely as Lincoln Logs.

Impressed, I handed it back to Gabby. He insisted that I keep it.

"Take that back to New York with you," he said, laughing.

My first thought was that it was the perfect remembrance of an old and endangered way of life that I caught a glimpse of this weekend. My second: trying to explain this thing to a state trooper who's pulled me over for doing 84 in a 65 mph zone.

"My grandpappy used to keep one around the house," Wayne explained. "He said it was the only thing that would keep the devil away."

That tipped the scales. I thanked Gabby and Wayne, put the foot add in the trunk, shook hands all around, and hit the road. I had six hundred miles ahead of me, a half-dozen I-need-it-yesterday messages on my answering machine, and a thousand deer ready to jump in front of my twelve-year-old Acura before I even got to the new Lowe's near the Interstate. But after this day, I had a few things that even Eric Clapton didn't: some wood with my name on it, a foot add in my trunk, and an open invitation to stop back anytime at the guitar shop on Tucker Road.

CHAPTER FOUR

All Solid Wood

IT'S THE MESOPOTAMIA of traditional music in America,"
said folklorist Nick Spitzer, host of *American Routes* on pub-
lic radio. He's referring to Wayne Henderson's extended neighborhood, the Blue Ridge Mountains where southwest Virginia
meets North Carolina, Kentucky, and Tennessee.

But what exactly do you call the music that Wayne Henderson and his friends play? It's not country music as the radio
defines it. Contemporary Nashville-style country is nothing
more than rock and roll with cowboy hats and a Southern accent.
"Bluegrass" is a better term, but it's a bit too narrow a designa-
tion. Let's call it old-time music for the moment.

When I embarked on a search for a brief history of old-time
music, Wayne suggested I track down Kinney Rorrer. Rorrer is a
professor at Danville Community College, the host of *Back to
the Blue Ridge* on WVTF, a local NPR affiliate and the author of
Ramblin' Blues, a biography of legendary old-time banjo player
Charlie Poole and his band, the North Carolina Ramblers.

According to Rorrer, old-time music in Virginia traces its roots
back to the 1740s and 1750s, during one of the first waves of immi-
gration to America. "The Scots-Irish were famous for their fiddling
and dancing and drinking," Rorrer explained, "and they brought a
lot of tunes with them that we still play under different names."
For example, one of Wayne Henderson's favorite instrumentals,

"Leather Britches," began life as "Lord MacDonald's Reel," although it's also known as "Four Nights Drunk." The popular "Billy in the Lowground" may have been named after William of Orange, the Dutch monarch who took the English crown in 1689.

The banjo came to America around the same time from a different continent. "In his diaries, Thomas Jefferson mentions blacks playing banjos in Virginia in the 1780s," Rorrer explained. What we know as old-time music today borrows from both of these traditions. "It's a melding of Scots-Irish fiddle tunes and African banjo music," said Rorrer. "The guitar doesn't show up until much later."

One of the hallmarks of old-time music has been its resistance to change. Because of a real physical isolation, and a culture that was socially conservative by nature, mountain musicians have dipped into a small common reservoir of tunes that hasn't changed very much over hundreds of years. Even today an old-time jam has the atmosphere of a campfire sing-along—everyone knows and can play the same couple dozen songs. "Once they latch on to something they hold on to it," said Rorrer.

Rorrer is quick to point out that old-time music is dance music, which is still evident in its incessant drive and toe-tapping beat. "It was homemade music, but it was also entertainment," he explained. In the days before radios and phonographs, when a band of musicians showed up, it was reason to put aside the farm chores for a while, and move the furniture out of the front room, because when the band left, the music went with them. Textile mills sponsored their own string bands the way that a factory might sponsor a softball team today. Old-time was, in many ways, the rock music of the day. While string bands played at square dances, with a caller and a selection of formalized moves like the do-si-do, most of the dancing was flatfooting—find a partner, move your feet, and dance till you drop. In spirit, it wasn't dissimilar to what you might see these days at a college dorm party on Saturday night.

By the time the twentieth century rolled around and outside influences like radio and phonograph records began filtering into these isolated communities, old-time music needed a preservationist, and got one in the person of Alvin Pleasant Carter of the legendary Carter Family. "A. P. Carter was good at ferreting out old songs that might have otherwise fallen by the wayside and putting them into some kind of singable, hummable form," said Rorrer.

Indeed, the Carter Family preserved more than just the music. On an early Carter Family recording, vocalist Sara Carter pronounces the word "sword" with the same "sw" as "swore." Rorrer noted this anomaly, but didn't complete the puzzle until he watched *The Story of English* on PBS. "Robert McNeil asks this Shakespearean scholar in England to read Shakespeare as Shakespeare would have read it. He does a scene from *Macbeth* and he comes to the word s-w-o-r-d and he pronounces it "*sword*" the same way that Sara Carter did."

A.P.'s sister-in-law, Maybelle Carter, was perhaps America's first guitar hero—Wayne Henderson is far from the only guitarist to cite "Wildwood Flower" as the first song he ever learned. Indeed, the appeal of Mother Maybelle's distinctive bass-melody style, coupled with the availability of cheap instruments from Sears and Montgomery Ward that could be mail-ordered to would-be musicians in isolated communities, contributed to the guitar's ascendancy as America's most popular instrument.

It's unusual that a genre of music can be traced back to a single artist and a single piece of music, but that's the case with the old-time spinoff, bluegrass. The Thomas Edison of bluegrass was a Kentucky mandolinist named Bill Monroe, and the Rosetta Stone was his October 28, 1939, performance of "Muleskinner Blues" at the Grand Ole Opry. Monroe combined stylistic elements of the blues with the repertoire and orchestration—mandolin, banjo, guitar, and bass—of old-time bands. Monroe's music featured keening tenor vocals—the high lonesome sound—and an overdrive tempo—his version of "Muleskinner Blues" is easily twice as fast as Jimmie Rodgers's original. "Bill Monroe took that song and made it soar," said Rorrer.

Despite their common roots, there remains some friction between the bluegrass and old-time camps even today. Part of it is a matter of approach. In an old-time jam, the fiddle is usually the lead instrument, and every other musician plays accompaniment, and a melody is played over and over again, with no solos, sometimes for fifteen minutes or more. The speed is moderate, and the groove is paramount.

Bluegrass music is not only far faster, it's also more competitive. Instrumentalists take turns taking lead breaks on a song, the flashier the better. Bluegrass musicians have also been much quicker to adopt songs from other traditions. For example, Del McCoury won an International Bluegrass Music Association award with Richard Thompson's "1952 Vincent Black Lightning," a modernized English bandit ballad.

The distinction between bluegrass and old-time is clearest among banjo players. Bluegrass players use loud resonator banjos to play fast rolls in the style of Earl Scruggs, a seminal member of Monroe's Blue Grass Boys, but perhaps best known for his playing on "The Ballad of Jed Clampett," the theme song of *The Beverly Hillbillies.* Old-time banjo players play quieter wood-rimmed banjos in a slower, droning style, often using a percussive clawhammer technique. A resonator banjo is about as welcome in an old-time jam as a Fender Stratocaster. These somewhat arbitrary distinctions manage to exclude iconoclastic artists whose style defies pigeonholing. "If a guy like Charlie Poole showed up today to play at the fiddlers' convention in Galax, he wouldn't be allowed into the bluegrass banjo contest because he didn't play bluegrass. And he wouldn't be allowed into the old-time contest because he didn't play clawhammer," Rorrer explained. "But he was as old-time as they come."

Wayne Henderson's rare in that he deftly straddles the divide between bluegrass and old-time camps. He can play as fast and clean as the fastest bluegrass players. But stylistically, his approach is more old-time. While many bluegrass players use the melody as a jumping-off point for wide-ranging improvisation, the way jazz great John Coltrane riffed on the melody of "My Favorite Things," Wayne is happy to simply play the song. And that makes him welcome just about anywhere there's an upright bass.

And that's also exactly how Wayne Henderson builds instruments. He's not interested in innovation. In just the same way that he's happy to play a version of "Sally Ann" the way it's been played for centuries, he builds his guitars like those turned out by the Martin factory seventy-five years ago. Call Wayne Henderson a traditionalist. He won't mind.

The world seems to be slowly coming around to Wayne's way of thinking. While traditional music has waxed and waned in popularity in recent decades, it's currently experiencing a renaissance. The local jams in Wayne's neck of the woods are populated with young players, some wearing Metallica T-shirts while playing an orthodox version of "Old Joe Clark."

And some of these modern old-time musicians have begun making remarkable contributions to this music. For example, about ten years ago, a group of young musicians showed up at the doorstop of Wayne Henderson's shop when their car broke down. They hung out and jammed. One of them was Gillian Welch. Although she comes from California, Welch writes murder ballads in a style that's old as dirt. "When I heard her songs I thought she had to be Carter Stanley's daughter," said Wayne, referring to the songwriting brother of Ralph Stanley, whose version of "O Death" in the *O Brother, Where Art Thou?* soundtrack propelled him to national fame.

Welch, who was also featured on the *O Brother* soundtrack and in a brief cameo in the movie, has since released four critically acclaimed solo albums, earned two Grammy nominations, but also returned to Rugby to headline the Wayne Henderson Music Festival.

"George Clooney did for old-time music what Bob Dole did for Viagra," Wayne Henderson is fond of joking. But while traditional musicians welcomed a little extra exposure that the Coen Brothers film provided, the reality is that this enduring tradition is the furthest thing from a fad. "There's a simplicity and a directness and an honesty to this music," said Rorrer. "It's unadorned. It has no veneer. It's all solid wood."

CHAPTER FIVE

1947

E VEN IN A PLACE where time is measured by guitar bodies
and fret jobs, a year can sneak by in a hurry. And by the
middle of June 2004, I was on my way back to Grayson County.
For the last ten years, the day before Father's Day has been also
the day of the annual Wayne C. Henderson Music Festival.

The festival is held at Grayson Highlands State Park, which
sits atop a five-thousand-foot peak in the Blue Ridge Mountains.
Stop at the scenic overlook—this rare view of the Blue Ridge
Mountains is prettier than any picture postcard—and you can see
Wayne's house and the guitar shop just a couple miles down the
road.

It all started simply enough. "Some people from the park
came down," Wayne recalled, "and said they'd like to have
another event and they said that I was well known enough they'd
like to attach my name to it. I thought that was pretty cool."

The festival soon took on a life of its own, with a board of
directors, full not-for-profit status, and an army of volunteers,
with just about everyone within a twenty-mile radius pitching in
in some way or another. The festival even has its own tiny
bureaucracy. The board meetings have printed minutes, and the
members bat around questions big and small, from who'll play to
who's in charge of carting the T-shirts from the storage bin to the
concession stands. While the board meetings are held in his din-

ing room, the event's namesake keeps it all at arm's length, making the coffee and avoiding the politics.

Wayne's job is to build the guitars. One of the highlights of the festival each year is the guitar competition, and Wayne builds a guitar for the winner, as well as one for the event's headliner. Some years, the lacquer's still drying on the third Thursday in June, but Wayne always seems to get the guitars done with at least a few hours to spare. The festival weekend also serves as a homecoming of sorts, an excuse for the lucky few Henderson guitar owners to return to Rugby. You can probably find three dozen of 300 Henderson guitars at the park on the day of the festival. It's an even more important day for would-be Henderson owners, like me. It's a chance to remind ourselves what we're waiting for, as well as to get some vital face time with the builder. Tony Rocci had flown cross-country from Seattle for five years in a row, and got his Henderson guitar in a near-record two years. Eric Clapton, who'd never been to the festival, was still waiting. If you expect a guitar within the decade you'd better be there. And so I was.

The 2004 festival—the tenth-anniversary event—generated a special buzz. The legendary Doc Watson, who played the first festival, would return as the headliner. And in addition to the regular guitar contest, there would be a tournament of champions, with each of the previous nine winners joining the new victor in the ultimate picking shootout. When I drove up to Chez Henderson the Friday before the festival, the yard was even more filled with cars than usual, with a couple of tents staked around the vehicles. And while the shop was quiet, the house was abuzz. A few local ladies were doing some last-minute cleaning for the giant after-party and Wayne's out-of-town houseguests were settling in. And two of the best guitar pickers on the planet had stopped by. Festival winners Robert Shafer and Adam Wright, the 2000 and 2001 national flatpicking champions respectively, were among those milling around in the living room.

But as usual the main attraction was the guitars. In the dining room sat three brand-new Hendersons: a mahogany dreadnought for the festival winner, a replica of a 1930s Gibson Nick Lucas–model for Richard Watson, Doc's grandson, and a special Brazilian rosewood dread for the Tournament of Champions winner. As if that wasn't enough, Wayne grabbed a trio of rare and valuable vintage Martins out of his collection, and Wayne, Adam, and Robert put the guitars through their paces ripping through "Sweet Georgia Brown," then "Arkansas Traveler."

I slipped into the room and put my own guitar down on the floor next to the fireplace. When there was a brief pause in the picking, I greeted Wayne. "What you got in that case?" he asked. Despite the houseful of company, and a small fortune's worth of his own guitars circulating around the room, Wayne was now fixated on the contents of an old, beaten-up Martin case. He laid the case flat on the hearth, fumbled briefly with the latches, and cracked open the lid.

"Nineteen forty-seven?" Wayne said in half a second, half-asking, half-telling.

I laughed out loud. In the same way that carnival barkers guess people's age or their weight, Wayne Henderson could start a little sideline dating guitars. I nodded, then shifted to shaking my head in amazement. Wayne had nailed the date of my new/old Martin D-18. It was virtually identical to thousands of guitars made over a twenty-year span, and yet he had pegged it to a particular vintage.

"How'd you do that?"

"Well, there's the Sitka top," he said. "And the pickguard." Did he sneak a peek inside at the serial number? I don't think so, but magicians never reveal their tricks. In truth, Wayne is a walking encyclopedia of American acoustic guitar history. He could tell you, for example, that for a few months in late 1947, the decorative heel cap on the back of the neck of most Martin D-28s were pointy, angular jobs, a feature not seen before or after. "Whoever was carving them must have liked triangles," he said with a laugh. "At least, until he got fired."

And then the conversation turned serious.

"That's a nice old guitar," he said, smiling, but his message was dead serious. "I'd like a guitar like that. I'd build you a nice, tight new one." Turns out Wayne was born in 1947 too, and one of the few missing pieces in his impressive guitar collection was a birth-year guitar.

At that moment I realized that Wayne suffers from GAS. GAS, short for Guitar Acquisition Syndrome, is an epidemic among guitar players. A victim sees a guitar, and immediately becomes fixated on it the way a two-year-old obsesses about Naughty Diesel from Thomas the Tank Engine. Somehow, possessing that guitar will bring joy to his world (victims are almost always male), cure him of his ills, and make him whole. Of course, once he gets that guitar, it doesn't quite work out that way. The instrument falls short of that Platonic ideal, or his paradigm of perfection shifts, so that once again, his reach exceeds his grasp. As Paul Simon once sang, "The thought that life could be better is woven indelibly into our hearts and our brains."

But, I thought, this was a special brand of weakness that was limited to us mere mortals, to the guys for whom a guitar could still be that magic sword. We seek a better guitar in the vain hope that it will make us better players. But Wayne could take a $100 plywood Yamaha and make it sing more sweetly than any of us could ever dream. And he routinely turned out guitars that any of us would trade our big toes for. Did the sword maker believe in the magical power of the blade? Clearly, here was one who did.

By comparison to the rest of Wayne's guitars, my D-18 wasn't special. I had bought it a couple of weeks before from an Internet acquaintance. Mr. Jody had put it up for sale in the classifieds of the Unofficial Martin Guitar Forum, a Web-based guitar bulletin board, needing the money to buy a house. In fact, he had also recently sold one of the few Hendersons that ever changed hands—number 72, a dreadnaught with a very skinny neck—that would find its way back to the house during festival weekend. I missed out on that one, but when a deal for the Martin with a guy from Alabama fell through, I sent Jody a check, and he sent me the guitar.

And truth be told, until I saw Wayne's reaction, I was still wondering about that old Martin. It had lots of heavy play wear. The top was rubbed to bare wood on either side of the soundhole, and there was a deep rivulet in the narrow gap between the pickguard and the bridge. The wood had been thinned to perhaps half its original thickness by a previous owner resting his pinky there as he picked a couple hundred thousand renditions of "Ragtime Annie." The heavy wear gave the guitar a certain mojo, and the neck was smooth and soft, all the finish worn off and the naked mahogany buffed by years of playing. The bridge had been replaced with a decent dark rosewood model, and the tuners with too–shiny modern copies. Tonewise, I was still taking its measure. It wasn't a particularly rare or terribly desirable guitar from a collector's standpoint, which was why I could afford it. Sure, it was more than a half-century old. But if guitars from that year represented a watershed for the Martin company, it was mostly in a bad way. Nineteen forty-seven was the first full year that Martin changed the tops of its guitars from old-school Adirondack red spruce from the East to the more plentiful Sitka variety that grew in the vast forests of the Northwest. The guitar was built differently too, with sturdy nonscalloped braces that were good for structural stability—Martins carried that lifetime guarantee—but prevented the top from vibrating as freely as the most desirable models from the late 1930s. My guitar was identical in most meaningful ways to thousands of D-18s that were made between '47 and '67. Still, we often measure the value of things— or at least I do—by the reaction of others. And Wayne's reaction was the last thing I expected.

The guitars in his collection were so good it was almost comical. A 1937 000-28 was freakishly clean, its yellow top still bright and cheerful as an egg sunny-side-up. It was roughly the same model as the guitar Eric Clapton played in his famous *Unplugged* concert, and two years older. But while Clapton's guitar had the finish worn off by years of playing, the top turned golden with age, this one looked more like a Martin reissue, a brand new Eric Clapton signature model fresh out of the box at Guitar Center. A little less clean, but even rarer, was a 1937 sunburst herringbone D-28. I picked it up, and while I wanted it, I wasn't gassing for it. I examined it with the resigned admiration I reserve for a Ferrari Daytona or a Vacheron Minute Repeater. This old herringbone was unattainable, a guitar that was worth more than my car, my wife's car, and all my guitars put together. Then Wayne pulled out his 1942 D-45. This was clearly the most valuable guitar I had ever touched, with a price tag usually reserved for real estate. Still, I got the impression that Wayne had mixed feelings about the guitar. He had paid $4,000 for it maybe twenty-five years ago, so it was the kind of investment that slaughtered the S&P 500. "A powerful deal," he explained.

But it also reminded him of the one that got away. A few years before he bought this D-45, Wayne was working at Gruhn Guitars in Nashville when Charlie Monroe's D-45 had come into the shop. Charlie is the brother of Bill Monroe, and he had, according to Wayne's recollection, sold the guitar to bluegrass pioneer Red Allen to pay his wife's medical bills, with the understanding he could buy it back when he got back on his feet again. But Allen sold it to Johnny Cash, who played it for a while, with his reckless strumming style. After a while, it ended up back at Gruhn's.

"Johnny Cash did that," said Gruhn disapprovingly, showing Wayne a few stray pick marks on this guitar.

And George told Wayne he could have it for four grand.

"I could have bought a Corvette for that," Wayne recalled. "I couldn't see how any guitar could be worth that kind of money." So he passed on the deal. Wayne was telling the all-too-American story of lost wealth, of near misses, about the lakefront property for five grand an acre, of Microsoft at $11, the Mickey Mantle rookie card that mom sold at a garage sale. A brief vacation in the land of what-if.

He even got a second chance at Monroe's guitar, after he had bought the D-45 he owned now. But since the guitar was on consignment at Gruhn the owner wanted cold hard cash, not just another slightly lesser D-45 and a player to be named later.

"It was a great guitar. Real balanced," Wayne recalled with a tinge of sadness.

"Nothing done to it. Had the original pickguard," he said longingly. This was a direct reference to the most significant flaw on his own D-45, a somewhat ugly oversized pickguard that covered part of the upper bout, applied at the Martin factory to cover some pickwear.

"What about this?" I pointed to a strap button applied in a slightly unusual position, on the side of the guitar, just at the edge of the neck block.

"I don't like that much," he said.

"How much does that bring down the value?" I asked rhetorically. "About that much," I said, pointing to my old '47.

This explained an awful lot. The guy with the best toys, the guy who made the best toys, wanted still more toys. He wanted *my* toy. Wayne understood his customers' yearnings, the aching as you wait for a guitar that's not quite yours yet. I understood now that he truly was one of us. And that's why he never said no to anyone asking him to build a guitar, although he knew that he probably should. That would be cruel, a crushing of dreams, and Wayne Henderson was too good a man to crush other men's dreams.

So Wayne passed the D-45 back to one of his houseguests. And he took one more look at the D-18 that was born the same year that he was. When someone called him from across the room—"Hey, Wayne"—we closed the case, literally and figuratively. For now, at least.

CHAPTER SIX

Third Saturday, Rain or Shine

THE WAYNE C. HENDERSON Music Festival, held every June since 1995, is an escape, a day for good times and forgetting your troubles. There's foot-stomping music, games for the kids, Kodachrome scenery, and a chance to catch up with old friends. But there is one solemn moment in the afternoon's proceedings: the presentation of first prize in the guitar contest. I remember the first time I saw it, in June 2003.

The finalists were lined up on the makeshift plywood stage like beauty pageant contestants, fidgeting while they waited for Herb Key to read the name of the winner.

"Roy Curry," Herb intoned.

Curry stepped toward the center of stage, as did Wayne Henderson, who was waiting in the wings with a dreadnought that he had finished building only a few days earlier. With five minutes of inspired picking, Curry had tapped into the only certain way to cut Wayne Henderson's guitar list: Win the contest, get a guitar. Wayne held out the shiny new instrument, proudly, but a little reluctantly at the same time. His face wearing a should-I-or-shouldn't-I grin, Curry reached for the guitar, and cradled it with both hands in the too gentle way you might hold a newborn baby.

Curry touched it reverently at first, almost afraid to mar its mirrory finish. And a few minutes later, just as appropriately, I saw him picking the living daylights out of his shiny new Excalibur. Fortyish, with a neatly trimmed mustache, a Hawaiian shirt, and a slightly goofy grin, Curry is everyone's brother-in-law, at least if your brother-in-law is a preternaturally gifted guitar player. He's won the National Flatpicking Championship twice. At one point, he recalled, he won thirty contests in a row. And since a single muffed note—a "clam" in guitarspeak—can torpedo a contestant's chances, that's a freakishly long run of clean picking. He'd won guitars aplenty in these contests, and had sold or traded every one, sometimes to pay for his trip to the festival, and at other times to raise some cash to repave the driveway or replace the dishwasher.

But his days of casually ripping through contests were past. Curry had driven from Chattanooga to Rugby in 2000. He finished third. He repeated the trip in 2001. Second. In 2002, second again. When he came to the 2003 Henderson festival, he was like the aging gunslinger, wanting just one last shot before he hung up his guitar pick for good. "I wanted to see if I had one more in me," he said to me still holding his prize. "And I said to my wife, 'If I win, I'm keeping the guitar.'" He did and he would.

To nonmusicians, the very idea of a guitar contest may seem strange. Music isn't a competitive endeavor. It's about the joy of self-expression. But players know better. On one level, it's about playing as well as you can. At another level, it's about playing better than the next guy. Most of the time the sparring is informal. One guy takes a lead break on a song, you take the next, and if the first guy nods his head—or better yet rolls his eyes—when you're done, you win. While there may not be a referee or a panel of judges, it's plenty serious. In the jazz and blues tradition, where it likely started with horn players, this informal competition is called, appropriately, cutting heads. (Indeed, this bit of jazzspeak probably gave rise to two popular bits of guitar slang: calling an instrument an "axe," which is especially common in the electric-guitar world, and referring to exceptional skill as "chops.")

In the world of American traditional music, the competition is often more formal, and that practice stretches back more than two centuries. As near as anyone can tell, the first American fiddle contest was held on November 26, 1736, as part of a St. Andrew's Day Celebration, and the winner took home a "fine Cremona fiddle" imported from Italy. By the mid-1920s, fiddle contests had gone corporate. Henry Ford was also an amateur fiddler who sawed out old-timey tunes like "Turkey in the Straw" on a 1703 Stradivarius violin that he had paid $75,000 for. Aiming to "revive the dances of our granddaddies, with all their innocent neighborly cavorting," Ford sponsored a series of fiddle contests at hundreds of his dealerships across the country. And in 1938, Joe Woods, the reigning national fiddle champion, looking for a business opportunity at the end of the Depression, started his own contest in Nashville, Tennessee. This event attracted twenty-seven fiddlers and a total of 9,400 spectators—who served as judges by means of an applause meter.

In 1934, at the first Old Fiddler's Convention in Galax, Virginia, a band featuring fiddler Walt Henderson won a yellow ribbon. By the mid 1960, Galax added a guitar contest to the long-standing fiddling, dancing, and band contests, and Walt's son, Wayne, began a ribbon collection of his own. Wayne Henderson won first place at Galax more than a dozen times—"Thirteen or fourteen, I don't remember"—and won more top-three ribbons than any other performer on any instrument.

So when the Henderson festival became a reality, Wayne's ambition was simple: to create a kind of dream guitar contest. The field would be small—twenty players on a first-come, first-served basis—so there wouldn't be much waiting around. It would be democratic: Anyone playing a guitar in any style with any implement could enter. In the late 1970s, Wayne traveled to the National Flatpicking Championship in Winfield, Kansas, he wasn't allowed to compete because he played with a thumbpick

and fingerpicks. ("I guess I could have snuck on, but they probably would have given me the hook," he said, laughing.) The judging would be impartial: The judges would be secluded in a tent,
where they can't see the contestants, and they can hear only the
lead guitarist's microphone feed. In the morning's preliminary
round each player does a tune. In the afternoon's final, the judges
cut the field to five, and each player rips through two tunes.

And the prize would be something worth fighting for. While
first prize at Galax is $110 and a ribbon, what's really at stake is a
year's worth of bragging rights. The first prize at the Henderson
festival is also priceless: a new W. C. Henderson guitar without
the ten-year wait. But once you win, you've got to step aside and
give someone else a chance.

Sort of. The 2004 festival had an added twist. For the tenth
annual festival there would be a second guitar contest. In addition to the regular contest, there would also be a Tournament of
Champions, in which each of the ten previous winners would
face off. The prize? A decade's worth of bragging rights. And a
Brazilian rosewood Henderson guitar. The real news was the
quality of the assembled pickers. Top to bottom, the field was
possibly the toughest of any guitar contest in history. Four of the
previous winners—Curry, Robert Shafer, Scott Fore, and Adam
Wright—had won the National Flatpicking Championship, and
two other champs, Steve Lewis and Brandon Bentley, had placed
at Winfield. This contest promised to be tougher than the
Nationals because there, players tend to win the title, maybe win
it again, and then retire from competition while the afterglow of
their achievement is still fresh in people's memories.

So while that Henderson guitar was a serious enticement, it
was hardly a given that all of the previous champions would
show up. In much the same way that winning a contest can buff
up a guitarist's reputation, losing tarnishes it. While the winner
got an amazing instrument, the losers got nothing more than a
hearty handshake, a barbecue sandwich, and a long drive home.

"It's a testament to Wayne," said Curry, summarizing the

sentiment that resulted in perfect attendance. "They wouldn't have done it for anybody else."

I ran into Curry in the mud backstage after the Tournament of Champions. He had just finished playing—a mid-afternoon rainstorm played havoc with the schedule—and was waiting for the judges to compile their scores. When I approached, he greeted me with a hearty handshake, remembering me from the previous year.

"I've been golfing more than guitaring," he said, laughing. "I spent all last week on a golf trip over near Asheville when I should have been practicing. When the nine other people you're playing against are all former champions, all the practicing in the world . . ." He stopped mid-sentence, and spun the negative into a positive. "You might as well go golfing." Curry was on vacation from his straight job. Being a two-time national flatpicking champion and the defending champ at the Wayne C. Henderson Music Festival only gets you so far. Curry works as a lab technician, Sunday through Thursday, with Friday and Saturday off.

"It pays the bills," he said with a shrug.

The talk, as it always does with Curry, turned to guitars. I asked him if, a year later, his Henderson was living up to his expectations. "The guitar I played last year was a really good instrument—a Nashville Guitar Company guitar. Marty Lanham makes them—and it's a marvelous guitar," he explained. "But when I won Wayne's and I took it home and played it in our little bluegrass band around Chattanooga, I sold that other one.

"I'm a mahogany guy," he concluded, saying that with the same kind of conviction that others might apply to "I'm a Baptist" or "I'm a Red Sox fan."

"I've got one old guitar and one new guitar," he continued. "I got a really good D-18. And I got a really good Henderson. So now I'm pretty happy."

I asked about his old Martin. "It's a '49. I knew it was the one when I brought it home and played it," he recalled. He had won a Collings guitar for taking second place at Winfield in 1999, and he traded that guitar and $900 for a friend's old Martin. "I've got the last D-18 I'll need for a while," he said with the half-smile of a committed bachelor who finally bought the ring and settled down.

"My wife said to me, 'I notice you don't look at any guitars anymore.' And I said, 'Yeah, you're right.' When I got my Henderson, I just quit looking. This is the first time I've been happy with two guitars." He paused for a long beat.

"It kind of sucks," he confessed, understanding that I would understand. "It's like a hunter who's got his limit."

How many guitars had Curry gone through in his career? "I counted it up once and it was ugly," he confided. "About twenty different ones over the years. Liking this one, liking that one."

"Do you mind?" I asked, as I got my '47 D-18 out of its case. I felt a little like the guy sipping a beer just outside an AA meeting, but I couldn't resist. I handed it over. Curry strummed a couple of chords, and launched into a little blip of "Blackberry Blossom."

He shook his head. "Boy, that's a good one," he said, as the last chord faded away. "That thing's *loud.*"

Curry spun it around, taking a quick look at the back. "It's in about the shape of mine," he assessed. "I don't have quite as much wear. And you've got the original case. Man, that's a nice guitar," he said with just a hint of longing in his voice. "You got lucky there."

As he handed it back just a little reluctantly, he knew he wouldn't be coming home with a second Henderson guitar today. He played with energy and drive and even humor—he snuck a riff from "Meet the Flintstones" into a medley of fiddle tunes. ("It kind of fit, and it was kind of fun.") But even with his Henderson-made Excalibur in his lap, he made a few too many mistakes to win a contest this competitive.

No trauma there. Curry's been trying to wean himself from the adrenaline rush of playing contests. Instead he's been spending his weekends closer to home, playing more gigs with his

group, the Lone Mountain Band, and delighting in the more sensuous pleasures of guitar playing. "A bluegrass band is a team,"
said the old gunslinger. "I like the rhythm aspect of the band
stuff better than I like contests. When you've got a good bass
player, a good mandolin chop, and a banjo, it's a bluegrass
orgasm."

TAKING THE STAGE as Curry and I conversed was an American legend.

Blind since childhood, Arthel "Doc" Watson, who hails from
nearby Deep Gap, North Carolina, all but singlehandedly made
the guitar a lead instrument in bluegrass and old-time music.
Until Watson came along, the guitar was relegated to providing
boom-chuck back up, punctuated perhaps by the occasional bass
run. During his stint in a rockabilly band in the mid 1950s, Doc
started playing fiddle tunes like "Black Mountain Rag" on a Gibson Les Paul electric, he's quick to remind you. Watson was discovered by Ralph Rinzler during the folk revival of the early
1960s, his clean, fast picking and deep baritone voice creating a
sound that was both new and totally familiar.

But before he was discovered, Watson struggled. He played on
the streets of Lenoir, North Carolina, grateful for the tips he got
from the factory workers flush from payday. Indeed, Wayne's
father, Walt, once shook his head when he looked at an early Doc
Watson album cover: "Someone ought to have told that poor
blind man that his fingernails were dirty."

At age eighty-one, Doc was still a force. His features were
rugged and angular, with a strong chin and a full shock of white
hair that's just a bit unruly. If you were to start Mount Rushmore
from scratch, with a broader eye toward honoring great Ameri-
cans, you could do worse than eliminate Teddy Roosevelt and
replace him with Doc Watson. And indeed, by the end of the
summer, Wayne had commissioned a more modest tribute to his
close friend and greatest influence: on his front porch is a magnif-

icent brick diorama of Doc and Wayne picking, built on site by Jeff Samples, a sculptor from Washington, in exchange for a Henderson mandolin. The shop wags have taken to calling it Mount Waynemore.

"Doc is my number one hero," Wayne often said. He remembered the first time he met him, at Gerald Little's Music Store in Boone, North Carolina, when he was little more than a teenager.

"Gerald handed me a guitar and said 'Play "Cannonball Blues"'."

As Wayne started playing, in walked Watson, and the young Henderson didn't know quite what to do—until Doc started singing. "That's pretty good picking, son," the legend told the star-struck fan. Doc and Wayne became friends and Watson is a periodic visitor to the shop.

Doc's performance that afternoon wasn't a concert so much as a musicology lesson. He started out with the George Gershwin standard "Summertime," then followed it up with "If I Needed You" by the late Townes Van Zandt. Van Zandt was the songwriter's songwriter—Steve Earle once said "Townes Van Zandt is the best songwriter in the whole world and I'll stand on Bob Dylan's coffee table in my cowboy boots and say that"—but to many he was remembered more for his carousing than for his craft. But as sung by Watson, this plaintive ballad earned a spot in the pantheon. Next up was "Louis Collins," a country blues ballad made famous by bluesman Mississippi John Hurt. Setting the song's oh-so-sad lyrics against a bouncy guitar line, Watson sang like a man who knew what it was like to lose a son. (His only child, Merle, a remarkable picker in his own right, was killed in a 1985 tractor accident.) As he sang the lines "Miss Collins weeps, Miss Collins moans" the skies opened up as if on cue and delivered a shower that was as delicate as teardrops. During the rain delay, Doc sat in the back seat of his maroon minivan, shaking hands and greeting fans with his special brand of down-home grace. When he returned to the stage, Watson launched into "Blue Suede Shoes." There wasn't an ounce of irony in his delivery. Instead of winking at Elvis, Doc's fresh and impassioned delivery focused on that lover who dared to dis him: "You can do anything, but lay off of my blue suede shoes," he growled. Watson's main set ended with that great old gospel tune "I am a Pilgrim." During his encore, he jammed on "Minor Swing" by the great gypsy jazzman Django Reinhardt, then ripped through "Bill Bailey," an old war song that had taken on new resonances at the turn of the millennium.

This set was remarkably eclectic, blind to every consideration of race, generation, or genre, music bound together only by one man's big heart and big ears. But Doc wasn't trying to lecture. He picked music he liked, and if it took his imprimatur to get the audience to listen with an open mind, then so be it. Louis Armstrong once said, "There is two kinds of music, the good and bad. I play the good kind." So does Doc Watson.

AFTER DOC'S SET, Herb Key announced the winner of all winners, Scott Fore. Fore was one of the favorites—he'd won Winfield in 2002—and he played clean and loud, ripping through a couple of classic contest tunes. As Fore walked to the front of the stage to collect the 2004 prize, his micro-cropped gray hair, immaculately pressed blue button-down shirt, and delicate rimless glasses gave him the air of the accountant that he, in fact, is.

To many in the crowd, Fore was the guy who played standing up. While most guitarists sit down when they play, Fore adopts a most distinctive posture on stage. He props one foot up on a folding chair and leans forward toward the microphone like a sprinter in the blocks. He looks like a man in a hurry.

"It started because I used to get so nervous in contests that my left leg would be shaking so badly it was shaking the guitar and it would mess me up," he explained just after he got offstage. "At home I had one of these folding chairs, and I wouldn't put the strap on, I'd kinda just throw my leg over the chair. I said, 'This feels comfortable. The guitar is at the right height for the mic.' So I started doing it in contests and because I could lean on my leg it stopped the leg from shaking. It kind of became a trademark."

"Contests are different than playing a show," he had confided to me earlier. "With a show you get to get onstage and warm up and get used to the mics and get used to the audience. You kind of warm into your best stuff. With a contest you have to jump up there cold, not sure what the sound system's gonna be, and you have to play your best tunes right off the bat. That's why contests are so hard."

Fore is nothing if not analytical. He sweats over each arrangement, deconstructing each tune, learning it in perhaps ten different positions on the guitar neck—from the lowest bass notes to the most tinkly trebles. He'll then take those basic melodies and mix in a variety of guitar techniques—harplike crosspicking, aggressive double stops, ringing open strings. "You might start out with twenty breaks and you end up with four that fit the time constraints of the contest," he explained. "Then you practice your arrangement until you can do it in your sleep." If you have time for sleep. When I asked him the secret of the afternoon's success, Fore didn't blurt an answer right out. "What's the secret?" Fore repeated the question, then pondered for another moment. "You have to play like yourself. Play your own stuff rather than copying someone else's tunes. You have to play really strong and clean and clear. And basically just play a song, not a lot of hot licks."

He paused, realizing that he had answered the question.

"You have to play a song, that's what you have to do."

CHAPTER SEVEN

A Bump in the Road

THE CLOCK OVER the door read 2:18 A.M. on Monday June 21, 2004. It was seven minutes slow, but Wayne Henderson didn't know this. He never wears a watch while he's working.

Eric Clapton is not the only one with an affinity for the hours after midnight. The wee hours of the morning, I learned quickly, are when things get done at the guitar shop on Tucker Road. The phone stops ringing, the visitors stop dropping in, and it's usually just Wayne and a pile of wood waiting to become a guitar. That's even the case on the third Sunday in June, the day after the festival. All evening the shop had been full of visitors, singing, playing, and drinking wine, bounding from Gillian Welch's "Orphan Girl" to Del Shannon's "Runaway." But now the population had dwindled to just three: Wayne, me, and Carmine Rocci—as Sunday night become Monday morning—a customer from San Diego who had flown in for the festival and was now getting the special opportunity to watch Wayne work on his guitar. Again. Wayne had started his beautiful Brazilian D-45 a year ago, gluing up the back, bending the sides, cutting the soundhole, and then put it aside like so many of the other half-completed guitars that litter the shop. It's easy enough to get Wayne Henderson to start a guitar, but getting him to finish one is another story.

This guitar had progressed far enough to earn a serial number:

the coveted number 300. And now Carmine was here, in person, so Wayne made magic. Working on only a few hours' sleep after the Festival party, Wayne buckled down and had between mid-afternoon and late night transformed a few pieces of wood into an almost completed guitar body. He was now sitting in his chair, savoring his favorite job, whittling on the braces on the underside of the guitar.

He scraped and talked and scraped and talked, and the talk, as it always does, turned to guitars. A few weeks before, I had met legendary bluegrass picker Tony Rice at the World Guitar Congress at Towson University and he gave me a little guided tour of his legendary 1935 Martin D-28. If there really is a holy grail among acoustic guitars, then the one that bears the serial number 58957 is it. After Rice's impromptu seminar, I had seen a group of grown men line up to genuflect before this guitar, and more accurately, to worship its provenance.

The great Clarence White had owned the guitar before Rice. In the 1960s, he took Doc Watson's flawless melodic picking to another level, adding modern influences to this traditional sound, in much the same way that a young Eric Clapton reinvented the blues. To listen to White's version of "Julius Finkbine's Rag"—a reinterpretation of the classic fiddle tune "Beaumont Rag" so radical it demanded a renaming—is to hear a genre being turned on its head. And his work with The Byrds, most notably on their country-tinged *Sweetheart of the Rodeo* album, presaged the alt-country movement of the 1990s. White's story, however, ends abruptly. In 1973 he was killed by a drunk driver while loading equipment after a gig, which, in the better-to-die-young-than-to-fade-away world of popular music, cemented his status as an icon.

When White bought it as a teenager at McCabe's Music in Los Angeles in the late 1950s, 58957 wasn't a valuable vintage instrument. It was just a beat-up old guitar. The previous owner had been a young woman folksinger from UCLA who had polio. She traded it in on a new guitar. You don't have to be Wayne

Henderson to see that 58957 is an example of improvisational luthiery at its most extreme. One of the early owners had a heavy picking hand, and literally wore out the wood around the soundhole. Some enterprising repairman took it upon himself to neaten things up, to smooth and even the soundhole, enlarging it by a half-inch or so. The fingerboard, which had needed to be replaced when the young Clarence bought it, is from a Gretsch, which features an nonstandard scale length, so it dangles over the soundhole like a gangplank. Before he died, White pawned the guitar to a friend to raise money for his wedding.

In the mid 1970s, old number 58957 ultimately ended up in the hands of White's friend Tony Rice, who more or less took over where White left off. Rice joined David Grisman's Quintet, and began employing the sophisticated harmonies used by jazz players. He took over the unofficial title of the picker's picker.

Hearing Rice's old Martin up close, it became clear to me why it sounded so great on record. Most dreadnoughts have a rich, bass-heavy tone, which makes them great for playing in jam sessions, or for backing up a singer, but this comes at a price. These unpredictable wolf tones are a recording engineer's nightmare. Number 58957, on the other hand is supremely balanced. The tone and volume stay even from string to string and up and down the fretboard.

When I mentioned my visit with Mr. Rice and his legendary guitar, Wayne said matter-of-factly, "It came in my shop to put a set of frets in it." He hardly looked up from the top braces he was sanding. "Tony Rice gave it to me at a show and had me refret it down to the fourteenth fret."

Wayne, as usual, was about to launch into a story that easily topped mine.

"When Tony Rice came through to pick up that guitar, all fourteen of those frets were laying on that old table there, and before he left he said, 'Did you throw those old frets away?'

"I said, 'Actually no, I've got them right there.'

"There are so many young players in the neighborhood who

are so crazy about Tony Rice that I done had the brainstorm that I was going to keep the old frets that were totally worn out and give them to the kids," Wayne recalled. "Like a souvenir.

"Tony Rice said to me, 'Well, I generally keep those.'

"That's the only time, in the thousands of fret jobs, that somebody asked for the old ones back," Wayne recollected, shaking his head. "I couldn't believe Tony Rice asked me for his frets back."

As for the guitar itself, Wayne searched high and low for the mojo.

"I looked at every brace and everything in it. Actually, it's about like my old guitar. The action is incredibly low and if you play it hard, it would buzz and rattle," he recalled. "I played it myself and listened to it as carefully as I could. It's a wonderful-sounding old herringbone," Wayne explained, referring to the top trim that distinguished prewar rosewood Martins. "Just sitting, picking on it, it didn't sound any different than any other really nice-sounding old herringbone. I think about 95 percent of it is in Tony Rice's touch," he concluded. "He just makes the tone come out so pretty."

The story about the reclaimed frets brought the talk around to money.

What's a guitar like that worth?

"I wouldn't be surprised if it sold for a million dollars or more," Carmine hypothesized.

"One of my guitars sold for $100,000," Wayne explained, and launched into a short version of the story of Tim Duffy's guitar, and the anonymous donor who wrote a six-figure check.

The story, of course, raised the legitimate question of why Wayne Henderson is the guitar builder with Eric Clapton still on his waiting list. Given that he can get a guitar done in a couple of weeks when he really needs to, why didn't he build the guitar ten years ago when he got the order?

Most other luthiers would drop everything to have the chance to build a guitar for a multiplatinum recording artist. T. J. Thompson, for example, turned a repair on Clapton's vintage 000-42 around in two weeks, motivated partially by the largeness of the shipping crate and partially by the importance of the client. (To be fair, a Thompson acoustic for Keith Richards remains unbuilt, a half-completed body in a rack of guitar parts owed to less famous guitarists . . . and stockbrokers and litigation attorneys.) Building Clapton's guitar was not going to make Wayne Henderson rich or famous, but it's more than faint praise when someone who can have any guitar on the planet wants one of yours.

But in a strange way, Wayne has always been somewhat ambivalent toward the whole Clapton guitar project. He really doesn't know Clapton's music and doesn't seem to care all that much. Once when "Layla" came on the car radio, I gestured toward the speaker. Wayne gave me a blank look.

"That's Eric Clapton playing that old Martin," I said.

"Oh, yeah," he replied, only thinly disguising his complete lack of recognition.

Indeed, while he'll sometimes tell people about the Clapton commission, he's wary about advertising it publicly. On the festival's Web site, Doc Watson is quoted praising one of Wayne's instruments: "That Henderson mandolin is as good as any I've had my hands on. And that's saying a lot, because I've picked up some good ones." But there's only a veiled mention of his most famous potential client. "There is a waiting list for Henderson's guitars made up of the famous (and not-so-famous)."

"Did you ever see that article in *People* magazine?" Wayne asked, almost rhetorically, about a two-pager on him that had appeared a few years before. "I told them I didn't want them to print that about Eric Clapton's guitar, unless they could verify it for sure, other than what I said. They said they would but they tried every way in the world to get ahold of him and they never could," he explained while sanding on Carmine's guitar top.

"I didn't want them to think I'm advertising I make guitars for Eric Clapton," Wayne said warily. "He asked for one, one time."

As he continued on the subject, I began to understand that there were several factors at work. The first variable factor is pretty obvious to anyone who has a glancing acquaintance with Wayne. It's the Squeaky Wheel Factor. If you want a Wayne Henderson guitar, you have to prod, cajole, remind, bribe, persuade, wheedle, prompt, and entice him. Eric Clapton, had done none of that.

"Did Eric ever call?" Carmine wondered.

"That's probably one of the reasons he never got a guitar," Wayne said with a chuckle.

And for a while, I think Wayne secretly took a bit of perverse pride in keeping a famous guitar player waiting while providing magnificent instruments for friends like Gabby who barely played at all.

But I sensed that that satisfaction faded long ago. The real issues keeping Eric Clapton from getting his Wayne Henderson guitar were now purely logistical: How does he get this guitar built and delivered to its famous owner? Practical problems never seemed to bother Wayne Henderson. If a guitar top is caving in, he'll devise a series of braces, cleats, and laminations to make it as good as new. But logistical problems are a different matter. If you want to make Wayne truly happy, just pick him up at the airport. Although he's traveled all over the world—from Sri Lanka to Nairobi—whenever Wayne Henderson is away from Rugby, he always seems a little wary about getting lost, stranded, or ending up in some sort of a mess. That's a big reason he's never adopted the motel-to-motel life of most musicians, where the only strange bed they sleep in is their own. He's only truly at home in the guitar shop, where the cast of characters is familiar and most problems can be solved with a band saw, a penknife, and the right piece of wood. But when it comes to the little bothers of the world, Wayne would just as soon delegate them to someone else, or simply avoid them altogether.

He recalled the roadblock that kept him from completing Clapton's guitar, and, fittingly, it seemed to revolve around a piece of wood.

"Tim Duffy discovered this stash of Brazilian rosewood that this speaker-building guy had," said Wayne. "At the time it was $400 a set. I thought that was outrageous. But, man, the quality of that stuff. They said it was actually from the 1930s. Perfect old Martin wood. They put these machines on it that measured how many vibration cycles it would do. I knew nothing about any of that, but it sure rang good.

"It had been handed down from a guy named Rudolph Zelnick, who was one of the most famous wood turners in eastern Kentucky," said Wayne, who couldn't name a single Eric Clapton song, but never forgets a source of wood. "He got to be eighty-something, and he decided that he's never going to use up all the wood that he had.

"Anyway, Tim found out about this guy's wood and made a deal with him and got enough to make a guitar. The piece had a big curl in it," he recalled.

Then the conversation circled back around to Clapton's guitar.

"I was going to *give* that guitar to Eric Clapton," Wayne explained. "I thought that would make Tim Duffy some points with him, that it would be some kind of a deal for their foundation. So I asked them to get me a set of that wood. They had a meeting and they decided that Eric Clapton didn't need to be given a piece of wood, he could afford to buy it himself."

We all laughed.

"Which is probably true," Wayne continued. "But if I got a piece of that wood I probably would have come closer to building it." And it was simple as that. With that simple refusal, this small bump in the road, Clapton's guitar got placed on the back burner indefinitely.

"I started bending some sides but I think I used them on somebody else's guitar," Wayne recalled. "I think the guy who was wiring my house got that set of sides. I glued up a top. I got a real pretty piece of Appalachian spruce from John Arnold," he added. "I have kept that top."

And with that little opening I sensed that Wayne hadn't

completely given up on the idea. His daughter, Elizabeth, would occasionally still prod him about it, not to mention the strangers who kept bringing it up, forcing him to hem and haw. "I always thought it'd be worthwhile just to make it," he said, as he continued to smooth the inside of Carmine's guitar with 220 grit sandpaper. "I could tell people, 'Yeah I made Eric Clapton's guitar.'"

Wayne didn't want much in return. "I'd want to see him get it. To give it to him or something," he added. "It would be cool if I had a letter or a note from him. If he sounded as nice as he did on that CD, I think he'd be happy to get it," said Wayne Henderson, half convincing himself to finish the guitar, half kicking himself for not having built it already.

I opened my big mouth. "Helen's JAM kids are always looking for money," I blurted, without thinking about what I was saying. His girlfriend started a worthy and underfunded music program—Junior Appalachian Musicians—for children in the Allegheny County school system where she works as a counselor. JAM was the rootsiest kind of grass roots program—where an eight year old can have a masterful musician like Wayne Henderson sit down for an hour and patiently teach him how to tune his instrument.

But the music was only part of the story. Many of the students in the program were at-risk kids, who lived in the kind of hopeless, violence-filled homes most people associate with the inner city. Helen told me the story of a troubled pre-teen whose father had committed suicide and whose mother was in jail. He learned to play fiddle in JAM, and he carries his violin around like a security blanket. That instrument has been his life raft in a sea of troubles. "We save lives here," Helen says without exaggeration. But like most worthy programs, there wasn't nearly enough money to help every kid who needed it.

"How about you make it some kind of a charity deal? You could build two guitars, give one to Clapton, and the other guitar, you could auction off to raise the money for JAM."

When he's really pondering something, I would learn, Wayne Henderson quiets down. Way down. For a good long moment the only sound in the shop was the ticking of the clock and the rhythmic scratching of sandpaper on spruce.

"That would be cool," he said.

And when he brought the question up to Helen at breakfast at Ona's the next morning, in front of Carmine and a dozen other witnesses, and she enthusiastically seconded the idea, I sensed that there was no turning back. At quarter to three the previous morning, I had just signed on to be the official liaison between Wayne Henderson, master guitar builder, and Eric Clapton, master guitar player, over the small matter of an instrument.

CHAPTER EIGHT

Lot 19

T WO HUNDRED THOWWW—SAND dollars. Thank you, sir," intoned the auctioneer, his tone crisp, British, redolent of money.

"Two hundred ten thowww—sand dollars. From the gentleman on the *phone.*

"Do I hear . . ."

Within moments, a 1939 Martin 000-42 bearing the serial number 73234 went from being a nice old instrument with an interesting history to the most valuable acoustic guitar in history.

The scene was the main auction room at Christie's auction house in Manhattan, the evening of June 24, 2004, just a few days after my late night heart-to-heart with Wayne after the festival. The event was the second Crossroads Guitar Auction. Five years earlier, on June 24, 1999, Eric Clapton decided to auction 101 of his guitars, with the proceeds from the sale to go to the Crossroads Centre, a substance-abuse treatment center in Antigua. Some fine instruments were sold in that first auction, most notably Brownie, the 1956 Fender Stratocaster electric guitar on which Clapton wrote "Layla," which brought a record $497,500. And that 1974 Martin 000-28 with a large bumper sticker on its side—aka the Rodeo Man guitar—that was used to record "Beautiful Tonight" brought $173,000. Indeed, it's possible that the idea of selling guitars as a fund-raising tool may have occurred to Clapton after the Henderson guitar he lusted after brought a cool one hundred grand for Tim Duffy's Music Maker Relief Foundation.

But that first Crossroads sale was just an appetizer to the second auction's feast of fine wood. "If anyone present today attended the last Crossroads Guitar Auction, you may be wondering where all these guitars come from," Clapton wrote in the introduction to the sale catalogue. "Well the truth is these are the instruments that I kept back from the last sale because I just couldn't bear to part with them. This is the A-team, the guitars that helped me shape my vision and taught me to play."

Among the treats up for sale at the second Crossroads auction were the 1964 Gibson ES-335 electric that he used when he played with The Yardbirds, and Blackie, the 1956–57 composite Stratocaster that was Clapton's main axe during his string of 1970s hits like "Cocaine" and "Lay Down Sally." Blackie would bring $959,000 (including buyer's premium), easily surpassing the half-million set by Brownie, and broken earlier in the evening by the $847,500 fetched by the Yardbirds ES. That said, Blackie's final sale price disappointed many who thought the guitar would be the first to crack the million-dollar mark.

But my eye was on that 1939 000-42, known in the catalogue as Lot 19. Lot 19 hardly needs an introduction to a Clapton fan, or even anyone with a passing interest in popular music. It's better known as the *Unplugged* guitar, the acoustic that Clapton played on his career-changing *MTV Unplugged* special in 1992.

"The picture of Clapton playing this guitar, which appeared on the CD cover for the multimillion-seller *Unplugged* album, has become one of the most enduring images of recent music history," said the catalogue description with only a thin veneer of hyperbole.

Specifically, Lot 19 was the guitar upon which Clapton played the loping version of "Layla" that struck a chord with so many aging baby boomers. Wearing a loose-cut dark suit over a gray checked shirt buttoned to the collar without a tie, a close-cropped beard, and horn-rimmed glasses, Clapton looked like the hippest English professor at NYU. And with Lot 19 on his lap as the accessory that completed the outfit, he smiled wryly and told the assembled faithful, "See if you can spot this one." The groove-heavy guitar riff was laid-back enough for Lite FM, and a clean and sober Clapton was giving it the smooth sell. (Eagle-eyed viewers will note that he kept flipping the bird to the audience, inadvertently one assumes, as he grabbed for a barred B-flat chord.) In the *Unplugged* version, the Guitarist Formerly Known as God still begged his beloved to "ease his worried mind," but at first listen it sounded as if he were stressed about the lease payments on his Mercedes and whether to max out his 401(k).

Still, this bouncy, even sentimental, blues moment was significant because it summoned the demons of a simpler time. The plugged version of the song, on the 1970 album *Layla and Other Assorted Love Songs*, by Clapton's band of the day—Derek and the Dominos—was a rock and roll touchstone. "There are few moments in the repertoire of recorded rock where a singer or writer has reached so deeply into himself that the effect of hearing them is akin to witnessing a murder, or a suicide," wrote rock critic Dave Marsh in the *Rolling Stone Illustrated History of Rock and Roll*. "To me, 'Layla' is the greatest of them."

On the plugged version, Duane Allman's tidy introductory riff bit like an angry rottweiler, and Clapton's vocal verged toward primal scream territory. The coda, with Clapton's and Allman's guitars soaring and searing over a piano groove laid down by drummer Jim Gordon, is an eloquent rebuttal to every self-indulgent guitar solo in rock and roll history. It elucidated everything that Clapton left unsung.

"Layla" aged better than much of the music of the day because it owed more to the primal blues of, say, Robert Johnson—the song's last line "don't tell me all my love's in vain" is an overt homage to the late Delta bluesman—rather than to the psychedelic stylings of Jefferson Airplane or Zager and Evans. Its message—I love you, but you don't love me—remained simple, but universal.

But heard twenty years later, it was also a reminder of a pre-tabloid age when one rock star (Clapton) could write a paean to the wife of another (Patti Boyd, who was married to George Harrison) without irony. "Layla, you got me on my knees," Clapton implored earnestly, and all of America let the double entendre slide past.

Martin Scorsese understood this music's power. He used the coda as mood music for perhaps the most memorable scene in his classic 1990 gangster film *Goodfellas*. The music soars over a montage that reveals one by one the final resting places of the fellow mobsters that Robert De Niro had whacked. It ends with the ill-fated Frankie Carbone—he had bought his wife a flashy white mink with the loot from a robbery—in the back of a freezer truck, hanging in poetic repose on a meat hook. "When they found Carbone in the meat truck, he was frozen so stiff, it took them two days to thaw him out for the autopsy," said Ray Liotta's voice-over, almost casually, as the music faded.

Clapton understood the song's backstory too in a different way. The years between the beginning of the 1970s and the beginning of the 1990s were especially unkind to the other members of Derek and the Dominos. Guitarist Duane Allman died of head injuries when he crashed his Harley only a year after the album's release. He wasn't wearing a helmet, and he was twenty-four. Bassist Carl Radle died in 1980 of kidney disease, probably the result of drug abuse, at the age of thirty-seven. Less than a year earlier, Clapton had fired Radle, sending him a pink slip by telegram. Clapton never saw Radle again and later admitted, "I hold myself responsible for a lot of that." He dedicated his 1981 album, *Another Ticket*, to Radle. In 1983 drummer Jim Gordon, suffering from schizophrenia, murdered his mother with a hammer and a knife and was sentenced to sixteen years to life, serving much of that sentence in a mental hospital.*

---

*Keith Relf, a member of Clapton's earlier band The Yardbirds, suffered one of the most ironic of rock deaths, being electrocuted by his own electric guitar. Some reports, probably apocryphal, suggested that he was soaking in his bathtub at the time, while a tamer version blames an ungrounded amplifier in his basement. Another advantage, perhaps, of unplugging.

As for Clapton himself, he fared better in facing down his demons. As the 1980s turned into the 1990s, he had conquered his addictions to heroin and alcohol, doing much of his rehab in Antigua, home of the Crossroads Centre.

Then in March 1991, he suffered his own personal tragedy. His four-year-old son, Conor, fell out a picture window on the fifty-third floor of the Manhattan penthouse apartment of his mother, actress Lori del Santo. The window was apparently left open by a housekeeper who had just cleaned it. It was the sort of accident against which fame and wealth provide no protection. Indeed, in the aftermath of the tragedy, Clapton admitted that he engaged in guitar therapy of a sort, putting the instrument down only to sleep.

One of the products of that period was "Tears in Heaven," a song of anguish as unvarnished as "Layla," but far more immediate. He performed "Tears" during the *Unplugged* show, putting down Lot 19, picking up a softer-voiced nylon-string classical guitar, lighting a cigarette and bearing his soul. "Would you know my name, if I saw you in heaven?" he sang just above a whisper. While few knew the song—at that point, it had only seen the light of day on the soundtrack of the low-profile movie *Rush*—everyone immediately knew what he was singing about. Even the background singers seemed choked up.

After hearing "Tears in Heaven," a twenty-year-old song about unrequited love had lost its urgency. But "Layla" hadn't lost its meaning. This acoustic version wasn't about passion and outrage, it was about sadness and acceptance. In short, "Layla," like the man singing it, had grown up. And the audience understood.

And in the hours before the auction, the guitar that distilled all of that lore into three minutes sat quietly on a stand atop a white cube, bathed in halogen spotlights in Christie's Gallery Six, dwarfing even the cedar-topped Juan Alvarez classical on which Clapton played "Tears in Heaven."

Lot 19 was the literal and figurative centerpiece of the collection of Martin acoustics that Clapton was ridding himself of.

And make no mistake, Clapton has great taste in guitars. This selection of Martins—nineteen guitars in all—formed a collection finer in its breadth and depth, for example, than those found at the small museum in the Martin guitar factory. There was a Martin 0–27, which featured abalone trim around the soundhole, and a rare, colored detailing in place of herringbone purfling on the far more common model 28. A 1915 0–42 featured a bridge carved out of elephant ivory. There was a 1929 00–45 that's only a few serial numbers away from Ella, my similar but plainer '29 00–28. There's a 1949 D-28, virtually identical to a guitar that looms large in Wayne Henderson's legend. And there was the Longworth, a 1966 000-28, adorned with pearl trim by Mike Longworth, a skilled luthier as well as the world's foremost Martin guitar historian. The so-called Longworth guitar, which is pictured on the back cover of Clapton's *461 Ocean Boulevard* album, can be identified by a tiny L inlaid in the fretboard below the eighteenth fret.

But in the center of it all was Lot 19, the *Unplugged* guitar.

While I stood there, nosing around the guitar, peering at its scars from six inches away, even sniffing its soundhole, a young Japanese man approached with a young woman from the Christie's staff in tow. He was wearing a T-shirt and trendy black-framed glasses and was armed with a digital camera that was in clear violation of the auction's no photography policy. He gestured toward Lot 19 a few times. She grabbed the guitar off its stand, holding it by the neck, and moved quietly through the crowded room, with the young man trailing behind.

It was a refreshing sight. In a guitar shop, these guitars would be treated like priceless artifacts, locked away behind glass and handled only with white gloves. At Christie's, where they're used to buying and selling truly pricey objets d'art—Picasso oil paintings and Stradivarius violins—even these astonishingly pricey guitars were treated casually. Indeed, the ultraconservative estimates on the guitars—$60,000 to $80,000 for Lot 19— seemed to say, "If you have to ask, you can't afford it."

Ten, maybe fifteen minutes later, the young woman returned with Lot 19, plopping it back up onto the stand. The young man had just played the holy grail of acoustic guitars. He seemed nonplussed.

"Too much pressure here," he said in English that wasn't much better than my nonexistent Japanese.

I guess the look on my face revealed my lack of comprehension. This wasn't some sort of wry commentary on his anxiety at the impending auction. He was trying to convey a simpler idea, and he resorted to sign language. He mimicked playing chords on the upper reaches of the neck, in the area near the soundhole.

"*Plays* better," he said pointing to a similar guitar on a stand across the aisle.

"*Sounds* better," he said, pointing back at the *Unplugged* guitar.

He was an electric guitar player, and he found the action—the height of the strings above the fingerboard—of this acoustic guitar too high for his liking. Still, his private audience indicated that he was clearly a serious buyer. He pointed to the lot card. "One more zero," indicating the $60,000 low estimate, upping it by an order of magnitude.

Indeed, the Crossroads auction came to be about the price of provenance . . . and magic. Lot 19 had a twin brother also on the auction block, Lot 20, the guitar that the young Japanese man was pointing to. Lot 20 is also a '39 000-42. The serial number is 73241, only a few digits away from the *Unplugged* guitar's 73234. According to the Martin guitar factory's records, both guitars were started on the same day, September 15, 1939.

To even an expert eye, these two guitars were virtually identical. Both sported similar blondish Brazilian rosewood backs and sides, and Adirondack spruce tops that had aged to a lovely pumpkin shade.

Lot 20 also had the same kind of modest play wear that gives a vintage guitar its vibe. In short, there was little to pick and choose from between these guitars. Lot 19 had five of its six original tuners—a minor consideration—while Lot 20 had a little less wear, and an even prettier pumpkin-colored spruce top. That said, these guitars were about as identical as two sixty-year-old guitars could be. They even smelled the same.

To better understand Lot 19, I visited my friend T. J. Thompson at his guitar shop after the auction. The world of high-end acoustic guitars is a small one, and it turns out that Thompson, who had repaired Ella, had his hands inside Clapton's old Martin long before it was the *Unplugged* guitar.

"I just thought it was a beautiful guitar," he recalled. "And I thought it was one of the nicest-sounding guitars I've ever heard. He laughs a little at the condition report on the guitar—one of his clients had bid a mid-six-figure sum for Lot 19, and his offer still fell short by the price of a modest house.

"It said it looks like the bridge plate may have been replaced. I actually did that work on the guitar."

With that, Thompson reached for a piece of wood that was hanging on the pegboard next to his workbench. It was the bridge plate of the Clapton guitar, a piece of maple that's glued to the underside of the spruce top, reinforcing the area so that the ball ends of the steel strings don't pull through the soft top wood. This bridge plate was beyond shot. There was just a single gaping hole where six discrete string holes should have been.

"There's just no stiffness to support this little thing," said Thompson.

He handed it to me.

Thompson had replaced the bridge plate, picking just the right piece of maple, and then kept it out on the windowsill in direct sunlight for a couple of weeks until it aged enough to match the rest of the guitar. The punch line was that Thompson not only replaced the bridge plate, which Christie's staff had detected by sticking a lighted mirror into the soundhole, he also replaced the bridge itself. It was a factory quality job.

How did Lot 19 end up at Thompson's shop in West Concord, Massachusetts?

"I think they knew that he wanted to have it for a long time, take it on the road, and they wanted to make sure it was road-worthy," Thompson surmised.

He still remembers the guitar's grand entrance. "It was kind of a funny scene," Thompson recalled, as he put the bridge plate back on the peg. "It arrived overnight express from London, in this huge shipping crate with G-force meters all over it so you could tell if it had been dropped or turned upside down."

"The guy couriered it out from the airport, and I met him out back, right by the train tracks. It's really scary back there," T.J. explained, setting the scene. "He was really nervous. I shook his hand and he couldn't believe it was me. I was dressed like this." He indicated his attire: a glue-stained T-shirt and a pair of ratty cargo shorts. "He was expecting a red carpet and a suit or something.

"I just let him stew." Thompson laughed. "After he'd had enough, I just kind of explained to him that we have a choice. We could go into downtown Boston and have a vault, like we were working on Stradivarius violins, or we could sequester ourselves in this funky little place with no sign in a building that no one would break into."

At the time, Thompson was more impressed with the way the guitar was handled than with the guy who owned it. "I was kind of a fingerstyle guitar snob," he recalled. "I didn't really know much about Clapton because it wasn't the music I listened to."

Others were more impressed, including a friend's girlfriend. "She found out that the guitar was here and she wanted to know if she could come over and rub her breasts on it."

"Did she?"

Thompson blushed. "I said she was welcome to, but I don't remember her actually doing anything."

What was more memorable was the way the guitar came together.

"I really like that guitar. And it's rare that I pick up a guitar and play a guitar that I want to keep playing and I don't want to put down. I was pretty impressed," said Thompson with characteristic understatement. "You could tell it was going to be a great guitar, but I didn't expect it would be a guitar I couldn't put down."

And that from T. J. Thompson, is saying something. He has repaired many of the world's best-sounding guitars—indeed, like a doctor with a particular specialty, he essentially limits his practice to pre–World War II Martins. When T. J. Thompson says that a guitar is something special, it is.

"It helped me to understand that Clapton knows what he's talking about when he picks up a guitar and plays it," T.J. continued. "My guess is that he kept it, held on to it, and played it because he knew that it was a great guitar. He wasn't just collecting. He was looking for a guitar that sounded great. And I happen to concur."

And so does the man who put together the Crossroads auction, Kerry Keane, vice president of musical instrument sales at Christie's. He remembered vividly the first time that he played Lot 19. It was October 2003 at Olympic Studios in London, where Eric Clapton was recording *Me and Mr. Johnson.*

"On Saturday we went into the studio to see the instruments that we were going to include in the sale but that Eric was still using," Keane recalled. "There's this rack of Martins and [Clapton's guitar tech] Lee Dickson hands me Lot 19. I sat down, and I fumbled through something like 'Deep River Blues.' I just said to Lee, 'Cancel my bus ticket, this boy is in love.' This was one of the finest guitars I've ever played."

Armed with that knowledge, I began to look at the results of that evening differently. Lot 19 brought $700,000, while the all-but-identical Lot 20 brought a mere $95,000, a modest amount when you consider that a similar guitar with no Clapton connection could easily command $50,000.

A cynic would say that it was all hype, the result of a celebrity-crazed society where a used piece of bubble gum chewed by a major leaguer can command thousands of dollars on eBay.

But there's another way to look at it. Lot 20 is a fine vintage guitar. But for some reason, Lot 19 has the magic that captivated T. J. Thompson, Kerry Keane, and Eric Clapton too. That magic is the reason he took Lot 19 up on that MTV soundstage to play "Layla."

Clapton made an appearance at the Crossroads auction, having slipped in through a side entrance, and watched the proceedings from a glassed-in luxury box above the auction floor, where he was invisible to most of the bidding floor.

When other guitars drew six-figure bids, like a Fender Strat that was worth a couple thousand dollars tops without his imprimatur, I could see him laughing, holding his hand to his forehead in disbelief. But when Lot 19 was auctioned, he smiled a sad smile, as a guitar he'd miss headed to its new home. As the gavel dropped at $700,000 plus buyer's commission, it was as if Eric Clapton was saying, "Someone just got a bargain." And perhaps, "I'm in the market for another magical guitar."

CHAPTER NINE

A Curse Reversed

"Y OU HAVE TO HAVE an angle," Donna confided to me, in the corner of Wayne's kitchen, while the world's greatest guitar maker was trying to decide whether to use the new microwave or the old one to heat up a sweet potato.

Donna Niemi lives across Tucker Road from Wayne. She's tall and cheerful, with a dark bob, a touch of makeup, and a welcoming smile. On one of my first trips to Rugby, Wayne had invited her and her husband, Doug, over to meet me; I somehow evolved from just another guitar customer to his best-selling writer friend who writes a sports column for *The Wall Street Journal*. But it turns out that the pleasure in meeting Wayne's neighbors was all mine. Donna is almost an honorary Wood Brother. The Wood Brothers were NASCAR's top pit crew, and propelled the late, great Jim Clark to victory at the 1965 Indianapolis 500. They were my heroes. I read and reread their exploits in *Great Moments in Auto Racing*—the book I hid inside my math textbook in fourth grade. Watching them change four tires in thirteen seconds was ballet in motion, but what captured my ten-year-old imagination was the way they sweated the details—polishing the hose connectors so that the fuel would flow faster on every pit stop. These guys were her uncles, and I was in awe. I had had my brush with greatness for the day.

But while Wayne was out of earshot, Donna also had some

practical advice for me. She'd seen plenty of people try to get guitars from Wayne Henderson, and she knew that just sending Christmas cards wouldn't cut it. What worked for her? "Pies. Wayne likes pies," she confided to me. So she took advantage of her talent and proximity. She baked pies and delivered them fresh from the oven. Cherry pies. Blueberry pies. Lemon pies. Especially lemon pies. And that is why Doug got his Henderson guitar sooner rather than later.

But finding just the right angle wasn't easy. Wayne can smell insincerity a mile away. Another would-be guitar customer tried to muscle in on Donna's turf and brought a lemon pie. It sat in the refrigerator, a quarter eaten, and he hasn't done a lick of work on the guitar since. What would my angle be? Well, on my first trip to Rugby in June of 2003, Wayne led me into his dining room.

"Let me show you something," he said excitedly.

He reached into the junk drawer of the buffet in his dining room, and fished out an old baseball in a plastic holder. He handed it to me. It was covered with ink, and the first signature I see is Dodger great Don Drysdale. Below it is Jackie Robinson. Pee Wee Reese. Duke Snider. Roy Campanella. Gil Hodges. Carl Furillo. Sal Maglie. Walter Alston. This ball is autographed by every member of the 1957 Brooklyn Dodgers, the team's last year on the East Coast.

"Is that Sandy Koufax?" I asked.

I scrutinized the signature more carefully and realized it's Sandy Amoros. The left-handed bonus baby's scrawl was there too, but it was smaller, crammed between two other Dodger vets. I'm not the kind of guy who gets all weepy about a game-used Don Mattingly bat, but touching this ball gave me chills. It wasn't merely that these were guys who could hit a line drive or throw a curveball for a strike. These were men of honor and integrity. Robinson tore down baseball's color barrier, then stoically bore a torrent of insults from fans, rivals, and even teammates. Reese, a man raised in the South, stood by his new friend, even though it cost him more than a little abuse. And Koufax, one of the few Jewish players in the Gentile world of baseball, refused to pitch a World Series game because it fell on Yom Kippur.

How did a ball such as this end up in Rugby, Virginia?

"A guy from Brooklyn gave it to me," Wayne explained. "His father owned a barbershop and all the players used to come around for haircuts." Like any number of shotguns, parts for his 1957 Thunderbird, and who knows what else, this remarkable ball was part of Wayne Henderson's elaborate barter system. Seven Hall of Famers = one guitar.

This is one story that doesn't have a happy ending.

"He was down for the festival, staying over at Gerald Anderson's, and he just dropped dead of a heart attack." Wayne shook his head. "Just about the worst thing that ever happened around here."

OVER THE COURSE of the summer, I began to see my angle. Summer is the time of relative inactivity at the guitar shop because most weeks Wayne is either playing music or teaching. In July, I caught up with Wayne at the Puget Sound Guitar Workshop, just outside of Seattle. I took his class and we sat outside the cabin under hundred-foot spruces, while Wayne taught us these age-old fiddle tunes the way he had learned them. He'd play a phrase, then we'd try to play it back. It was music teaching in its most organic form. And in these sylvan surroundings, even a halting version of "Wildwood Flower" played in shaky unison by a bunch of neophyte pickers took on a certain timeless beauty.

In August, I saw Wayne at the Penland School of the Arts. A half-dozen students, most of them young and having only the vaguest idea of what a great guitar sounded like, much less how to build one, worked sixteen-hour days trying to get a guitar done in two weeks. Wayne was the mother hen, fixing problems both little (chipped lacquer around the holes drilled out for a tuner) and big (a student who started scalloping the wrong braces). I was there when these instruments were strung up, and every one of them sounded like a Henderson.

On those trips, a pattern emerged. One of the first questions Wayne asked me was, "You been to any baseball games?"

"A couple."

"I'd like to see Yankee Stadium sometime," he said. "But I sure would like to see Fenway Park."

I assured him he had an open invitation to the Bronx anytime he could get up to New York during baseball season. Boston? That was a different matter. Red Sox tickets are tough to come by at any time of the year. For the last couple years Wayne has been teaching at Old Time Music Camp North near Boston in the middle of October. That would be playoff time. Those are the kinds of tickets for which New Englanders mortgage their house—or their firstborn. Every time I called, Wayne kept talking about the Red Sox, and I kept hemming and hawing. As the summer drew to a close, he wore me down. I finally said, "I'll see what I can do."

It was the most qualified promise of my life. *If* the Red Sox make the playoffs. *If* they win their first-round matchup. *If* they're playing at home. And the biggest if of all: *If* I can score tickets.

All the ifs came to pass. When it was clear that the Red Sox would be playing at Fenway the week that Wayne would be in Boston, I started asking around. I called a guy I knew at Major League Baseball. He was, at best, an old acquaintance, someone I once worked with on a book.

Now, I don't normally do this. I don't like asking for favors, even small ones, even for myself. I've never called and tried to score tickets to anything for anyone—not best friends, not editors, not my own kids. But the pursuit of a Henderson guitar makes people do strange things. I picked up the phone.

My MLB contact was having his calls screened.

"What is this in reference to?" asked a polite young woman.

I couldn't bring myself to come right out and say.

"He'll, um, know what it's about."

"Can you please tell *me* what it's about?"

"Well, it's, um . . . well, about my media credentials." I would be covering some of the games for the *Journal*.

"Let me transfer you."

"Uh, wait"—and before I could even hang up I was talking to an assistant in the PR office. I concocted some pretext about checking to make sure my application was in order. He checked, and it was all good.

"Oh, yeah, I was also wondering about the possibility of getting a couple of tickets for Game 5 if Boston makes the ALCS and—"

"You'll have to talk to Heather, her e-mail is . . ."

Likely the woman who had screened my call.

But I'm smoother in an e-mail that I am on the phone. I sent her a missive, mostly explaining who I was, who I wrote for, and parenthetically explaining who the tickets were for, to give the request an air of legitimacy, so that she wouldn't assume that I was going to scalp the tickets on eBay.

Within minutes, a reply popped up in my e-mail.

"Wayne Henderson? THE Wayne Henderson?" the e-mail emoted. It turns out that Heather was one of a tiny handful of devoted Wayne Henderson fans in New York City. She *loved* bluegrass and old-time music. She'd be happy—no, *honored*—to help Wayne out.

"We don't always get the best tickets," she apologized. "But I'll do what I can." I rearranged Wayne's plane tickets. We were going to Fenway.

I carried those tickets around for a week and felt a warm glow every time I caught a glimpse of them in my wallet. But I also had visions of getting my pocket picked, leaving my wallet in the washroom, one of my kids choosing this moment to try out the paper shredder. I carry around my laptop, my cameras, and valuable old guitars, all without so much as a second thought, but somehow these two pieces of printed cardboard took on an unexpected gravitas. I hid them at the back of my wallet away from the cash, next to the receipts from the video store.

The first two games of the playoff series at Yankee Stadium were ugly from Boston's point of view. It started with Boston's ace Curt Schilling pitching like he was throwing batting practice and went downhill from there. The Yankees won the first two games, setting up the very serious possibility of a New York sweep. Which meant there would be no game five at all. With a few well-timed swings of a Yankee bat, these tickets could be transformed into useless rainchecks procured at great cost.

But the afternoon Wayne and I arrived in Boston—I picked him up at Logan Airport—it began to rain. Biblically. As the puddles overflowed and merged and the gravel-covered parking lot at the Old-Time Music Camp became a pond, then a lagoon, we were only a few minutes away from gathering the animals two by two. Which also meant that game four was officially rained out and our game five tickets would become game four tickets. Come hell or, more likely, high water, Wayne and I would see a baseball game.

On Saturday night, the Yankees beat the Red Sox 19–8, setting official records for runs, hits, and homers and an unofficial mark for whup-ass piled upon a hated opponent. On the jam-packed T after the game, the normal "Yankees Suck" anger had given way to an air of frat boy resignation. "Well, at least we got the Patriots, duuuuuuude!" shouted one college student wearing a blue Sox sweatshirt and a Boston cap turned backward. "Go Paaaaats!"

The pall over the city was palpable. Tickets that would have brought more than $1,000 apiece earlier in the week—not that I was really thinking about selling them—were now being fire-saled for a couple hundred. Game four was a deathbed vigil for the Sox, and fans were looking for any excuse to avoid it. No one wanted to be there when the hated Yankees performed the coup de grâce.

But there was no pall over Wayne Henderson. He had spent

fifty-eight years on this planet and never seen a big league baseball game. All that was about to change. As we drove past the
back side of Fenway's Green Monster, his eyes lit up like a little
boy's on Christmas morning. Making small talk, the conversation turned to the Clapton guitars.

"Well, I guess I could get them done if I put aside three weeks
or a month," he said. "If you think that you can get them to
him."

"No problem," I fibbed. "What's your wood supply like?"

"It's hard to get good Brazilian, and what I've already got is
mostly spoken for." And with that, we pulled up in front of the
hotel, and that conversation was put on hold. Time to dump the
luggage and head to the ballpark. I fished for the tickets. Still
there. We stopped for a quick photo op at the giant bronze monu-
ment of Ted Williams, the notoriously cantankerous slugger posing beatifically with a little boy, and went inside. We wandered
through the bowels of the dumpy old ballpark, heading toward
right field. The corridors of Fenway, dingy, crowded, and confus-
ing, were thoroughly underwhelming. I could see that Wayne
was a bit uncomfortable, no doubt wondering in graphic detail
what might happen if we got separated. A missed flight back to
Rugby? A night in a Boston jail? Or worse? I took a quick peek
back every half-dozen steps just to make sure he was following
me, but he was right on my tail.

I had a plan. This stadium deserved an unveiling. We headed
out to Section 35 in center field, site of not only the best view in
the park, but simply the most magnificent vista in all of baseball.
As you emerge from the staircase, the drab concrete of the stadium walkways gives way to a vast expanse of perfectly mani-
cured Kentucky bluegrass.

"Awwww, heeeeeck," Wayne said just above a whisper, drawing out both syllables. He intoned it about as reverently as you
can say a phrase like that.

The October air was crisp and clear, the fading twilight blend-
ing with the cool white glow from the light towers. The skeleton

of the old stadium was green and the field was even greener. Even the bright-red Budweiser sign that loomed above home plate somehow looked like God had put it there.

We headed out to deeeeep right field to Section 42, Row 37, Seat 21, a single bright-red seat in a sea of green. On June 9, 1946, Ted Williams hit a titanic home run off Fred Hutchinson of the Detroit Tigers. It landed 502 feet away, supposedly crashing through the straw hat of the gentleman sitting in that very bleacher seat. Wayne sat and smiled, I snapped a picture. Wayne was happy to be at Fenway, a first visit a half-century overdue, and I was happy to take him, but a little sad that the game wouldn't mean more. How wrong I was.

We headed out to our seats down the left field line, in the shadow of the Green Monster, the most famous wall in baseball. I slipped into the press box and snuck out with a plate of lobster rolls and a container of clam chowder.

"I'm stuffed," he said as I waved some jumbo shrimp under his nose. But he ate them anyway.

We watched the warm-ups as Manny Ramirez, the Boston left fielder with the Sideshow Bob hair, played catch with center fielder Johnny Damon. Manny, baseball's ultimate idiot savant, can hit a baseball better than just about any human alive, but ask him to do anything else and he turns grotesquely human. He tried to throw the ball up to the well-connected customers in the prized seats atop the Monster. He aimed. He fired. The ball made it barely halfway up the wall and caromed into the corner. Manny walked slowly and sheepishly to where the ball sat mocking him. He picked it up without rancor, finally delivering it to its intended destination on his second try. It had been that kind of week.

The game was preceded by a moment of silence for former Red Sox catcher Ray Boone, who had died at the age of eighty-one. Exactly one year earlier, his grandson Aaron, then playing for the Yankees, hit the game seven home run that beat the Red Sox. Out of respect for Boone's memory—and the chorus of boos that would have followed—the PA announcer declined to mention his progeny. The Kingston Trio sang "The Star-Spangled Banner" and followed it up with their hit about Charlie on the MTA. Wayne leaned forward to look at Nick Reynolds's Martin tenor guitar. "We had one of those in the shop a while back," he said.

The crowd was subdued, not wanting to expose their hearts for fear of getting them crushed again, like just another beer can. At least most of the crowd was subduded.

"C'mon, get up," shouted a young man with a goatee, two rows up, hoisting his brew. "This could be the last game of the season. They're *your* Red Sox," he bellowed. Two stylishly dressed thirty-something women took their cue—and possibly some beer—from him. They banged incessantly on the railing in front of them with their bongo sticks—two-foot-long inflatable cheering devices that looked like nothing so much as Brobdingnagian sex toys. When two young men wearing Yankee caps tried to walk past down the aisle, they began bopping them on the head and chanting "Go A-Round! Go A-Round!"

Even the grim goings-on on the field couldn't dampen their spirits. In the third, Yankee third baseman Alex Rodriguez—the highest-paid player in baseball—launched a moonshot over the Green Monster out onto Lansdowne Street to put the Yankees up 2–0.

"Throw it back," I yelled half-jokingly.

I can't imagine that someone heard me, but lo and behold, the ball came flying back over the wall, and it landed in center field. Johnny Damon picked up the ball and threw it back over the Monster. Ten seconds later, thinking it was another Yankee home run, some despondent Red Sox fan tossed it *back* over the wall. Damon and some drunk were playing catch over the Monster, which put Manny's pregame gaffe in some perspective. This time, however, the umpire picked up the ball and put an end to the silliness.

In the fifth, the Sox mounted a small offensive to take a 3 to 2 lead. A young woman two rows in front of us—sixteen, there with her father—put on a tan woolen cap over her long blond hair to ward off the chill. Just as she did, Orlando Cabrera slapped a single to right and the Sox were on the scoreboard.

"It's a rally cap! It's a rally cap!" shouted her father teasingly, rubbing her head with every base runner.

The Yankees struck back in the sixth to take a 4–3 lead, and the natives were getting testy. Beer Guy was kvetching ever more loudly about the general apathy. An older guy in our row told him to sit down and shut up, calling him an asshole almost parenthetically. Beer Guy hurled the epithet right back. The guy's son, a not particularly martial-looking fellow, felt the need to defend dad's honor. "Hey, you can't say that to my father!" Hard words begat hard looks. Wayne looked at me. I looked at Wayne.

"Which way do we go?" he asked.

"Away," I quipped.

A security guard came over to broker a tentative peace. And then they all left. The Bopping Women. Beer Guy. Mr. "What Did You Say About My Father?" and his dad. All of them. They were cold and they had drunk too much and suffered even more for their Red Sox. And they will be haunted forevermore by their failure of faith. Not that it wasn't tempting to leave. Facing Yankee closer Mariano Rivera down by a run was as close to dead as you can get in the game of baseball. It was midnight on death row in Texas, the last meal had been eaten, the witnesses were in place, and the guards were ready to start the IV. And while everyone in Fenway was looking at the red phone, there was no call from the governor, as Mariano set the Sox down in the eighth. It was three outs away from a long winter.

And then I spied something. I nudged Wayne. "Rally Cap Girl nearby doesn't have her hat on." I nudged her father.

"C'mon, you gotta put it on," Dad pleaded. The girl rolled her eyes, but she knew that her father wouldn't give up easily, so she undid her ponytail and donned the rally cap. Within moments the mojo began working. Kevin Millar walked. The pinch runner, Dave Roberts, stole second. I high-fived Wayne.

He high-fived back, tentatively, perhaps worrying about his picking hand, and perhaps just being a little too old-school for all this. When Bill Mueller singled and Roberts scored, all hell broke loose.

"Ral-ly Cap! Ral-ly Cap!" we chanted and we all rubbed the blond girl's head for luck.

Thus began a nail-biting journey into extra innings. We knew full well that one mighty swing of a Yankee bat against an arm-weary Red Sox reliever could still send us all home disappointed. At the end of the tenth, we watched the scoreboard operator walk out onto the field, take the numbers down from the ancient wall and replace them with a fresh set of zeroes.

In the twelfth inning, around the time that this became the longest game in postseason history, I glanced at Rally Cap Girl. The hat was still on, but the little Ralph Lauren Polo emblem was askew, facing back toward the stands.

"The logo's got to face the field," I kidded.

She knew better than to argue. Before Dad could utter a word, she spun her cap around. Not ten seconds later David Ortiz launched a home run into the right field bleachers, and suddenly it was Christmas and the Fourth of July at Fenway. The whole section crowded around the Rally Cap Girl and dozens upon dozens gave the cap a rub, hoping to capture some of the mojo. Wayne jumped, he yelled, he beamed, he turned beet-red. "Don't that beat all?" he said breathlessly. Did he hug the blond girl? Did he hug her dad? Did he hug me? I'll never tell, but in a post-season postgame celebration anything goes.

"That cap contains great power, so use it wisely," I said to the blond girl with mock solemnity.

I had been to hundreds of baseball games—Opening Day, All-Star Games, World Series clinchers, contests featuring heroics of every stripe—but from beginning to end, I had never been to a better one, and even though it was 1:30 in the morning, I didn't want to see it end. So Wayne and I, we lingered. Partially it was practical—thirty thousand people who had to get up for work the next morning pressed toward the exits. But it was more than that. We were in a sacred place at a magic moment. I wouldn't have traded places with anyone on earth, and judging from the grin on his face I could tell Wayne Henderson felt the same way. When the guards gently prodded us, we headed out into Kenmore Square, where the cars gave the right of way to pedestrians and even the riot cops were smiling. We even got a cab.

And if this was a moral victory that did nothing more than prevent a Yankee sweep, it would have been a great night. But after Wayne Henderson's first visit to Fenway Park, the Red Sox didn't lose again that October, winning seven straight games and their first World Series since 1918. The Rugby Hillbilly, who'd never seen a big league team play in person, ever, had reversed the curse.

CHAPTER TEN

Picea rubens, Dalbergia nigra

L ET'S DWELL FOR A MOMENT on Wayne Henderson's
favorite joke, the one about how he builds a guitar.

"You start out with a pile of good wood. Some nice Brazilian
rosewood, some good Appalachian spruce. And then you get
yourself a sharp whittling knife. And you cut away anything that
doesn't look like a guitar."

It's a good joke (and a nice homage to Michaelangelo), but it's
also about as good a description of the process as you're likely to
get in 37 words. Notice that the whole process begins with getting the right wood.

And as Wayne hinted to me earlier, the key hurdle in turning
the Clapton guitars from concept to reality is getting the right
pieces of wood. So that is where we'll begin.

A steel-string acoustic guitar consists of different woods,
from different parts of the world, each contributing in its own
way to the instrument's sound. The top and the bracing are made
of spruce, which is light, yet strong and resonant. That's the reason the Wright brothers used it to build the frame of the first airplane, and Howard Hughes, during wartime metal shortages, used
a similar wood, laminated birch, to craft his legendary wooden
cargo plane, the *Spruce Goose.*

But not just any spruce will do. Consider the Ice Age Theory
of the Stradivarius violins. A nineteenth-century astronomer, E.

W. Maunder, documented a centuries-long lull in solar activity, which resulted in a cold snap that gripped Europe from the mid-1400s to the mid-1800s. A few years ago, a Columbia University climatologist named Lloyd Burckle noted that the coldest period of this mini–Ice Age—known as the Maunder Minimum—occurred between 1645 to 1715, which coincided with the so-called Golden Age of Violin Making.

Burckle took his hypothesis to one of the word's foremost experts on tonewood, a University of Tennessee dendrochronologist named Henri Grissino-Mayer. He plotted a five-hundred-year chronology of high-elevation forests in Europe, and discovered a period of unprecedentedly slow growth between 1625 to 1720 caused by the long winters and short summers. The result? The trees from this period featured tightly spaced growth rings, which made the resulting tonewood both denser and stronger. This Super Spruce theory gained surprisingly rapid acceptance in a violin world that spent much of its time focusing on the varnish applied by Stradivari and his pals.

And the spruce that Stradivari used is essentially the same as the wood used by Wayne Henderson, a variety of *Picea rubens*, or red spruce. A red spruce is a relatively plain-looking tree with short needles and tiny cones, hence its nickname "the she balsam." It grows at medium to high elevations from the Adirondack Mountains south through the Appalachians—which is why the Martin guitar factory refers to it as Adirondack spruce, while Wayne Henderson calls it Appalachian spruce.

"It pretty much looks like a Christmas tree," explained John Arnold, the luthier who has probably cut more guitar-quality red spruce than anyone in the last 50 years, including the tops for many Henderson guitars. Cutting red spruce is no easy task. It grows among other species of evergreens, and once you find one, only perhaps one in a hundred red spruces is suitable for guitar tops. While limb height and straightness are considerations, size is the biggest hurdle. Arnold explained that a tree must have a diameter of twenty-four inches at a person's chest to yield good guitar wood.

And as Stradivari probably knew, there's a lot to be said for finding just the right piece of spruce. T. J. Thompson, for example, recalled the time he was turned loose in Martin's wood room to hand-select tops for a high-end guitar project.

He picked up each top and tapped it to listen for the overtones.

"The first fifty or so, I didn't really know what I was doing," he admitted.

He soon began to divine the very real differences between tops. Some rang when he tapped them. Some merely thudded. By the end of the afternoon, Thompson found that he could predict what a piece of wood would sound like just by picking it up. The best-sounding pieces of spruce were harder, smoother, and cooler to the touch.

Appalachian spruce represents a modest ecological success story. In the 1930s and 1940s, the old-growth forests were logged to near extinction, with the vast majority of red spruce trees made not into guitar tops, but into two-by-fours and pulp for the day's *The New York Times*. That's why in 1947, Martin stopped using Adirondack spruce in favor of the more readily available Western-grown Sitka spruce. But almost sixty years later, the faster-growing second-growth trees have become large enough for use in guitars. And Arnold has been working with the U.S. Forest Service to try to ensure a steady supply of tonewood for future generations of luthiers. He's marked selected red spruce trees for a sixty-year growth cycle that would allow them to grow large enough to become guitar tops. But he's not sure that this will represent a lasting victory. In a government bureaucracy where decisions are often driven by politics, that extra twenty years is an eternity.

The good news is that Wayne Henderson lives right smack in the middle of a forest still dotted with red spruce. In August 2004, he returned from a trip to find a giant Appalachian red spruce log sitting in his front yard. The foresters in the area had culled a number of trees to prevent the spread of southern pine beetle infestation, and someone had the good sense to bring the wood to Wayne rather than feed it into a wood chipper. So between these random acts of generosity and the wood cut by his friend John Arnold, Wayne has a steady supply of good Appalachian, given his very modest output of guitars. When I asked him, he said he had a top he could use for Clapton's guitar.

The same cannot be said for Brazilian rosewood. *Dalbergia nigra*, as it's known to scientists, is the world's most valuable tonewood, having been used for the back and sides of many of the best guitars ever made. Whereas a good set of the more common East Indian rosewood can be had for $150, a nice set of Brazilian will go for ten times that amount or more.

And while guitar builders are ordinarily not a particularly sentimental lot, that changes when the topic turns to Brazilian rosewood. Wayne Henderson often plays the Carter Family tune "Little Rosewood Casket," and when introducing the song he often says, "Whenever I play this one, I feel kinda sad thinking about how many guitars you could have made out of that wood."

Pick up a piece of Brazilian rosewood, and it's easy to see what makes it special. The first thing you'll notice is that it's remarkably dense. Heft a big piece and you could almost be convinced you were carrying a piece of steel. Tapping it lightly unleashes a remarkable cacophony, a high-pitched metallic chime. Sound, yes, but not music. Taming this high-strung wood, which is brittle and prone to cracking—that's where Wayne Henderson comes in.

"Nothing sounds quite like that," he is fond of saying about the sound of a good piece of Brazilian.

Brazilian rosewood grows not in Brazil's Amazon rainforest, but in the coastal forest of Bahia. What was once a lush, diverse ecosystem, home to exotic birds and lion tamarinds and capuchin monkeys found nowhere else on earth, has now largely been developed. Less than two percent of the forest remains unscathed. While some of the timber was made into furniture, and the tiniest percentage into guitars, the reality is that most of this valuable wood was burned, some for energy, some to use as fertilizer for pastureland (a gambit that worked only temporarily), and most simply to make way for progress.

By the mid-1960s, the supply of Brazilian reached a crisis point. In 1969, Martin began making its production-line rosewood guitars out of the more commonly available Indian rosewood, which is grown as a shade tree on tea plantations. (The company continued to make some limited editions out of Brazilian rosewood, and in 2004, with the supplies tightening further, the company raised its minimum price for a Brazilian rosewood guitar to $25,000.)

In 1992, the Convention on International Trade in Endangered Species of Wild Flora and Fauna (CITES) was passed, which banned export or import of Brazilian rosewood, except for those pieces that had been harvested before the ban went into effect.

I knew that scoring a couple of sets of truly high-quality old-growth Brazilian rosewood was the crucial missing link between Wayne Henderson and the Clapton guitars, one for Eric and one to be sold for charity. I knew that it wouldn't be easy.

Luthier supply houses sold some wood—largely harvested from stumps—but the wood was often slab-cut and needed seasoning before it could be turned into a guitar.

I asked around and located a source. Top quality old-growth Brazilian would have to be acquired through informal channels. He preferred to remain anonymous, so we'll call him Deep Trunk. He's not a luthier, just a guitar player who became obsessed with the world's finest tonewood. Deep Trunk came of age around the time that Martin stopped building with Brazilian rosewood. He acquired a few random sets for his own personal guitars. But he wanted more. So before the CITES ban went into effect, he and a couple of partners bought a portion of a Brazilian rosewood tree—at a time when this was still legal—and had it imported into the United States. There was some disagreement as to how the wood should be cut, so one morning, Deep Trunk arrived with a chainsaw and a Ryder van and simply took his share of the wood. That valuable timber sat in his garage for a while, until he rented a Wood-Mizer, a specialized thin-bladed band saw, and resawed the log right in the street in front of his house.

The supply that's been sitting in his garage for over fifteen years isn't Deep Trunk's nest egg so much as his personal stash. Several sets have been made into spectacular guitars, while others are in progress. Better than almost anyone, Deep Trunk understands this organic link between good wood and great music, so it took only a little persuading to convince him to supply a couple of sets for Clapton's guitars. And a week later, when two sets of beautiful straight-grained chocolate-colored old-school Brazilian arrived at my doorstep, the final piece of the puzzle for Clapton's guitars had fallen into place.

CHAPTER ELEVEN

Reading the Grain

T HE LAZY AUTUMN SUN was just beginning to set behind largely leaf-free hills, as I turned off Route 58 onto Tucker Road in early November. I drove past the hillside neatly dotted with adolescent Christmas trees. I hung a quick right just beyond the big elm tree, drove up Wayne's gravel driveway, and parked on the grass.

Sandy, Wayne's sweet and ancient mutt, raised her blond head, stretched deliberately, and ambled out of the plastic dog-house beside the shop to greet me. She no doubt smelled the five pounds of barbecue sitting in a paper bag on the front seat. When I entered the shop proper, things were almost as I had left them in the spring. Gabby wasn't there, but Ralph Maxwell was sitting in his usual spot in the oak swivel chair in front of the joiner. A bag of now cold Hardee's burgers he had brought that morning was sitting on the thickness planer. Gerald Anderson, the instrument maker who shares the shop, was hunched over in the small maple chair beside his workbench, carving the scroll on a mandolin. Wayne was poking around inside an old Martin guitar owned by Steve Kilby, a local picker looking to get a few tips about guitar repair. Just the same, this wasn't business as usual. There was the aroma of anticipation in the air, and it wasn't for the smoked chicken and pulled pork.

"How *you* doin?" Wayne said, with just a little more than usual animation.

I said my hellos, shook hands all around, and brought in my computer bag, my camera bag, and my old '47 D-18 in the burnt-orange fiberglass flight case. Then I went back out to the car for the trip's raison d'être: a box containing two sets of Brazilian rosewood ready to become Eric Clapton's guitars. I removed the box from the back of the hatchback, carried it inside, perched it atop the thirty-five-gallon plastic Rubbermaid garbage can that was overflowing with junk, and sighed with relief. In truth, I had been a little paranoid about the wood ever since it arrived at my home in Montclair. I played show-and-tell with my kids, telling them a little story about the rainforests and how guitars get built, demonstrating the wood's heft and the way it rang when you tapped it. They were, I soon discovered, interested enough in the wood but truly fascinated by the Styrofoam peanuts that filled the box. From then on I had nightmares about them sneaking up into my office and tossing aside thousands of dollars worth of old-growth rosewood in an attempt to get at a buck's worth of packing material. And my worry continued even after I loaded the precious wood in my car to head south toward Rugby. In my overnight stop at a Quality Inn outside Harrisburg, I took the box inside my room, not wanting to leave it in my trunk overnight, exposed to the elements and would-be wood thieves. I now grabbed a knife from the workbench and slit the packing tape, as everyone gathered around.

At 3:37 P.M. on November 11, 2004, I carefully handed Wayne eight pieces of Brazilian rosewood, each still lightly swaddled in clingy wrap. Work on Clapton's guitar, and its twin, had officially begun.

He unwrapped the lumber—two back pieces and two side pieces for each guitar—and gave them a quick once-over. At first, Wayne scanned the wood casually, forming a first impression. He looked them up and down the same way the rest of us did, admiring the straight grain, wondering what the chocolate color might look like under a few coats of lacquer. "That's real purty," he pronounced, followed by nods of agreement all around.

Indeed, the pieces of wood were spectacular, at least from a guitar builder's point of view. The color of a piece of Brazilian rosewood can range from a golden pumpkin to a greenish gray to a striking brick-red, and the grain can be mazelike in its complexity. These sets didn't have that eye-catching beauty. The center was dark brown, almost the color of bittersweet chocolate, the result of a fungus that attacks the oldest rosewood trees from the center outward. Near the edges, the wood lightened to a milk chocolate hue with some subtle greenish streaks. But in guitar wood, beauty is more than a veneer. The darkest-colored wood is usually the densest and most resonant. While straight-grained stock such as this may not make a stunning coffee-table, it's easy to work with and sounds the best as well. Indeed, this was old-school instrument-building wood that the guys at the Martin factory sixty years ago, who built Lots 19 and 20 from the Crossroads Auction, would have been more than happy to make into a guitar.

Lying on the floor, however, with a light coat of sawdust on its new black case, was evidence that you don't need noble and pricey materials to make an amazing guitar. That is, if you're Wayne Henderson. The back and sides of guitar number 324 were built from boards of reclaimed cherry, which had, in its previous incarnation, been a part of Rose Kirby's chicken coop. While some inexpensive guitars are being built from cherry, as manufacturers search for alternative materials to exotic imported hardwoods, George Washington's favorite timber is hardly considered a front-line tonewood. Other top guitar builders have used humble materials for guitars, but mostly to make a point. The Spanish guitar builder Manuel Torres once built an instrument with sides formed from papier-mâché to prove the primacy of the guitar's top, and California builder Bob Taylor cobbled together the infamous Pallet Guitar out of packing crates found on the company's loading dock, and then sold a limited edition of similarly knotty instruments for more than the company's best Brazilian rosewood guitars. But these were more rhetorical devices than instruments. Not so for Wayne's first cherry guitar. To Rose Kirby's nephew these old planks from his aunt's chicken coop meant something. Seeing this battered wood on the back of his guitar would be a trip in a time machine, and that was reason enough for Wayne.

As I opened the case to inspect it, I found that the cherry guitar was pretty enough, with a pale warm glow, somewhere between maple's pale complexion and the caramel color of unstained mahogany. The top was an ordinary piece of store-bought Sitka spruce, clean and stiff but nothing special, not something from Wayne's special stash.

But I began to change my assessment of the instrument when Steve Kilby picked it up and casually picked a couple of fiddle tunes. Although Kilby was barely touching the strings—he was noodling, not performing—the guitar responded, ringing clean and clear. Then again, Steve was the kind of player who could make any old box sing. I didn't take this guitar's true measure until I picked it up. I strummed a chord, and it felt almost alive in my lap. I couldn't reconcile its bold tone with the humble materials.

"When did you finish this?" I asked.

"I strung it up this morning," Wayne said casually.

Within eight hours this guitar had taken on the assertive voice that most instruments never quite achieve. There were mitigating circumstances—Sitka tops need less break-in than guitars topped with the stiffer Appalachian spruce—that made this guitar more like a *vin de table* that should be opened right away than a great Bordeaux sent to the cellar. Still, here was further proof that the magic in a Henderson guitar lies with the chef, not the ingredients.

Wayne carried the pieces of fine Brazilian rosewood across the shop to the table saw and separated the wood into two small piles. After he put on his reading glasses, he gently laid his hands on the rosewood for a few long, quiet moments, almost as if he were taking its temperature. It wasn't a premeditated ritual, some kind of self-conscious communion-with-the-wood kind of thing. Wayne doesn't do touchy-feely. If he thought about it at all, he would have dismissed it as a practical gesture; he just liked the warm rough touch of raw wood better than the cold smooth steel of the table saw. But viewed from a distance, it was more profound than that. Wayne understood that this wood was three pounds of pure potential, waiting to be tapped. This represented a beginning, a brief interlude in the land of boundless hope and infinite promise. Touching the sides, and then the backs, feeling the fibers pass between his fingers for the first time, grounded those great expectations, brought that reverie into the here and now.

He flipped the boards over one more time, making his first decision of how to turn these pieces of exquisite raw wood into the best of all possible guitars. "I believe the wood just wants to point in this direction," he announced after a long moment of deliberation.

After a few moments of coming to grips with the wood, he got to the real work of laying out the pieces. Although the slabs were numbered, he ignored the markings. Instead he read the grain.

"You need to make sure it's in the right direction, the way it came off of the log," he explained. "This side of the tree which is closer to the bark is more perfectly quartered than anywhere else." He laid the halves of the back flat, edge to edge, as if they were the pages of a book. The edge with the straightest grain would be in the center of the guitar back, or, if you prefer, the spine of the virtual book.

"You see these little knots?" he said, pointing to a couple of small pin knots. "They're way closer to being exactly the same than if you laid it the other way."

Wayne launched into a brief seminar about how wood is cut. You can tell most everything you need to know about a piece of wood by looking at its edge, he explained. If the grain lines are running perpendicular to the direction of the slice, it's quarter-sawn. If it's running along the length of the slice, it's slab-cut. Mills hate quarter-sawing wood—it's time-consuming because you have to rotate the log with each cut, and expensive because there's a fair amount of waste. The alternative—slab-cutting—simply consists of running a log through the egg slicer of the gods and letting the grain fall where it may. The bottom line is that quarter-sawn wood yields straight-grained planks that ring like crazy and are more predictable to work with. This wood was very close to being perfectly quartered.

Wayne flipped the flitches of wood one more time, then flipped them back again. "I believe the wood just wants to point in this direction," he repeated.

After he was satisfied with the orientation, Wayne brought out a template for a Martin-style triple-ought body. This tool, like so many in the shop, had seen its share of use; it was formed of simple plywood, painted white, and the top layer had begun to splinter around the edges. Wayne moved it around a bit, up and down along the length of the wood—the lateral orientation was decided by the center seam of the wood—the binding of the figurative book. He shifted it up and down a bit, dodging a few slabby places in the center. He stood back for a second, then scribed the back's circumference with a silver pencil, all the better to be seen on the dark rosewood.

Wayne repeated the ritual with the sides. Since the sides have to be bent, practical considerations trumped aesthetic ones there. He looked for the straightest, most uniform grain he could find. The features that catch the eye were also the place where a crack might start.

"You're looking for the cleanest wood," he said. "Even though that thing might be pretty"—indicating a beauty mark where the grain changes color—"it's likely to cause trouble."

Silver pencil in hand, he pulled out the template for the sides. While one edge is relatively straight, the other edge was alarmingly crooked, as if it had been made on Friday at some factory ten minutes before quitting time. While this cock-eyed edge looked strange—and worrisome—at the moment, Wayne assured me that this baroque geometry would all make sense when the sides were bent.

"That's how you get the arch in the back," he explained. "It's a funny-looking thing. It goes flat for a while. Then crooked. Then back flat. And then it actually goes back up the other way a little. It's a weird-shaped thing, but when it gets bent into the shape of a guitar, the arch ends up being where the hump is."

He took the sides to the band saw, and roughed around the outside of the silver line. The shop filled with a sweet, slightly spicy smell that wouldn't be out of place in Starbucks. The smell of Brazilian rosewood. "Nothing smells like that," Wayne said, taking a little extra sniff. Indeed, that smell is one of the best ways for wood merchants to tell the difference between rare Brazilian rosewood and the more common and far less expensive East Indian variety.

Wayne slid the other side through the saw and brushed the pieces onto the floor, just another addition to the shop's great heap of scrapwood. Steve Kilby, a bear of a man with glasses and majestic sideburns that make him look a bit like a nineteenth-century statesman, snapped to attention. "You ought to pick up all those scraps," he said. "You can cut them up in little pieces and sell them on eBay. Tell them they're from Eric Clapton's guitar and people would buy them, I guarantee."

A fine picker in his own right, Steve had recently discovered the power of the Internet. He built his own Web site, where he markets his CDs and his lessons, both in person and on tape. And the guitar he and Wayne had been working on, a 1963 Martin 000-18 in need of a neck reset, had been won in an eBay auction. Wayne smiled, but I bent over, picked up the scraps, and casually dropped them in the box where the wood had come from. I didn't need Steve Kilby to tell me that these scraps of wood shouldn't go in the garbage.

Wayne turned his attention to the thickness of the wood. These sides are plenty thick. Too thick, in fact. He looks at them kind of wistfully. They were almost thick enough to slice each piece into two sides.

"With a perfect blade and a perfect saw you could make each one of these into two sets," Wayne said. "Or, you could ruin 'em too."

With me standing over him, he took the coward's way out. He ran them through the thickness sander, turning a sixteenth of an inch of Brazilian rosewood into a thick coating of sawdust on the concrete floor. As he sanded, the wood came to life. The sandpaper skimmed the oxidation off the wood, leaving it lighter and its figure more striking. The lighter sections of the wood, formerly kind of grayish, revealed even more of that subtle green hue. A thin black stripe, with some tiny spider veins that are so typical of Brazilian rosewood, emerged, becoming more vivid with each pass, like an image coming to life in a photographer's developing tray. After a few passes, Wayne handed me the side and pulled a small caliper out of the draw.

"About eighty-six thousandths?" he announced casually.

It was eighty-six thousandths of an inch *exactly*.

"When was the last time you used that?" I asked.

"I don't know."

"Are you doing this for my benefit?"

"Yeah."

We all laughed. "I do it by feel," he admitted. With thirty-five years of guitar building behind them, his fingers have always been more sensitive than any caliper.

It was in moments like this that I came to the conclusion that Wayne Henderson is a genius. His brand of genius harks back to the word's unsullied origins: the Roman term for "begetter." In the days of Caesar, a genius wasn't something you were, it was something you *had*. A genius was a vaguely protective being like a guardian angel, but most of all this Roman version of a genius was a maker, a conjurer, a genie, who could create very real things out of thin air. And in that old-school sense of the word, Wayne Henderson has a certain genius, an ancient forest nymph that sits on his shoulder and whispers directions every time he picks up a piece of wood. Wayne Henderson doesn't analyze his gift or even attempt to, any more than Charlie Parker sat around and wondered why he could blow a horn. Too much questioning might scare it away.

Ralph got up to leave and Wayne had an ADD moment. Along with the barbecue, I brought a blackberry pie I had bought on the way, and there are few things that Ralph likes better.

"Why don't you have a piece of pie before you go?" Wayne implored.

I searched around for a kitchen knife. Steve Kilby offered me a jeweler's saw, only half-jokingly. I politely demurred.

"I'll make a knife," Wayne offered.

All of a sudden, the Clapton guitars were completely off the radar screen and the only thing that mattered was Ralph and the pie.

Before I could intervene, Wayne picked up a piece of spruce from the floor and free-handed it on the band saw into an elegant little utensil, one that looked like a pickle fork on steroids. He took it over to the belt sander and gave it a few quick licks to hone the edge.

I asked if he wanted to do the honors.

"Wait, I'm gonna make a getter-outer," he replied.

Three rips of the band saw, a few whirls of the sander, and voilà, a perfect little mahogany pie server.

Why spruce for the knife and mahogany for the pie server?

"It tastes better that way," Kilby deadpanned before Wayne could formulate a response.

As Ralph devoured the gooey pie off a napkin—given another minute, I'm sure Wayne would have made a plate too—I concluded that this is the kind of helpful impulse that makes Wayne a great friend. It's also what makes him a guitar builder a decade behind in his orders.

Satisfied with the back and sides, Wayne headed over to a pile of half-completed guitar pieces and fished out a paper-white spruce guitar top. As he put it down on the workbench, I noticed the words "Eric Clapton" penciled in right above the already marked soundhole. He tapped it once, twice, pulling his left ear close and really listening. Wayne then pulled down a set of folding stairs, and disappeared into the small crawl space above the shop. He came down with a handful of guitar tops, and quickly zeroed in on one in particular. This sister piece was silky in texture and creamy in color with just a couple of caramel-colored swirls. More important, the grain was uniform, the flex was stiff, and when you tapped it, it hummed like a dial tone.

It was big though, too big, in a way. The other top was barely big enough, with merely a thirty-second of an inch to spare. When Wayne saw that this one was big enough to make a much larger dreadnought guitar and then some, part of him was sad that he was going to have to waste so much of it to make a smaller guitar. He tapped it, then tapped the Clapton top, then tapped it again. Tonally, they were sisters. This was the right piece.

"I guess we could use this one for a special guitar," he announced.

As he sized up this second piece of spruce, he focused on a couple of tiny pin knots, little imperfections you could cover with a pencil eraser. His first instinct was to slice out the middle section, but he reconsidered. He was more concerned about keeping the piece intact. These beauty marks would stay.

With the plotting done, Wayne fired up the jointer and got to work, smoothing and evening the edges so that they can be glued up. The jointer is a noisy and potentially dangerous beast. The fact that the knives in the cutting head, which are spinning at 10,000 rpm, are hidden from view makes it all the more fearsome. On an instrument builders' forum on the Web, one particularly gruesome post told the story of a luthier who got his fingers too close to the blade and wondered for a split second what that red stripe on the wall was, before the pain had a chance to register.

Wayne doesn't pay this any mind. When Wayne draws one edge of the rosewood past the blade on the first pass, the sound is staccato, as the blades bite into a piece of wood, then rests for a millisecond as a high spot passes over the blade. By the tenth pass or so, those high spots are gone, and one uniform rrrrrrrr-rrrrripppp announced the arrival of a perfectly flat and smooth edge ready for gluing. The building of Clapton's guitars was now fully under way.

"How long you think it'll take us to make this into a guitar?" Wayne joked as he turned the machine off.

"Who's this *we?*"

CHAPTER TWELVE

Dangerous Curves

THE FAR CORNER of the guitar shop, behind the gangly multiuse Shopsmith machine, near the sawdust-choked humidifier, is a testament to human ingenuity. Or at least Wayne Henderson's ingenuity. I ignored the scraps of wood and God knows what else on the floor and waded in toward where Wayne was standing. It was cramped and dusty, yes, but it was also a chance to steal a quick peek into the magician's bag, stand backstage while Penn and Teller rehearse. As Wayne began rummaging around, I knew I needed to pay close attention.

Wayne accidentally knocked a block of plywood to the floor and snapped me back to the here and now. The twilight had slipped toward evening, and the shop had cleared out except for Wayne and me. It was Veterans Day 2004, and the local radio station was playing a string of patriotic favorites. As the overnight DJ cued up Johnny Cash's "Ragged Old Flag" for the second time in as many hours, Wayne got down to the serious business of guitar making, of turning a plain old pile of not-so-plain wood into a two star-worthy guitars. And that first step was a doozy.

Look at the silhouette of a guitar with a curious eye, and the first thing you might wonder is: "How exactly do they get a piece of wood to bend like that?" Follow for a moment the left side of a guitar as you're looking at it from the front. At the bottom is a calligraphic S with a graceful flowing bottom and a much tighter top, geometry that would impress any font designer or Grayson County road builder. That's followed almost immediately by a tight reverse left-hander that dead-ends into the neck. The other side—a guitar's perimeter is made of two pieces—sports a set of mirror-image arcs. When the Museum of Fine Arts in Boston did a major exhibit a few years ago on the guitar as a design object, they entitled it "Dangerous Curves." It's easy to see why.

Side bending is the step of the guitar-building process that scares amateur builders and small children. As I picked up one of the fragile Brazilian rosewood sides and then looked at the intricate curves of an already bent guitar side, I couldn't help but think that somewhere in the middle would be a loud crack followed by a louder string of four-letter words. There had be a trick, I thought, to transforming a slab of brittle wood into a series of sinuous arcs.

"Just add water," Wayne said with a smile, as he proceeded to demonstrate.

He approached a small bench, which held a stainless steel trough three feet long and about nine inches wide, sitting atop a small two-burner hot plate of the kind you'll find in only the best single room occupancy hotels. He picked up the trough, carried it to the tiny, filthy bathroom just through the doorway—when Wayne, still a country boy at heart, feels the call of nature, he'll usually just walk outside to do his business—and filled it up with ordinary tap water.

He plopped the trough back down on the hot plate, and cranked the dial clockwise. How hot? "It's almost hot enough to boil over by that one eye," he explained as the water began to bubble and churn. Turns out that one heating element was dead.

"Maybe I'll invest in a new hot plate," he said with a laugh. "That'd be big."

When the water seemed hot enough to, say, boil hot dogs, he dunked a piece of koa wood into the trough, where it would soak for fifteen minutes or so. This was the first time he'd used the side bender in a while, so he proposed a trial run using a less irreplaceable piece of tonewood. I got the sense that he was doing this for my benefit, that I'd rest a little easier if we used someone else's wood as a guinea pig.

Before he bent Clapton's sides, he soaked and bent a piece of koa destined for another OM-sized guitar. When I asked him about the guitar, he bristled just a bit.

"I took a total screwing on that one," he grumbled.

In exchange for not one, not two, but three hand-built Wayne Henderson guitars, the luthier received a rather nice 1966 Martin D-35. The guitar had a retail value of around $3,500. But even though it was made of rare Brazilian rosewood, this was a guitar model that was falling out of fashion by the minute. The guitar's mellow voice suited a certain kind of sensitive singer-songwriter whose best days have long past. (Dan Fogelberg was the D-35's poster boy.) The guitar's three-piece back, which allowed the use of smaller pieces of wood, was a reminder of the dwindling supplies of Brazilian rosewood. It wasn't a terrible guitar—really no worse than the D-28s or D-18s of the day—but since there were no great prewar D-35s, the model reminded people of the bad old days. The D-35 was the guitar world's answer to the Gerald Ford administration. In essence, Wayne had traded three of his guitars for the instrumental equivalent of a Whip Inflation Now button.

This almost comically bad barter deal said quite a lot about the way Wayne Henderson conducts business. Wayne and Henry both knew what the D-35 was worth if a dealer sold it, and they both realizeded how little Wayne charged for one of his guitars.

"I sell my guitars at wholesale," Wayne calculated. "But they're pricing the guitars they're trading at the highest possible retail."

So as he popped a piece of koa into the side bender, he continued his good-natured rant. "I don't know what I was thinking," he said, referring to the one-sided deal he'd agreed to. The beneficiary of this powerful deal, certainly did. He asked Wayne to sign an elaborately detailed order form that outlined the parameters of the one-sided trade.

"I just want to get those guitars done so I don't have to think about it anymore," Wayne said with only the slightest trace of rancor.

So while the trial side was in the side bender, we popped over to the house to eat some of the barbecue I had brought from the Galax Smokehouse—a guest bearing food is always welcome chez Henderson—and wait for the results of the trial run.

Stomach full, and the koa bent, it was on to the Brazilian. The first trick of side bending? The miracle of water. "It gives the wood amnesia," Wayne explained. This brief hot bath atop the hot plate acted like a shot of Sodium Pentothal they might administer in an ambulatory surgery suite. You might have been awake enough to roll over or say ahhh during the procedure, but as far as your long-term memory is concerned, you might just as well have been out like a light.

Same with the wood. As soon as those fibers touch the hot water, they forget that they once formed a tall, straight tree and instead relax into a docile and compliant blob. Wayne explained that commercial side benders often come with directions that suggest simply spraying the sides gingerly with water from a little squirt bottle, kind of like preparing a cotton shirt for a hot iron. That's a recipe for cracking, he claimed. For Wayne, the wetter the better.

Then Wayne showed me the side bender itself. Like most of the jigs in the shop, he built it himself. Until he constructed the device, he bent his sides the old-fashioned way—heating a piece of pipe with a blowtorch and very carefully bending the thin wood over the round pipe and removing it before it scorched. While that old method sounded plenty medieval, the new side bender, a collection of springs, clamps, and hot metal plates, was an object that the Marquis de Sade could surely relate to. It starts with what looks to be a heavy plywood guitar body, split in half lengthwise, with a dozen thick metal bars separating the top and bottom in lieu of wooden sides. Inside the body are buried three ordinary incandescent bulbs—the heat source for the device.

By this time, the rosewood was just about fully soaked, and the fun began. Wayne picked up the side and handed it to me. The transformation was remarkable. The rigid, brittle, high-strung piece of tonewood had become downright relaxed, about as flexible as a pizza box doubled over.

He grabbed two flexible curved aluminum plates that looked like the side of a metal guitar. He placed one of the metal sides down on the wooden form. Then he laid the softened rosewood on top of the metal. Next, he completed the sandwich—rosewood on aluminum—by placing the other metal side gently on top of the rosewood.

Then it was time to apply the pressure. Above the form was suspended a big clamp. Wayne turned down the clamp gradually, pushing the rosewood-on-aluminum sandwich up against the wooden form, the luthier's answer to a panini press. Wayne then grabbed a block attached to two giant springs anchored at the bottom of the form. He struggled a little as he slid the block around the outside of the form. As he pulled, the block pressed the sandwich firmly against the form. He repeated the sliding and pulling on the other side until the wet rosewood was right where he wanted it to be, snug up against the hot form, the light bulbs working just like an incubator to keep the sides hot as they dried out and took shape.

All that was left was to wait. Not that the waiting is without its dangers. Only a few weeks later, Wayne was bending a set of Brazilian sides for another guitar. He headed to the house to get something to eat and zoned out in front of the television, mesmerized by the Weather Channel footage of the tsunami in Southeast Asia, forgetting about the side bender. When he returned to the shop, smoke was billowing out of the red-hot side bender. "You couldn't see across to the other side of the shop," he said. He unplugged it and doused the incipient blaze.

"When I poured water on it, each of those bulbs exploded like three shotgun blasts."

When the smoke cleared, there was a hole burned clean through the side bender. Wayne opened the sides expecting to see charcoal. What he found was a perfectly bent piece of Brazilian rosewood with only a couple of small and easily sanded scorch marks as evidence of the near-conflagration. Five more minutes of tsunami watching and the shop likely would have burned down. Now the side bender has a timer.

Watch Wayne work for a while, and you can sense the inventor's heart in action. The guitars he builds are near perfect and have been for years but he's always looking for a better way to build them, and in that way, there's a little bit of Ben Franklin in him. He changes things up just to amuse himself, it seems. Faced with the prospect of stripping the rosewood sides to the proper thickness, for example, he improvised. The first set he ran dutifully through the thickness sander again and again and again. For the second set, he got a bright idea. *Maybe I can saw it off*, he thought. He adjusted the big band saw to act like a deli meat slicer. There was no real upside to this process—the sides turned out to be too thin to split in half—and a small but nonetheless real chance of making a disastrous mistake. A small slip of the saw could turn the side into expensive scrap wood.

But Wayne pressed on, taking the time to adjust the saw so that it would take the slightest skim off the surface of the wood. I was nervous, but he wasn't. The saw rumbled to life and Wayne was perched precariously atop a pile of scrap wood, ready to feed the rosewood into the blade. It worked fine—in Wayne's World these flights of fancy invariably do. The result was a series of saw marks on the inside of the wood. You'd find these dark diagonal scorches on Ella and other old Martins, evidence of the waste-not, want-not way that the wood was sawn at that legendary old guitar factory. The marks on the sides would be sanded away, but perhaps this was just another of Wayne's invisible nods to the way things used to be done.

WHILE THE ROSEWOOD SIDES were undergoing their meta-
morphosis—the whole process takes about forty-five minutes or
so—Wayne turned to the evening's other task. At first glance it
appeared far less demanding. Glue together the two halves of the
back. Seems simple enough, conceptually. Smear some glue on
the edges. Clamp it up. Job done.

Not so fast. Actually, this is like that other kind of parlor
trick—the seemingly simple task you ask someone to perform
only to have them discover that it's nearly impossible. The wild
card in this task is the gluing surface, or lack thereof. In assembling a back, Wayne has to glue together three pieces of wood—
the two halves of the back and a decorative back stripe in the
middle—that are each less than an eighth of an inch thick. The
smearing of the glue? That's easy enough. If any squeezes out,
the sanding later on will take care of it. The pressure's the thing.

"As you clamp them together, the pieces want to buckle,"
explained Wayne. Not to mention shift, slip, slide, and twist.

Back in the day—as little as seven or eight years ago—Wayne
used to perform this tricky task with a piece of thin rope and an
abundance of patience, simply winding some twine back and
forth carefully across the width of the wood.

But now Wayne's got the Squeezer. Or at least that's what he
calls the device he and his friend Don Wilson built especially for
this task, one of the knottier little problems of guitar making.
The Squeezer, which sits on the bottom shelf of the bench, below
the side bender, is an elegant piece of design. The wood to be
glued sits on a perfectly flat metal plate covered with a piece of
ordinary waxed paper to keep any excess glue from sticking the
wood to the plate. Suspended above the plate are two bars holding three clamps each.

The next part of the puzzle is a piece of heavy flat aluminum
bar stock, a flattened I-beam that lies on either side of the back
stripe. On either side—lying atop of the rosewood back—are two

foot-long pieces of two-by-four that will bear the pressure of the clamps and transfer it to the rosewood. Wayne tightened down each of the six clamps a little at a time, moving from one side to its opposite, the way you might tighten the lug nuts on a spare tire.

"This way it can't buckle," he explained.

Then he moved to the side. In the lateral direction, the Squeezer was essentially a giant vise. One side was fixed, but the left side had three giant clamps that would press the tightly bound wood together along the narrow joint.

"Now you can squeeze it as tight as you want," Wayne said with the pride of a man who had dug a thorn out of his own side.

As he got the Squeezer loaded, the stream of patriotic hits on the radio was interrupted by a special announcement.

"On Saturday night at the VFW Hall in Hillsville, there'll be a fund-raiser featuring Wayne Henderson and Friends . . ." This was maybe the third time this evening I had heard the announcement, and while I did a little double take every time I heard Wayne's name on the radio, he ignored it until now.

"I don't believe there was more than twenty-five or thirty people there last year," he said.

"If they don't show up this year, you'll know why," I jibed.

Let's focus for a moment on the wood that Wayne was clamping. The two pieces of Brazilian rosewood had their edges run across the jointer to keep them smooth, so there's no reason he couldn't simply butt the two pieces of Brazilian together and glue them up. But Wayne didn't do that. It's not the Martin way.

The reality is that rosewood doesn't grow wide enough to make a guitar back out of one piece. The back stripe, a piece of decorative wooden marquetry about a quarter inch wide, has been traditionally used in the best guitars to accentuate this seam. This thin sliver of wood doesn't, as far as anyone can tell, affect the sound of the finished guitar. It's part of the tinsel of the instrument, a small nod to the hidden difficulty of this part of the building process, a way to celebrate the skill required to make three thin pieces of wood act as one.

Wayne reached into a drawer and picked up a couple of pieces of back stripe, with a red, white, and black arrow pattern, that looked vaguely American Indian in motif. These were the last two strips in the bin that mimic a vintage 42-style Martin, like Clapton's *Unplugged* guitar, which is what these guitars will aim to replicate. Wayne could make the back stripe himself—it's a process of carefully bundling linguine-size strips of wood, gluing them together, thinly slicing the resulting roll like olive loaf, and then gluing the slices together into a strip. This of course would take many hours, so Wayne bows to expediency and buys the premade strips, fabricated in a German factory, from a guitar builder's supply catalogue for five bucks apiece. However, he bows toward frugality by splitting each strip in half to double its effective yield.

The bisected back stripe is just a little bit thinner than the two halves of the back it will join. So Wayne bends down and finds a strip of mahogany on the floor and glues it to the back of the back stripe to shim it to the same thickness as the rosewood.

Why? Because that's the way it was done on the great old Martins made during FDR's day. This is a fact known only to a select few. In a completed guitar, the underside of the back stripe is covered completely with a wide spruce brace. So only someone who'd seen a guitar stripped completely naked—as Wayne Henderson has—would even know about that stealthy piece of mahogany.

Does it matter that it's mahogany? Wayne doesn't know. "I've never tried it any other way," he said. If it's good enough for a Golden Age Martin, it's good enough for him.

Wayne looked at the clock—it was well after 1:00 A.M.—and pulled the first cooked side out of the side bender. The process of mesmerism was now complete. What was once a straight piece of timber, with no other goal than to reach straight up toward the

sun, had taken on a different shape in the service of another form
of exaltation. The side traced a subtle sinuous curve that would
have sent Brancusi back to the drawing board.

The bent side was now a virtual rosewood spring; press the
top gently and it pushed right back. Wayne picked up the first
side, balanced it so that it hung from his index finger, and drew it
close to his ear. He tapped the lower curve with a fingertip. The
initial ping faded quickly, and Wayne smiled as the hummy,
thrummy overtones seemed to hang in the air almost forever like
the long slow fade at the end of "A Day in the Life."

CHAPTER THIRTEEN

Playing with Knives

LET ME TELL YOU about Wayne's first guitar. Both of them. Propped in the corner of Wayne's first-floor gue-stroom, with its deep blue paint, its springy old bed, and its unsurpassed view of the guitar shop, is the guitar that bears the serial number 1. It's made of light-stained mahogany, with a spruce top that has darkened to a rich caramel brown. The neck is as big around as a Louisville Slugger. At a casual glance, this looks very much like any ordinary guitar.

It's only when you investigate more closely do you notice that the inlays around the edge of the top have been cut by hand, and each sliver of this thousand-piece mosaic was inlaid one piece at a time. Poke around a little more and you'll notice that the script on the headstock of the guitar reads not C.F. Martin, but W.C. Henderson.

Pick it up and strum it, and you'll quickly conclude that it may not be the best guitar you have ever played, but it's far from the worst. What makes it remarkable is that it was built by a 14 year old who'd hardly ever seen a quality guitar, much less seen one built. A teenager who would, one day, grow up to become perhaps the world's finest guitar maker.

In the other corner, by the couch, is the prototype—made by a prepubescent Wayne Henderson out of a cardboard box with wooden neck attached, frets drawn on with pencil, fiddle-style tuners that actually worked, and tensioning strings made of twine.

"I had to change the box every so often," Wayne said with a laugh when he saw it. The last change was to a box from Dental Scotch Snuff.

Examining these two instruments is like peeking into a time capsule and seeing Pablo Picasso's crayon drawings, listening to a young Igor Stravinsky noodle on the family piano, or reading Thomas Wolfe's fourth-grade book report. Love a good creation myth? Sit back and listen.

"My grandfather made caskets and that's bound to be where I inherited my guitar making from," Wayne will joke. "They're all boxes."

But more to the point, his father had the practical woodworking skills that you needed when you grew up poor on a farm in rural Virginia. The Hendersons didn't go out to Wal-Mart to buy things. If it was something that could be crafted out of wood, they made it. But even in a do-it-yourself culture that preceded *This Old House* by a quarter-century, Wayne was something special. "While the other boys were playing cowboys and Indians," his mother, Sylvie, recalled. "He'd be sitting somewhere by himself with a knife making his own toys."

Wayne had a small side business of carving his classmates' names into their pencils (Think about *that* for a second.)

"How much did you charge?" I wondered.

"Usually nothing. Maybe an apple or something. None of us had any money."

Wayne had once shown me a small wooden toy that now sat in the china cabinet in the dining room. It was a ball-in-a-box about four inches long, shaped roughly like a box kite, with four struts connecting two solid end plates. A small ball was suspended by the struts, and when you tipped it, the ball would roll smoothly from one plate to the other. At first glance, it looked like the sort of precisely finished tchotcke that factories in Thailand or Sri Lanka turn out by the thousand and sell for $6.99.

"I guess I was about eight years old when I made that," Wayne said matter-of-factly.

I thought about my own son, who was almost that age, and then rolled through a mental list of all the preteens I knew. I couldn't think of another with the combination of patience and dexterity to turn out something so precise. Then the other shoe dropped.

"The hard part was trying to figure out how to carve the ball inside there," he said casually. I assumed that the toy had been assembled—first shape one plate, then the next, fabricate the struts, smooth the ball, a few dabs of glue and it's done. Wayne had crafted this toy from a single piece of walnut. The ball was perfectly round and smooth, just small enough to roll freely, but not so tiny that it rattled around. The frame was Shaker-square, full of clean lines, sharp edges, and perfect ninety-degree corners. It was a little piece of art. I couldn't fathom how I—or anyone of any age—would start such a project, much less pull it off so perfectly. But for Wayne it was simple. He would see something and replicate it, usually with precocious accuracy.

One of Grayson County's sacred objects when Wayne was growing up was E. C. Ball's 1949 Martin D-28, a guitar not dissimilar to one sold at the Crossroads Auction. A distant cousin of Wayne, E.C. drove the school bus, owned the general store, and played music, not necessarily in that order. Ball and his wife, Orna, sang and played gospel-tinged tunes—he on guitar and she on accordion, and earned a fair measure of fame outside of Rugby. When folklorist Alan Lomax met Ball at a Galax fiddlers convention in the early 1940s, he came back to record E.C. for his historic Library of Congress recordings. The session took place on the porch of the Henderson household because they were the only ones in the area with electricity.

Ball's guitar, which he played every day at the store, was a constant in young Wayne Henderson's life for as long as he could remember, and he knew that there was something about that guitar that separated it from the hand-me-down Sears Silvertone that his brother, Max, left lying around the house.

But a Martin like E.C.'s cost maybe $500, used car money. For a farm boy from Grayson County, he could have just as easily been lusting after a Rolls-Royce. So he approached the problem with the kind of practical hubris that only young teens possess. "Aw, heck, a guitar's just made out of wood," he reasoned. "I can make one myself."

One night, he swiped the drawer out of his parents' dresser, removed the bottom, and left it in the creek overnight to soak off the veneer. This was Wayne Henderson's first tonewood. Over the course of the summer, he lavished every spare minute on the guitar, the instrument taking shape secretly in a shed on a corner of the farm. He whittled the neck with his knife, used chicken wire for the frets, stole the tuners off the Silvertone.

"By August I had something that looked like a guitar," he recalled.

Only one problem. He used some old black rubbery glue that his father had used to seal weatherstripping on the car. This would prove to be a fatal flaw. One especially hot summer afternoon, young Wayne walked into the out building to discover that his guitar had exploded. "Like a morning glory," he recalled more than four decades later, still with a tinge of sadness. His guitar-building career could have been over even before it began. But Wayne's father sensed his blue mood and asked him what was the matter.

Wayne spilled it. Walt Henderson, who doted on his son more than he let on, made him a deal. "He felt real sorry for me and told me that he would take me to see Albert Hash." Hash was a master violin maker who had a small shop just over the North Carolina border, and while it's only a hop and a jump now, to the teenaged Wayne it could have been a trip to Jupiter.

"It was only a couple of weeks, but it seemed like forever," he said.

Hash found Wayne a piece of mahogany from the back of a door, ordered a spruce top and a fingerboard from an instrument maker's supply catalogue, and gave him a primer on the basics of instrument building, although Hash himself had never built a guitar.

When Wayne returned with the finished instrument, Hash was more than impressed, he was astonished. "If I knew you were going to do this good a job," he said, "I would have given you some better wood."

Walt encouraged his son, albeit guardedly. Dad gave him the six-foot-long bench that Wayne used as his first de facto workshop. "When I was about eighteen years old, as soon as I got out of school, I opened a checking account with the money I got from a calf," he recalled. "I wrote a check for $75 for enough lumber to build a shop. My dad helped me, but I did a lot of the work myself. I had a place to work with lights. I was so proud of that." The building still stands near his mother's house, filled to the rafters with wood and assorted junk. But Walt still expected that his son would go to work on the farm.

And part of the reason was Robert McNamara. A farm deferment would keep Wayne out of the Vietnam War. "The local draft board would give me deferments as long as I stayed around and took care of my parents," Wayne recalled.

"And at that time that was pretty important. It was right smack in the middle of the Vietnam War and I didn't want to be in that mess. When I had to go be examined for the Army, I tried to figure out everything in the world that could be wrong with me. But when I got to the examination place, one of them doctors would look down your throat and the other one up your ass and if they didn't see one another they'd pass you," he said with a laugh.

There was one other reason to stay on the farm. At that particular juncture in history, there wasn't any such thing as a guitar builder. Steel string acoustic guitars were made in factories the same way as chairs, or piano benches. The best ones came from factories like the Martin plant in Nazareth, Pennsylvania, and the Gibson factory in Kalamazoo, Michigan.

A few luthiers—like Elmer Stromberg and John D'Angelico—who made the expensive archtop guitars favored by jazz players worked in small shops producing instruments in small quantities by hand. And a few classical guitar makers, most of them trained in Spain, had moved to America and continued building fine instruments in a traditional bench-work manner. But steel string flattops were built on an assembly line.

In the mid-1960s this began to change. A Greenwich Village classical guitar builder named Michael Gurian branched out into steel string guitars. A New Jersey barber named Augustino LoPrinzi, who built a guitar on a bet in the back of his shop, decided to quit cutting heads and build guitars full-time. J.W. Gallagher, a cabinetmaker in Wartrace, Tennessee, took up guitar building. These shops schooled a number of apprentices who ultimately set out on their own, and inspired plenty of others who began to understand that you didn't need a factory to build a guitar.

What was the catalyst of this change? By then, the Martin and Gibson factories were making the worst acoustic guitars in their history, and discerning guitar buyers began looking for a sound they couldn't get from factory-built guitars.

The other part of the equation was blowing in the wind. Don't forget, this was the heyday of the counterculture. Playing a guitar that you built yourself—or at least by someone you shook hands with—was yet another way to thumb your nose at the establishment. Look inside a Gurian guitar from the early 1970s and you'll find a hand-drawn label that pokes gentle fun at the C.F. Martin Co./Nazareth PA/MADE IN U.S.A. insignia branded inside every guitar. It reads: "Gurian Workshops. Earth. Third planet from the Sun."

How did this fledgling craft movement affect fledgling guitar maker Wayne Henderson? Hardly at all. Keep in mind that in the days before satellite dishes, Wayne would have to go over to the next county just to watch a World Series game. Nineteen sixties or no 1960s, the only thing they smoked in Rugby, Virginia, were Salems and Raleighs. At the beginning at least, Wayne built guitars because he needed a guitar, and his friends needed guitars, and the guitars that he made were far better than store-bought. And the more things change . . .

CHAPTER FOURTEEN

Filing on Elvis's Nut

T HE FIRST FULL DAY of the Clapton guitar project at the
Wayne C. Henderson Guitar Company had dawned a rainy
slate gray, but surprisingly balmy for mid-November in the
mountains of Virginia. And rain in these parts is actually a good
thing, and not only for the way that it makes the rolling Blue
Ridge peaks look like the heathered hills of Scotland. It keeps the
humidity up, and guitars and tonewood like it moderately warm
and generally moist.

Having knocked off at 2:00 A.M. the previous night, Wayne was
getting a rolling start to the day. Up at 11:30, he slid into his shop
uniform—a pair of Carhartt jeans, a festival T-shirt, a baseball cap
from the Palestine Old Time Music Festival—Texas, not the Middle East—and a pair of New Balance running shoes that had never
seen anything more than a hurried trot. He wolfed down a bowl of
Cheerios with a banana cut up in it, puttering around the kitchen
quietly so as not to wake me, although I'd been up and banging
away at my computer for a couple of hours even more quietly.

Wayne Henderson was ready for his morning commute—
thirty-six steps across the front yard to the shop. He made a bee-
line to the side bender and the Squeezer, plugging in both, as well
as the hot plate, and plopping in the first of the two remaining
sides as soon as the water began to warm. Wayne was putting in
a little extra effort this morning.

He had commitments. Robin Kessinger, a masterful flat-picker with a Paul Bunyan physique and a laugh to match, was driving up later in the afternoon. He was bringing his Henderson guitar—number 237, circa 2000—to be refretted. He had played it so much and so hard that he was literally wearing it out. Later on that Friday night Wayne would be playing a gig at the Ashe Civic Center with Jeff Little, a remarkably talented piano player whose frenetic style channels the young Jerry Lee Lewis. And on Sunday morning, after the VFW show on Saturday Night, Wayne would be leaving for Silver Spring, Maryland, a six-hour drive, where he was scheduled to do a workshop and a concert with Kessinger. A busy man.

Knowing that there was much to be done and not much time to do it, Wayne loaded up the side bender. Then he grabbed one of the sides he had bent last night, carried it across to the belt sander, and he rubbed it back and forth against the fast-moving belt with a rolling and rocking motion. It was a tiny ballet, and also purposeful. Although the sides had been sanded smooth before they were placed in the bender, the soaking and the heating had raised the grain again, and the wood felt like it had a five o'clock shadow. A couple of quick passes on the belt sander, and the rosewood was glassy again. At the same time, Wayne was doing luthier's liposuction, buffing out the small wrinkles and irregularities that the side bender left, rendering the remaining curves perfectly smooth and sensuous.

The shop was crowded this morning. Gerald Anderson had the day off from his mail route. Steve Kilby was back to finish up the repair on his guitar, and he had brought along his wife, Penny, a former schoolteacher, who quickly retired to the house to make some phone calls. Steve, as usual, was in a teasing mood, yanking Wayne's chain about his famous client.

"Who's going to play you in the movie, Wayne?" he asked. "Dudley Moore's dead."

"Robert Redford ain't," Wayne countered.

By a little after noon, Wayne's older brother, Max, and his

wife, Pat, showed up, bringing lunch. There was some food left over from a funeral at the church the previous day—Kentucky Fried Chicken, beans, Pat's homemade orange slaw, and sweet tea supplemented with a batch of fresh biscuits. Even when he wasn't here bearing food, Max was an invisible presence in the world of the W.C. Henderson Guitar Company. A retired machinist, Max made the truss rods that hold the neck straight in every guitar. And he has had a hand in many of the tools that are as much a part of the landscape in the shop as the piles of sawdust. The fretting hammer he made is a particular beauty, forged from brass with a multicolored Bakelite handle that just begs you to grip it.

And then there was the soundhole cutter. Putting the freshly buffed sides down, Wayne turned his attention to the guitar tops and installed the soundhole cutter on the Shopsmith. It was Max's masterwork. This elegant device consisted of a disc of precision-milled aluminum, with a small drill bit in the center to precisely mark this most crucial of measurements, and three sliding channels that hold a series of wider cutter bits. The outermost bits make a shallow groove for the decorative rosette that surrounds the soundhole. The innermost one scores and slices the soundhole clean and true. With one quick pull of the lever, Wayne had popped a hole in the top with three perfect concentric circles around it.

"That's quality work," I said to Pat, indicating Max's invention.

"He didn't even sign his name to it," she said with a smile. "Did you see the cannon?" Sure enough, under the bench, hidden by a cardboard UPS box, was a miniature cannon about a foot long. Made of sold brass, atop a metal frame, it was fully functional. Stuff it full of black powder and it's the War of 1812 all over again. Max had made it for Wayne as a Christmas present. They were both grown men by then, but they both had enough little boy in them to revel at the sight of something blowing up real good. Max stuffed it full of powder, boxed it, wrapped it with a bow, and put it under his little brother's Christmas tree.

"That was good powder," Max recalled, with a faraway look in his eye. "I left the fuse hanging out of the box."

On Christmas morning, Wayne dutifully took his cue, and like Yosemite Sam in any of a hundred Warner Bros. cartoons, he lit the fuse. Kerboom! There was corrugated cardboard and Christmas wrapping all over the yard. It blew the box to smithereens.

"It's no wonder they both have ringing in their ears," said Pat indulgently.

"He told me that was the best Christmas present he ever got," Max said, still beaming.

THE MORNING HADN'T STARTED out so auspiciously for me, or for Gerald Anderson. Gerald was working quietly at his own little workbench in the corner when I arrived at the shop. His space is an oasis of order amid the shop's general chaos. Tall, trim, and looking closer to thirty five than his actual age of fifty, Gerald even manages to keep his clothes clean. After I walked in the door, he showed me what he had completed the night before. It was an elaborate abalone fern inlay that would grace the top of the mandolin's neck. He handed it to me.

"That's sweet," I said.

I instinctively turned the neck over to inspect the back of the peghead. The only problem was that the abalone and mother-of-pearl inlays weren't yet glued in, so half of them tumbled to the floor which was covered with two inches of sawdust. I began apologizing profusely as I started sifting through the mess. Gerald was unfazed. He joined me on the ground and we found most of the pieces within a couple of minutes. The last two shards probably bounced under a pile of wood never to be seen again. "Aw, don't worry about it," he said as he got up. As he began recutting the missing pieces, he told me that Spencer Strickland, his young apprentice, had done the same thing the night before.

Gerald has known Wayne since they were both in school, although their eight-year age gap precluded a childhood friendship. Gerald went off to college and got a degree in anthropology, but one day he showed up at Wayne's old guitar shop, and essentially never left. He started out doing repair work under Wayne's supervision and then graduated to building guitars. Realizing that the six-string niche was well-filled, he slid over into building mandolins. Gerald is also an accomplished musician. Although his guitar picking is good enough to have won a blue ribbon at the Old Fiddlers' Convention competition, when he plays gigs with Wayne, Gerald usually plays mandolin.

Gerald is a skilled mandolin maker, but while Wayne can just sweet talk a piece of wood into becoming an instrument, Gerald sometimes has to prod, cajole, and even coerce the raw materials to do his bidding. Whatever he may lack in natural talent, Anderson makes up for it with pure work ethic. "I never saw anyone who was so determined to build instruments," Wayne said.

The proximity of genius is both a blessing and a curse. While Gerald gets gigs and orders because of his relationship with Wayne, there's also a flip side. Whenever Wayne's around, Gerald becomes the second-best instrument builder and the second-best picker in the room.

"I figured I'd have a job in an office," Gerald confessed as he reglued the last piece of inlay. "And a house with a picket fence and a yard full of kids. But it didn't work out that way."

HOW MUCH WAS WAYNE feeling the pressure? Well, the ultimate one-man band was ready to delegate some of the tasks of guitar building.

To me.

During my early days at the guitar shop, I had been what Wayne calls a General Loafer. Someone like Gabby or Ralph, who brings food, laughs at jokes, marks time, and monitors progress. A spectator.

Granted, I didn't have an assigned seat—Ralph set up camp in the old oak swivel chair in front of the jointer, while Gabby always sat in the tiny maple chair on the other side of the thickness planer in front of Gerald's bench. I just grabbed whatever stool was available at any given moment when I wasn't wandering around aimlessly. "They also serve who only sit and watch"— that's one of the unofficial mottos of the guitar shop. Right alongside "Opossum: the *Other* Other White Meat."

Granted, during those first days I was a General Loafer with a tape recorder in hand, and a silly question always at the ready. Still, I was a spectator. I'd answer the phone or head over to the house to round up some food, but the actual work of guitar making was left to the professionals—the professional, I should say. But the night before, things had begun to change.

Fumbling with the mahogany neck and tail blocks he'd just cut—the sturdy internal braces that will hold the two sides together at the top and bottom of the guitar body—Wayne gave me a long look over the top of his sawdust-coated reading glasses. "You want to do something?" he asked.

We had already eaten dinner, so I was a little puzzled.

"You want to sand these blocks?"

"Sure?" I said, with more trepidation than conviction.

He handed me the two blocks and pointed to a large sanding block with some coarse 60 grit paper attached to it. "Even at the top and the bottom, a guitar isn't completely straight," Wayne explained. The goal was to make these two blocks ever so slightly convex, so they sit completely flush against the subtle curve where the two sides meet, a real-life rendering of the elusive asymptote, those lines from junior high geometry that converge but never meet. "A lot of guitar makers just put 'em in flat, but I like doing it this way," said Wayne. That is, of course, Waynespeak for "This is the right way to do it."

Wayne's trick is to use a sanding block that has the faintest trough in the middle, making it ever so slightly concave. Rub a flat heel block against this concave sanding block, and the result will be a tail block that becomes just convex enough to fit snugly against the guitar body. He puts a mark in the center of the tail block with a pencil. When the mark is gone, voilà, then the block has the appropriate curve.

Why me? Why this? This task took a fair amount of just plain muscle, and although he didn't let on, Wayne's shoulder was probably aching a little. And it was a soft-fail situation. If I screwed it up, he'd just pick up another piece of mahogany and cut a couple more, no big loss of time or materials. At worst, it'd be a good story: "After the way he butchered that poor neck block, I think we're going to have to demote old Allen here from General Loafer to Colonel Loafer," he'd announce.

He did, however, wait until the shop cleared out to ask me. I'd get to make my world guitar-building debut in relative privacy.

Wayne always made it all look easy, telling jokes and listening to stories while he worked, but I was soon to discover that even the simplest guitar-building job was far from mindless. I started rubbing the tail block against the sandpaper and saw the soft mahogany dust pile up around the edges. It was grunt work, but it was precision grunt work. The strokes needed to be straight and down the center. The pressure needed to be even, front to back, so I wouldn't create an unwanted complex curve. And I needed to rotate the block occasionally just in case it wasn't.

I sanded. I showed it to Wayne. I sanded some more.

"That looks pretty good," he said.

He gave it a few more stiff strokes for good measure.

"Does this mean I'm an apprentice?"

As a matter of fact it did. He then clamped the neck block, which not only holds the sides together but attaches the neck to the body, into a vise, with the unsanded side up. He had already taken the block over to the table saw and made the two critical cuts that define the sides of the dovetail joint into which the neck will fit. What still needed to be done was to clean out the wedge in the center with a chisel. The precision work had already been done, but I had graduated past sandpaper. Wayne demo'd, and I followed. I drove the narrow chisel into the smooth, hard mahogany, tapped it gently with the heel of my hand, and felt the grain split with a silent crack. I scraped first from one side, then the other, until my neck block looked pretty much like the one he had made for the other guitar.

When it was done I felt like a second-grader bringing home his latest art project.

"Hey, look at what I did," I wanted to shout.

"That's pretty good," said Wayne, but his biggest compliment was that he didn't feel the need to tweak the job himself.

I also came to realize what Wayne was doing. Sure, he could save a little time by delegating the no-brainer jobs to me, so he could concentrate on the real job of guitar building. Given that his typical quitting time was 2:00 A.M., every minute saved meant a few extra minutes of sleep. But it was also something else. He was giving me a gift, or shall I say, *another* gift. A few weeks earlier, I had asked him to name some of the celebrities whose guitars he worked on.

"Oh, Tony Rice, Doc Watson, Stephen Stills, Neil Young . . ."

Anyone else?

"When I was at Gruhn's we had Elvis Presley's guitar in the shop. We all took turns filing on the nut"—the slotted piece of bone at the top of the neck which holds the strings apart—"just so we could say that we worked on Elvis's guitar."

So here I was, filing Clapton's nut, in a manner of speaking.

And so in the days to come, Wayne would hand me little jobs, usually ones involving nothing sharper than sandpaper, ones with no possibility of affecting the overall quality of the instrument. For example, most old Martins have these fabric reinforcements on the inside of the guitar's sides, but they've largely fallen out of favor among new-school builders. Many eliminate them completely, while others go the opposite route, fashioning a system of thin wooden braces—mahogany usually—where the cloth strips would have gone. But Wayne's old school.

He uses a special satiny ribbon, almost exactly the same shade of brown as a good piece of rosewood. There are nine of them at slightly irregular intervals, running the width of the sides from top to bottom. They serve the same function as a levee, designed to minimize the damage if the guitar should crack along the side, as they're prone to do. Wayne did the first side on the Clapton guitar, and feeling the time pressure, with three still remaining, he made me a proposition.

"Do you think you could do this?"

"Um, yeah, sure."

He spread a thin layer of glue on a piece of scrap spruce. He dragged one end of the ribbon deftly through the shallow pool of Titebond, applying the lightest of pressure with his fingers. "You can't be slopping glue around on these, because you can't just sand it off." While they are visible, these reinforcements aren't structural, so he was willing to be pragmatic.

He cut a bunch of the strips and I started gluing, placing them precisely on the pencil marks he'd drawn. After I had a few on, I picked up another one and realized that it was too short. It now dawned on me that each ribbon was a slightly different length because the side varied in width, and Wayne had cut them to fit and laid them out in order. I had started grabbing randomly, and had already used the ones meant for the longest sections. So much for the system. I cut a few more strips and dealt with the other challenge, walking the tightrope between not enough glue and too much. I wiped the excess glue with my free hand, and then realized I needed that hand to be clean to press the ribbon in place. So I grabbed a paper towel, which stuck to my gluey fingers and so it went. But when all was said and done, the job I did wasn't noticeably worse than Wayne's. The ribbons were straight, with a minimum of glue on the ribbon or oozing out the side.

And during these moments of filing Clapton's nut, I gained a first-hand appreciation of the craft of guitar making. Sure, it was harder than it looked—that was a given. But I began to understand the payback. Partly, it's a sensual thing. There's a rhythm to the sanding and filing and chiseling and smoothing that's not unlike playing music. *One . . . two . . . three . . . four . . . One . . . two . . . three . . . four . . .* And then there's the scorekeeping aspect. Even the incremental accomplishments in building a guitar are real and tangible. Five ribbons down, four to go. That little pile of sawdust and woodchips, and that freshly rounded and chiseled neck block, served as evidence of your labors. If you needed some positive reinforcement, simply pick up the piece of wood, show it to someone, and they'll oooooh and aaaaah as surely as Pavlov's dog drooled.

"Whadya think?" I asked Wayne.

"That is pretty good work," he said. "This one's a little crooked."

"You did that one," I lied.

"Oh."

THE IRONY WAS THAT while I fussed over the little pieces of ribbon, Wayne seemed to be channeling my clumsiness. He was gluing the rosettes around the soundhole of one of the guitar tops and for the first time in all the hours I've watched him work in the shop, he was visibly struggling.

This was a bear of a job to be sure. Wayne was managing nine little pieces of hair-thin wood purfling—imagine a piece of extra-thin linguine—each soaked in Duco cement, wrapped around a springy coil of Teflon, which is a place holder for the brittle abalone shell inlay that needed to be installed in tiny half-inch sections. It's an ingenious process—the glue won't stick to the Teflon, so after the glue dries, it can be pulled up, leaving a perfect little channel for the pearl. However, the combination of the tough, thick Teflon and the delicate wood purfling made this job a special challenge. "In the factory, they'd just use pieces of plastic and pound it in with a hammer," Wayne explained.

And today the willful Teflon was not cooperating. The little strips of wood were playing hide and seek, getting twisted and out of order. For the moment, these uncooperative pieces didn't

seem to want to become part of a guitar, and like a defiant tod-
dler who splatters the peas all over the floor, they seemed to have
the upper hand. But Wayne didn't cuss. He didn't growl. He
didn't hurl the top across the room like a giant wooden Frisbee.

He just winced. He sighed. He furrowed his brow. "Is lunch
almost ready?" Wayne asked, in search not of day-old Kentucky
Fried Chicken, but of a reprieve.

I watched for a moment and I asked him if he'd like me to
leave him alone.

"I don't get distracted," he said. "If I got distracted, I'd be
fucked." I gave him some space anyway, that not-so-casual pro-
fanity expressing what his words did not. And when he was done,
the guitar top was, well, a mess. There was glue smeared all over
the bindings, black stains on the top, and a couple of little places
where a black line of purfling was missing altogether.

"Time for lunch," Max announced.

Wayne put the top down on the top of the table saw to dry. It
was far from the prettiest work Wayne Henderson had ever done.
But after lunch—and after refretting Robin Kessinger's guitar,
and just before getting ready for tonight's gig—the top of
Clapton's met with a few passes from a razor-sharp scraper, and a
brief interlude with the belt sander, and those moments of angst
became nothing more than proof that Wayne Henderson is
indeed human.

CHAPTER FIFTEEN

Exactly Somewhat Between

W**HAT IS HARDER**, building a violin or a guitar?
I posed that question to Kerry Keane over lunch at the Sea Grill in Manhattan's Rockefeller Center, just around the corner from Christie's New York headquarters. Keane is well qualified to speak to this question. In addition to being vice-president of musical instrument sales for Christie's, and the man who made the Crossroads Guitar Auction a reality, he is also a classically trained violin maker and a guitar builder who worked under the pioneering luthier Augustino LoPrinzi.

"Building a guitar is a lot more difficult than a violin," he said without hesitation. "And if the American Federation of Violin and Bow Makers ever heard me say that, I'd be dead in an alley somewhere."

With close-cropped grey hair and an impeccable dark grey suit draped perfectly over his trim frame, Keane is the very definition of the word dapper. He is that rare individual who can wear a bow tie without affectation. But along with that polish, so necessary in his line of work, comes a sly smile and a dry, subversive wit. He took a sip of water. "Violins, violas, and cellos are carved. They're sculpture," he explained. "A guitar is fabricated. It's a construction project."

His answer went to the heart of the matter.

"You complete a guitar, you set the neck, you string it up,

and the very first thing that happens is that the bridge wants to move to where the peghead is and vice versa. They want to meet in the middle, and they're doing all they can to get there," Keane explained. "And your job as a maker is to make sure that doesn't happen." Or as master guitar builder John Greven once explained to me, "Every good guitar is right on the verge of blowing itself apart."

In the world of classical music, where instruments are narrowly defined, the guitar is considered a member of the percussion family, along with the tympani and the triangle. Indeed, guitar builders tend to think of a guitar body as a wooden drum. The guitar top is the drumhead—it vibrates and produces sound. The sides support the top, like the rims of a drum—indeed, luthiers often call them rims. But acoustically speaking, a drumhead has it much easier than a guitar top. The impact of a drumstick may be violent, but it's also over almost before it starts. Not so with a guitar top.

It must withstand the constant pull of six steel strings. And unlike a violin or other classical stringed instruments, where the strings push down on a bridge that sits on a heavily arched top further braced by a sound post, a flattop guitar's strings pull *up* on a bridge at an angle that's designed to tear the thin spruce top right off.

On the other hand, the guitar's none-too-simple task is to amplify the minuscule amount of acoustic energy provided by plucking a string into a sound that can fill a room. (To get an idea of how little, try plucking a string on a solid-body electric guitar. When it's not plugged in, its voice is barely a whisper.) Like the bumblebee, the acoustic guitar shouldn't work, but somehow it does.

"To be able to build a box that is to vibrate at its optimum level when aggravated by six strings that are exerting 200 pounds of pressure on it, yanking on it, that's a huge challenge," said Keane. "And for it to even stay together for two years, let alone twenty, fifty, or a hundred, that's quite a feat."

But a great guitar rises above the forces that would destroy it. To keep it from pulling apart, the spruce top is reinforced by a system of braces glued to its underside. And that's the instrument's paradox. The very same braces that keep a guitar from imploding also impede the top from vibrating, inhibiting its volume and ultimately strangling its voice.

"In violin-making school, the rule was 'the least amount of material for the required amount of strength,'" explained Keane. "And that rule is even more important in guitar making."

A guitar that's braced too heavily will last forever—and sing as sweetly as a deck chair. A guitar that's braced too lightly will astound you with its sound—for a moment, and then implode in your hands.

This delicate balancing act, between strength and stability on one hand and tone and volume on the other, is at the very heart of guitar building. Wayne's instinctive grasp of this dichotomy extends to the terminology he uses. He calls braces tone bars. "That's what they're called in mandolins," he explained. Sure it's a cool phrase, but it also reflects an understanding that a guitar body is a house of cards, but one that's supposed to last for a hundred years. And the ability to strike that balance between beauty and longevity, between a guitar's voice and its bones, is what separates a master like Wayne Henderson from other guitar builders.

IT WAS ABOUT 10:30 in the evening when Wayne returned to the shop from his gig over at the Ashe Civic Center just across the North Carolina state line, and he was pumped up.

"That was the best show I've played in a long time. The sound was real good. I could actually hear my guitar over Jeff's piano," he announced as he strolled into the house. I was sprawled on the battered leather couch in the front room half-asleep with a guitar in my lap and an instructional DVD playing on my laptop. "You should've come."

And I guess I should have, but I needed a little decompression time, a few minutes of *doing* in the middle of a week full of *watching*.

At an hour when most musicians would be hitting the bar or

heading to bed—perhaps not unaccompanied—Wayne headed back to the shop, wearing the same baseball cap, T-shirt, and clean Carhartt jeans that he'd worn to the show. As the clock crept toward midnight, the bracing of Clapton's guitars began.

Wayne pulled down his old bracing pattern, a guitar top made of now splintering plywood, headed straight to the wood pile, and picked out two pieces of clear white Appalachian spruce. He scanned the grain for obvious flaws, but the serious inspection began when he examined the cross section to see how well quartered the wood was. "I like it to be nice and straight," he explained.

Wayne made all the bracing on a guitar from the same piece of wood. The builders at Martin didn't do it this way back then and they certainly don't do that now—at modern guitar factories braces are roughed off on a CNC machine by the dozens. But his theory is sound. Pieces of wood from the same tree are likely to vibrate in the same way. And because the guitar is more likely to react to changes in temperature and humidity in a uniform way, expanding and contracting at the same rate, it should help the guitar's structural stability.

"It can't hurt nothing," Wayne said with his characteristic modesty.

He headed to the band saw and began ripping the soft clear wood into quarter-inch strips. On Internet guitar bulletin boards, there's much debate over bracing—much of it by people who have never seen the inside of a guitar builder's shop. Some pickers swear by five-sixteenth of an inch bracing, and others tout the slightly narrower quarter-inch bracing used in some vintage Martins.

"I just go by eyeball," Wayne said. Sensing that this reply was a little too vague, he added, "These are somewhat between."

I snatched a piece of the completed brace stock, and I fetched a caliper from the drawer and measured—it was exactly nine thirty-seconds of an inch. Exactly somewhat between.

Ripping the braces to size was the easy part. Then came the tightly choreographed ritual of brace shaping. Wayne picked up a piece of brace stock, laid it on the wooden template, marked it with a cursory stroke of the pencil, then walked over to the belt sander and bisected it, shaping the end of the brace to match the curve of the guitar. Not even turning the saw off, he walked back, put the completed brace on the table saw, snatched another piece, placed it quickly on the template, and without bothering to measure, walked to the band saw and cut it to length. He repeated this a dozen times, the big saw whining the whole time.

Then he took the braces to the belt sander and he began the dash of sculpture that spices up this architecture project. He pressed the soft pale spruce against the spinning belt, fishtailing the stick one way and then the other like a car on an icy road, rounding the chunky brace stock into something far sleeker.

Each completed brace looked a bit like the kind of crew racing sculls that compete in collegiate regattas. The braces are long and thin, reasonably tall in the center, and feathered down to a sliver at each end where they meet the guitar body. They're also carefully shaped in cross section, almost flat where they'll be glued to the top, but converging to a near knife-edge at their apex. Clearly, the shape that allows efficient human-powered travel on the Charles River must also offer little impedance to soundwaves as they try to escape from the inside of a guitar.

Wayne was on a roll now. He grabbed each piece of brace stock and rocked it back and forth gingerly on the belt sander, flipping each one casually from side to side and end to end. A plume of white sawdust billowed from the sander and settled slowly on the builder. After a few minutes, Wayne looked like he'd been out for a short walk in a fierce snowstorm, his gray beard now whiter, covered in a skim coat of ivory-colored spruce dust from the tip of his cap to his shoes. He didn't pay any attention, except for stopping to wipe his drugstore reading glasses before he worked on the X-brace, the large, crucial brace that intersects between the bridge and the soundhole. Each guitar had a dozen braces on the top, and four on the back, a grand total of thirty-two. In fifty minutes he had taken a couple of pieces of spruce and turned them into a guitar's skeleton. That's less than two minutes per brace. He stood back, looked at the pile of guitar bones, and pronounced himself satisfied.

Then it was time for the Lucky Stick. He walked over to the bench by the telephone to find one of the few hand tools in the glorious mess of a shop that's actually afforded its own dedicated resting place, a nail on the side of the bench. It's a bright green promotional yardstick that announces "So much more in Roten's Furniture Store." It will now have the honor of marking off the bracing on Clapton's guitars. "This yardstick has measured off the bracing in just about every guitar I ever made," Wayne explained. "I've had that since the 1960s when my guitars numbered in the single digits, no doubt." Lucky or not, this stick is showing its age—it's been glued back together in a couple of places. This heirloom tool was sometimes pressed into service for nonmeasurement purposes. "Back in the old shop we had bees," Wayne recalled. A bit of overly exuberant bug swatting snapped the promotional yardstick in half, but instead of making a new one—it would take him all of about ninety seconds—he glued it back together. "I've broken that thing I don't know how many times." He then indicated a notch that went almost all the way through the wood. "It got laid on the sander one time and almost ground the end off it. That would have done it in."

And if the yardstick had seen better days, the same could be said for the template, which had far more than a patina of wear. "You really can't see the lines on it good," Wayne admitted. "It's like the old men who used to play checkers over at the general store. They'd play with pop caps and after a while the black on the checkers was totally worn off. I always wondered how they kept from thinking the other one is cheating, but they knew where it used to be." He paused. "Same with that old pattern, I guess. I use it so much that I just know where the lines used to be."

Wayne's built his first few guitars almost by feel, after reaching inside the soundhole and under the top of a still-intact guitar to estimate where the braces were and transfer its placement to the top of a new guitar, an impressive bit of guesstimation.

"My guitars got so much better after the first time I got ahold of an old D-28 top that'd been smashed," Wayne recalled. "That old guitar, I still remember it. It had been played by a guy named Gene Mead. He was one of the greatest rhythm guitar players I ever heard, but he was really hard on guitars and that old Martin was beat all to pieces. Somebody filled the top with Bondo and painted it with yellow house paint."

When old Gene's guitar arrived at the guitar shop, even Wayne couldn't save that guitar top. But that cadaver gave him a peek under a guitar's skin to its bones. In a way, Gene Mead's old guitar died so that Eric Clapton's could live.

With the Lucky Stick and a razor-sharp pencil, Wayne continued his elaborate game of connect the dots, transferring the exact placement of the braces from the template to the clean spruce top. He lined up the notches at either end of the template with the center seam of the top. He scribed the perimeter and carefully marked the outer edge of each brace, then inserted the pencil into each of half a dozen pinholes in the template, marking through to the top.

With the saw and the sander off, conversation was again possible. Wayne started off with a few stories of his concert tours, short stories with clear punch lines. For example, Wayne played on the Masters of the Steel String Guitar tour, a national venture that found him playing nightly with musicians like Jerry Douglas, Albert Lee, John Jackson, and Eddie Pennington, an amazing Merle Travis–style thumbpicker and an even better jokester.

"One time after the tour Eddie had his wife call the shop pretending she was the desk clerk from the hotel. 'We've got $200 in charges for adult pay-per-view movies. We contacted Mr. Pennington and he said they were yours.' She had me going pretty good. 'I wasn't watching no porno movies. I was watching the Animal Channel.'"

As he settled into the rhythm of drawing and marking, Wayne eased into another story, a more resonant one, the one about E.C. Ball's old Martin.

"He had a 1949 Martin D-28 that was totally gorgeous. And I

think the reason it sounded so good was that he played it every day," Wayne recalled. "That was the first good guitar I ever saw, and sometimes when I was little he would sit me down where there was nothing I could bump and let me play it. I couldn't believe how great it sounded."

As Wayne grew up, E.C. would come over to the shop to pick with him and to let Wayne work on his guitar. And one day Ball broached a sensitive subject.

"He was getting old and he and Orna didn't have any kids, so he asked me if I wanted his guitar. He told me I could have it if I would take care of his funeral. So I told him I'd be glad to do that, but that's something you don't want to talk about or think about."

One day Wayne was out running his mail route, and when he dropped the mail off at the store, a couple of the loafers came out to the box. "Bad about old Estil, wasn't it?"

"What happened?"

E.C. was on his way to Albert Hash's and about halfway down the hill he had a heart attack and they found his car in the ditch at the side of the road and Ball slumped behind the wheel.

"E.C. had this nephew, who was also a cousin of mine," Wayne recalled. "I guess he wanted that guitar too, and somehow or another before E.C. had a chance to get cold, he come over and he had taken it."

That great old guitar was gone, if not forgotten, for a decade or more.

"This fellow Carl Caldwell used to come into the shop, and he liked to tell tales about old instruments—old Martins and Lloyd Loar mandolins in somebody's barn or something—but usually I didn't believe anything he said. One day, he told me he saw E.C. Ball's guitar in John Arnold's repair shop in Tennessee. I didn't even consider believing it, but I got to thinking, 'How could he have possibly made that up?' Carl said the guitar belonged to Ray's Music in Lenoir, North Carolina, so I went ahead and called the store.

"Ray got on the phone and said, 'Yeah, we got a guitar like

that, a guy came in and sold it. I'm supposed to send it to Oregon on Monday on approval.'

" 'Is the serial number 112020?'

" 'How did you know that number?'

" 'I knew that guitar since I was five years old.'"

Ray was a preacher and he wouldn't open the shop on Sunday. Monday was a heavy mail day for Wayne. And while Ray agreed to hold the guitar until Tuesday, he had a revival meeting after work so he wouldn't stay one minute past five o'clock.

"I hustled that route," Wayne recalled, "I just made sure that everybody got some mail even if it wasn't theirs—and I drove like crazy to get to Lenoir. I got there ten minutes before the store closed." There, in a tiny music store three counties away, Wayne Henderson was reunited with the guitar that meant more to him than any other.

"He wanted four thousand dollars for E.C.'s guitar. I told him that was a lot of money and it was. I asked him to get his heart in the right place and tell me what was the least he'd take for it. We agreed on $3,600, but I guess I'd have given him $10,000 if that's what it took."

Just as he told the story's happy ending, Wayne made the last of the bracing marks on the top. He put the wood and the template aside, and walked over and fished out a tatty guitar case from the mess in front of the pop machine. Inside was an old D-28 that was beautiful enough to bewitch any young boy, and powerful enough to transport a grown man back to the days when he was barely bigger than the guitar.

"That's a slim chance accident that I heard of it," Wayne said, as he closed the case. "In another day or two it would have been shipped to the other end of the country. It must have been some kind of fate, if you believe in any kind of stuff like that, but I think old E.C. would be happy that I have it."

CHAPTER SIXTEEN

The Buzzard's Revenge

OSTENSIBLY RETIRED, Wayne Henderson pretty much works every waking hour on those days when he's home, his fifteen-hour days punctuated by brief interludes to visit with the General Loafers, answer phone calls from guitar seekers, and have a quick bite to eat. The television doesn't get much of a workout.

But some days life intrudes, and Saturday, November 13, was one of those days.

First, there was the question of his forthcoming gigs. Wayne had a workshop to do in Silver Spring, Maryland, the next afternoon and a concert the day after that, both of which would keep him out of the shop for the bulk of the next three days. That evening, he also had a benefit show at the VFW in Hillsville, about forty twisty miles down Route 58. Ralph, who is his de facto road manager, was trying to convince him to drive straight from Hillsville, only a mile or two from the Interstate, get a hotel room somewhere north of Roanoke, and complete a leisurely drive on Sunday morning. It was the smart move, but Wayne still clung to the idea of stealing a few hours late Saturday night and early Sunday morning to work on the Clapton guitars.

And then there was the matter of the broken laptop. Wayne's ex-wife, Carol, called. She told him that one of his guitars—a thirty-year-old D-45-style with an elaborate tree of life inlay in the fretboard—had sold for $10,000. She also informed him that his daughter Elizabeth's laptop was broken. The upshot? He needed to drive to the Mouth of Wilson post office to put a check in the mail so the money for the new computer got there sooner rather than later.

As we turned out onto Route 58 in Wayne's Ford Focus, it became apparent that Wayne knows these roads like a palmist knows her favorite client's hand. Wayne drove that mail route—eighty-two miles a day—for thirty-five years, a good three quarters of a million switchback miles from one holler to the next. "Nothing but checks and love letters," he'd chirp cheerfully to everyone he saw on his route, as he dropped off the bills and the junk mail. Still, it's not the rain or snow or sleet or hail that's a mailman's worst enemy. It's boredom. The challenge of the day was to find a way to shake up the routine, as I discovered when I made an innocuous comment about the fact that the odometer on my old Acura Integra was only a few hundred miles away from turning 100,000.

"What's the mileage now?" Wayne asked.

"Ninety-nine thousand seven hundred something," I replied.

"That'd be a good serial number for a guitar," Wayne announced immediately. "A nice Brazilian '47 D-28 maybe." Talk about a one-track mind. "That's the kind of thing I'd think about when I was driving the mail route," he explained as he negotiated the next hairpin turn. "One of the fringe benefits of that job was riding around through the country looking at animals," Wayne said as he turned down the NPR station on the car radio. "I'd stop and mess with every snake I'd see and look at deer and turkey." Which brings us to the decade-old story of the buzzard's revenge. This is not a tale for the weak of stomach.

"One day I was running my mail route and I was coming up the road and a hundred fifty yards away in the middle of the road was a big old buzzard sitting on top of a dead possum, having lunch," Wayne said with a smile.

"I got up a little closer but he was paying so much attention to that three-day-old possum that he wasn't paying much attention to me," he recalled. "I got to within fifty yards and I said, 'I'm going to give him some excitement.'"

Wayne floored the accelerator on his small car of the day, an old Ford Escort, and within a moment he was right on the bird's tail.

"Buzzards can't fly fast at all, especially taking off, so I floor-boarded the car and I'm having the best time chasing him up the road."

And while buzzards may have some admirable qualities—William Faulkner once said that if he were reincarnated he would want to come back as a buzzard—grace under pressure is not one of them. Instead of merely veering into the woods, the flustered bird flapped furiously but kept following the road. "He's going with everything he had. He didn't know enough to turn off," said Wayne. "He was like right there," he said, pointing to the sky just above the windshield.

"All of a sudden that thing cut loose and he puked up two-thirds of that dead possum." This was Proust in reverse. If old Marcel's sense memory was that of freshly baked madeleines, Wayne was conjuring up the indescribable odor of road kill recy-cled. "I thought I was going to have to stop and throw up myself.

"I'd always heard that a buzzard, if you disturb them or con-front them or get in a fight with one, they'll puke on you," Wayne recalled. "Being a country boy I'd always heard that, but I didn't hardly believe it. How could they do that?"

He became a believer in a hurry. "It landed dead center right on my windshield. I've never had such a mess in my whole life. I couldn't see where I was going. Buzzard puke absolutely all over the hood and the windshield. I had to turn my windshield wipers on so I didn't run off the road, and that just made it worse. Luckily there was enough in the windshield washers to clean a little bit of it off. If you've ever seen anything nasty, that there just about takes the cake," said Wayne by way of under-statement. "Man, I had a hard time doing the rest of the route."

He dumped the car at the post office for the weekend and prayed for rain. "It did rain," he recalled, "but there were still chunks and hunks of that stuck on the roof and the hood. Took the paint right off. That mess stayed there until I wore that old car totally out."

We finished the errand, skipped lunch, and Wayne started to work again on the guitar backs. The inside of the back stripe was reinforced by a narrow piece of spruce, with the grain running perpendicular to the grain on the rosewood back. He went over to the bench and unearthed a spoke shave—essentially a plane that you pull toward you rather than push. But this one was downright Lilliputian, only a little bigger than Wayne's finger. He grasped it delicately between his thumb and forefinger, the way a socialite might hold a tea cup, and scraped off delicate curlicues of spruce.

"That's one of my favorite jobs," he announced.

"Where'd you get that spoke shave?" I asked.

Wayne paused for a second as he shifted from the here-and-now of this guitar to the there-and-then of acquiring the tool.

"Lenny got that for me," he recalled. "He was a disabled Vietnam veteran. He had an awful time in Vietnam," he said. "But he came out pretty lucky, I guess. He didn't look like he was any more disabled than me. But he had every bone in his body broke, a big hole in his head, everything on him shot through once.

"This guy come took my guitar-building class at Augusta West Virginia, couple of times. He even came down here and worked with me for a spell. The Veterans Administration paid him for coming and paid me for teaching him a little."

WAYNE TURNED HIS ATTENTION back to the pleasant, easy job in front of him. "It's just a fun thing to do," he said. "If I ever got a job in a guitar factory, this is the one job I'd want to do."

"You'd be feeding it into a CNC machine," I said. He frowned a little and kept on scraping. The truth is that Wayne Henderson was the last person who would flourish in today's Martin guitar factory. Located on the outskirts of Nazareth, Pennsylvania,* the company's sprawling single story building houses a state of the

---

*In the Band song, "The Weight," the line "I pulled into Nazareth/I was feeling 'bout half past dead" is not a reference to the place where Jesus plied his trade, but a description of Robbie Robertson's trip to the Martin guitar factory.

art manufacturing facility. On one of the daily factory tours the company offers, I saw how Martin guitars are made today, and it is a far cry from the Wayne Henderson method.

The assembly line consisted of dozens of individual workstations, most nicely personalized with family pictures and NASCAR calendars. Each worker had a specific job, from grading wood to stringing up finished guitars, and they did that job all day long. The shop was clean and modern—I saw hardly a speck of sawdust or a scrap of wood—and many of the messiest and most repetitive jobs had been automated. The goal here was consistency, to make each guitar exactly like the one before it. And that left little room for guitarmaking, at least as practiced by Wayne Henderson, tweaking each instrument to get the most out of a particular piece of wood. Only a handful of the hundreds of employees could have made a guitar from start to finish. In fact, an increasingly large percentage of the company's workers are women who came to Martin after the garment factories moved out of the area.

Still, the general consensus is that over the last decade or so, the company has begun to reconnect with its past. Prodded in part by keepers of the flame like Wayne Henderson, Martin is building the best guitars since the company's glory days of the 1930s and '40s. What's the explanation for those great guitars of the Wartime Era? Probably a glorious accident, caused by a confluence of top grade materials and the glut of skilled labor caused by the Great Depression.

And indeed, the relationship between Wayne Henderson and the Martin factory is a walk backward on the path of commerce. The story of capitalism has always been about finding a way to take hand-crafted objects and make them cheaply and efficiently in large quantities. Wayne Henderson does exactly the opposite, working alone in a small shop, crafting instruments that capture the best qualities of remarkable guitars built on assembly lines in factories fifty years earlier. Adam Smith would surely scratch his head.

The weather turned colder, and the sudden chill had Wayne a little worried. A guitar is a bit like an old man—its mood, and indeed its very configuration, can change with the weather. A flattop guitar isn't flat. The back arches slightly along its length from the top to bottom as well as across its width, and that's to allow the wood to expand and contract with changes in humidity.

The braces for Clapton's guitar had all been roughed out, and gluing them down to the top and the back was a quick job that would take a pile of wood a long way toward becoming a guitar. But the humidity had been dropping along with the temperature. If Wayne glued the braces and left them unattended for a couple of days while the humidity dropped sharply and quickly, there was a chance that the fragile rosewood of the body and the spruce of the top could develop cracks even before they're built. He resisted the temptation to take one small step forward and risk several large steps back.

Wayne put one of the back braces down on the back. It rocked like a runner of a rocking chair, balancing perfectly on the back stripe. He notched out its future home, cutting that inner spruce strip carefully with his sharp penknife. Tolerances? The braces press-fit so perfectly into the back stripe that when Wayne grabbed a brace between his thumb and forefinger, it held the entire weight of the back without a speck of glue. And that's the way it would stay for the time being.

As Wayne grabbed his bag and his guitar and prepared to leave for three days in Washington, there was a perfect build-a-guitar kit sitting on the workbench.

"You could start selling them," said Ralph as Wayne headed to the door.

"It'd be a box with a pile of wood and a sharp knife," said Wayne as he picked up his overnight bag and pulled the door shut. "And if you order before midnight tonight, you get a picture of a guitar, so you know what parts to cut away."

The story begins: Eric Clapton playing Tim Duffy's Henderson OM-28, in 1994 (COURTESY OF MARK LEVINSON/TIM DUFFY).

The cubicles at the guitar shop where Wayne Henderson files his guitar orders.

Raw Brazilian rosewood before it has been cut into guitar-sized planks.

The Brazilian rosewood sides for Eric Clapton's guitar.

Gluing a rosewood back using the Squeezer. The side bender (top center) and the hot plates on the workbench (right) are used for shaping guitar sides.

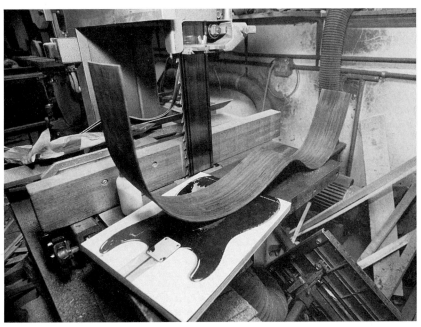

A Brazilian rosewood side after it has been bent, sitting atop the Christie's catalogue for Eric Clapton's Crossroads Guitar Auction.

Wayne Henderson tapping a bent side to assess its tone.

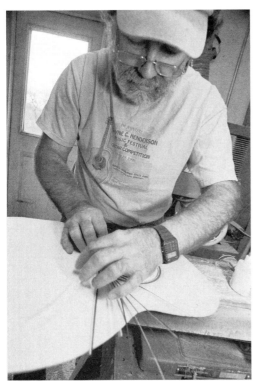

Finessing the thin pieces of decorative wood and plastic purfling for the rosette around the guitar's soundhole.

The finished rosette on an Appalachian red spruce top.

Cutting the soundhole from the spruce top.

Rosewood guitar sides with the neck and tail blocks glued on.

Gluing the mahogany kerfing onto the rosewood sides, using binder clips as clamps.

Sanding guitar sides on the belt sander.

Branding the back stripe with a red-hot branding iron.

The brand found on every Henderson guitar.

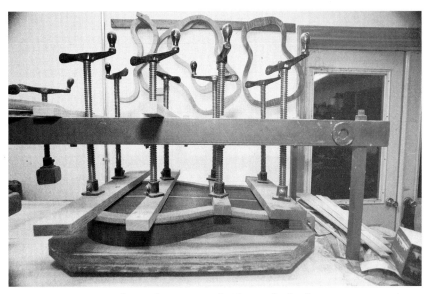

Gluing the rosewood sides to the back.

Inspecting the nearly completed
guitar body.

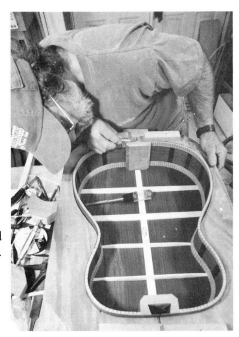

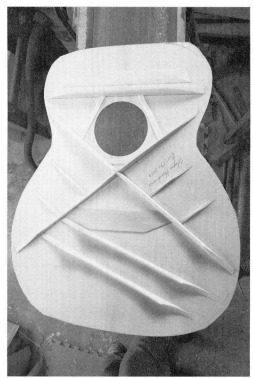

The bracing on the underside of a completed guitar top.

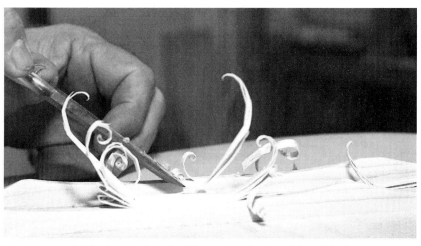

Scalloping an Appalachian spruce brace with a chisel.

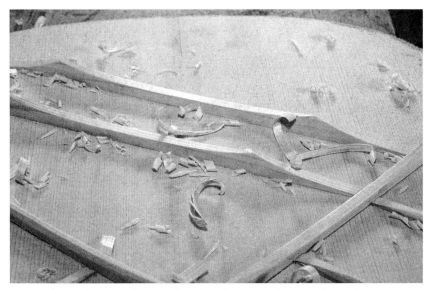

The peak-and-valley profile of scalloped top braces allows the top
to vibrate freely.

Shaping the maple bridge
plate on the sander.

Gluing the bridge plate to the guitar top.

A small tone bar after final shaping with a carving knife and fine sandpaper.

Signing the underside of the top before it's glued to the body.

The signature and date of guitar 327.

The serial number stamped on the mahogany neck block, inside the guitar.

Gluing the top on the completed
guitar body.

The dovetail joint at the bottom of the mahogany neck block, which attaches the guitar neck to the body.

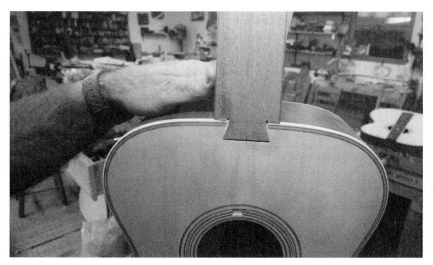

The front of the dovetail joint.

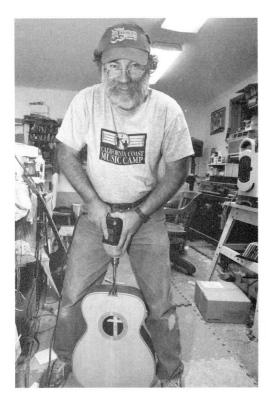

Drilling a hole in the neck block for the truss rod.

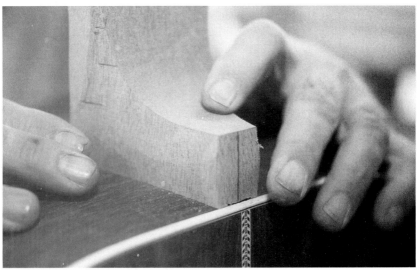

Fitting the rough neck block to the guitar body.

Shaping the profile of the neck
on the belt sander.

Shaping the neck heel where the neck meets the guitar body.

Whittling on the neck, Wayne's favorite part of the guitar-building process.

Testing the shape of a nearly completed guitar neck.

Polishing the edges of the newly fretted guitar neck.

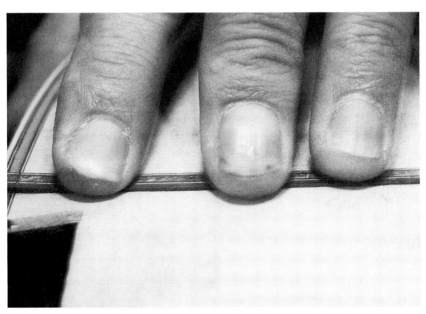

Inlaying the fretboard extension with greenheart abalone.

The front view of both Clapton guitar bodies before finishing.

Back view of both guitar bodies before finishing.

Everything that isn't a guitar: the guitar shop's scrap pile.

The completed guitars on the workbench.

A young Wayne Henderson playing guitar number 7
(Courtesy of Elizabeth Henderson).

Wayne, his mother, Sylvie, and brother, Max, in front of the shop.

Wayne Henderson playing
Clapton's guitar.

Students from the Junior Appalachian Musicians program in the nearby Allegheny County school system will benefit from the proceeds of the sale of guitar 327 (COURTESY OF HELEN WHITE).

CHAPTER SEVENTEEN

Four Hours That Way

WHILE WAYNE AND RALPH headed north to the suburbs of Washington, I pointed my old Acura south and west for a couple of days in Nashville. Part of my motivation was practical. I had never been to Nashville, it was only four hundred miles away, the weather was clear, the tank was full, and I had three days to kill. And Bill Frisell was playing at the Exit/In. But it was also a pilgrimage of sorts. The informal education of Wayne Henderson, guitar maker, began at Gruhn Guitars on Broadway in Nashville, just across the alley from the Ryman Auditorium, the original home of the Grand Ole Opry. And this story, and indeed Wayne's, might have taken a very different turn if not for a spur-of-the-moment decision some forty years ago by George Gruhn, the founder and proprietor of Gruhn Guitars.

Before my trip to Nashville I had heard lots about George Gruhn, most of it in the form of the typical, gently humorous stories that Wayne loves to tell.

"One time, I stayed over at George's house, and old George had a houseful of snakes," Wayne began. "He had this big snake in a box with just a screen laying across the top. Now I was worried about the snake getting out of that box, but he assured me that the snake would not get out of that box.

"So that night, I took my britches, my clothes, everything I had and packed them in the crack under the door. I wasn't all that worried about the snake, but I didn't want it in there when I was asleep."

"Didn't want no strange bedfellow?" Gabby interjected.

"But the next morning, we got up and the screen was off the top of the box and the snake was gone. George could not find that snake anywhere. And the next time I saw George, he said it was six months before he found that snake. It was coiled up inside the couch eating mice all that time."

Then there was the time that George stayed over at Wayne's mom's house. Wayne's mom showed him the freshly made bed. George asked about the bathroom. "Out there," she said, pointing him toward the outhouse in the pitch-black barnyard.

"Whay-errrr?" Gruhn is said to have replied, Wayne doing an amusing but not particularly accurate imitation of the flattened consonants that typify a Chicago accent.

Wayne and George are complete opposites, the Oscar Madison and Felix Unger of Six-String Nation. Gruhn is the city mouse, and Wayne is his country cousin. Wayne builds and plays guitars while George knows everything there is to know about them. Wayne can make friends with anyone, while George likes to keep to himself. Wayne Henderson is all about instinct; George Gruhn is pure intellect.

Armed with a few of these stories, plus the reputation that preceded him as the guy who literally wrote the book about guitars—*Gruhn's Guide to Vintage Guitars* and *Acoustic Guitars and Other Fretted Instruments*, to name two—I headed from the Best Western on Music Row to Gruhn Guitars to meet George Gruhn.

One of the salespeople showed me to the elevator and punched the security code—all the better to keep out the tourists who flock to the shop, attracted by the shiny, expensive guitars—but didn't feel the need to escort me up. While the large anteroom on the second floor is filled with tastefully displayed high-end guitars and violins, Gruhn's corner office was filled with cages housing a variety of snakes and reptiles. What kind? I didn't ask, but I did take a quick but careful peek to make sure that the lids were on tight.

Gruhn will tell you that he knows as much about reptiles as about guitars—when he was twelve years old he had a subscription to *Copeia: The Journal of the American Society of Ichthyologists and Herpetologists.* "I think I was the only one who read it who didn't have a Ph.D." he said casually. He later studied zoology and psychology at the University of Chicago (my alma mater, as well) and did graduate work at Duke.

Gruhn applied this same obsessiveness to his instrument collecting, which he began in earnest when he was a college student.

"For me collecting was very much an addiction," he explained. "You get up in the morning, and if you haven't gotten an instrument yet, you have withdrawal symptoms. When I started out I was buying a guitar every ninety days. Then it was once a month. Then once a week. Then every other day. Then every day. About the time that I ran out of room in my apartment is when I decided to open the shop.

"When people collect instruments, it's always erotic," he said.

"Erotic or neurotic? I asked.

"It's a little bit of both," he concluded.

George is bearded and about the same age as Wayne, tall but with a slightly stooped way of walking that minimizes his height. Gruhn has adopted the slow and slightly imperious speech of a professor, speaking at a deliberate cadence that suggests that he thinks you should be taking notes. When I walked in he was holding a tape recorder, dictating an appraisal of a Gibson Birdland archtop electric. The guitar was a clean example, but with one big problem: "The neck appears to have been replaced, since the binding on the headstock and the configuration of the heel conform to the specifications of a later model."

He put down the recorder and we walked to lunch at a nearby Japanese restaurant. I wondered how exactly George and Wayne, these two seemingly polar opposites, had been attracted to each other.

"I met Wayne Henderson at the Galax fiddler's convention," George said without hesitation. It was 1966 and Gruhn was still a student on summer vacation, and he headed south on a guitar-buying mission. "I decided I'd come down to Nashville because maybe there would be good guitars there. Old Martins and old Gibsons. There was nothing." He stopped into a store called Hewgley's, and the guy behind the counter told him about a man in Chattanooga named Mike Longworth who had a great collection of vintage instruments.

George called Longworth. No answer. He figured that he must be at work and would be back by the time George got there.

"How far is it to Chattanooga?" George asked. "It's four hours that way," came the reply.

When he arrived in Chattanooga, Longworth's wife answered the phone, and said that although her husband was out of town, he could come over and look at some of the guitars. Longworth, it turned out, was at a music festival in Asheville, North Carolina.

"How far is Asheville?" George asked. "Four hours that way," came the reply.

"I arrived at 1:00 A.M. and they were still picking. It was just an amazing thing because there were all these neat old instruments and people playing music. And it wasn't just Yankee boys playing music they heard off a New Lost City Ramblers record, it was the real thing."

George spent the weekend there and learned that there was another festival the next weekend in Galax, Virginia.

"Where's Galax?" Gruhn asked. "Four hours that way," came the reply.

Galax is where George Gruhn and Wayne Henderson first crossed paths. While George doesn't remember the exact moment that they met, Wayne Henderson does.

"The first time I ever laid eyes on him, I had no idea who he was, no clue, but he had a prewar D-45 slung over his shoulder," Wayne remembered. "I saw that all the way across the field." He ran over before Gruhn could disappear into the crowd.

"Is that what I think it is?" Wayne asked.

"Why, yes, it's a prewar '45," George replied casually.

Wayne ogled this holy grail of a guitar, but in a way that appealed to George's analytical side. Sure, he reveled in the sheer beauty of the pearl-bordered instrument, but he also looked at the inlay with an eye toward replicating it. And he wondered what made it tick.

"He let me play it," Wayne recalled as if it were yesterday. "He let me look inside a guitar I never dreamed I would ever be able to touch. The first thing I wanted to look at was the bracing. You could look right in the soundhole and see that somebody had repaired it. There was an extra piece laid alongside of the X-brace. I saw that first thing."

George said to Wayne, "Of all the people who've looked at this guitar, you're the only one who's ever seen that."

That was the beginning of an important, if not exactly beautiful, friendship. George and Wayne kept in touch, and when George opened the shop in Nashville a few years later, he asked Wayne to come to Nashville and work for him. Wayne turned him down; the draft board's farm deferments and his natural affinity for Rugby's slower pace made it a relatively easy call. But as the shop flourished, Gruhn made Wayne an offer he couldn't refuse.

"If you come down here for three weeks, you won't have to touch anything but a prewar '45," George told Wayne. So Wayne headed to Nashville, twelve hours or so the other way. And if Wayne was a mere footnote to the history of Gruhn Guitars—he was there for maybe three months total in the thirty-five-year history of the shop—Gruhn Guitars was to Wayne Henderson what Princeton was to the young Scott Fitzgerald.

During his brief time there Wayne got to play and work on some of the finest acoustic guitars ever built, in an environment that was dedicated to doing things right, a place that was among the first to recognize that great vintage Martins were more than just old guitars.

"My basic business model is to do for guitars what Hill and Sons of London did for violins for over a hundred years," said Gruhn. "They treated the instruments with respect."

And if Wayne ever had a country boy's fear of working on guitars that cost more than his dad's tractor, he got over that in a hurry. He recalled the time that he spent hours working carefully with a palette knife to remove the top from a vintage D-45. He had gotten the spruce top loose from the Brazilian rosewood sides everywhere except for the area where the top is glued to the fretboard. Wayne asked Randy Wood, another repairman in the shop who has since gone on to become a successful instrument builder, for some advice on how to proceed.

"It's loose everywhere but here?" Wood asked him.

"Yeah," said Wayne.

Wood grabbed the top of the old pearl-topped guitar with both hands and simply yanked. "Bamm!" Wayne shouted, mimicking the sound. "It made the biggest pop you ever heard. I just about swallered my tongue." Like a sleight-of-hand artist yanking a tablecloth out from under a setting for six, that stomach-churning rip left a perfectly clean seam on the spruce, better than anything he could have achieved with a jeweler's saw. The trick is being quick and decisive, and it's a lesson Wayne Henderson hasn't forgotten.

Wayne's time in Nashville also broadened his view of the world.

"George took me backstage at the Grand Ole Opry, which was almost next door, and he introduced me to Sam McGee," Wayne recalled. McGee, a hot guitarist whose version of "Buck-dancer's Choice" has been called the national anthem for aspiring fingerpickers, was then the oldest member of the Grand Ole Opry. "I sort of hit it off with him. He had a small farm outside

of Nashville and he'd almost rather talk about farming than guitars. And he seemed to enjoy picking with me."

One Saturday night, McGee was about to take the stage for
his weekly instrumental number at twenty after midnight and he
said to his new guitar buddy, "Why don't you come out and pick
with me?"

"Lord, I was in shock," Wayne recalled. "A million thoughts
ran through my mind." One of them was the fact that he had the
chance to live out a dream. Another was the fact that while
McGee was spiffed out with a fancy Western shirt and a bolo tie,
Wayne was wearing the same dusty jeans he wore to the shop.
And third and most prominently, there was a woman stationed
at the stage entrance writing notes and taking names.

"I did look pretty grungy but Sam wouldn't have cared, but I
was afraid he might get in trouble. So I chickened out," Wayne
admitted. "I still regret not doing that. I guess if they threw me
in jail I would have gotten out sometime or another."

Wayne isn't the only guitar builder who learned life lessons at
the repair shop at Gruhn Guitars. In addition to Wood, John
Greven, Kim Walker, Marty Lanham, archtop builder Mark
Lacey, and mandolin maker Steve Gilcrest are among the well-
known craftspeople who honed their chops at this shop, working
on fine old instruments day in and day out.

"So many modern builders have not studied vintage," Gruhn
explained. "They're extremely arrogant in thinking they're better. They may be neater and cleaner. They may do prettier miter
joints or do neater, cleaner inlay. But no, they're not better. They
never did learn what makes the old ones tick."

It's a daunting challenge—and in many ways a losing battle—
trying to build a new guitar that equals the best vintage instruments. Some, including Gruhn, claim it's never been done.
Which is why many modern builders sidestep this issue entirely.
Instead, they build a guitar that conforms to a sound that's in
their head—Irish luthier George Lowden claims that the design
for his most popular model came to him in a dream.

Gruhn then told the story about a mandolin maker who came into the shop with the second instrument he had ever built.

"It was a piece of shit. It was crude. It was ugly. It didn't play well," he spat. "You could see the chisel marks. Now, you can see chisel marks on a Guarneri violin that brings $4 million, but some chisel marks have artistic flair and some are just sloppy work. This was just sloppy work."

Gruhn paused, downed his last spoonful of seafood soup, and zipped up his black fleece.

"He claimed he turned down $5,000 for it," Gruhn explained. "And he said that's because it's a real handmade instrument, not some slick factory job.

"Being factory-made doesn't mean it's not as good as hand-made," Gruhn argued as we left the restaurant. "Martin was still a factory in the mid-1930s. They did lots and lots of handwork but it was still an assembly line. One guy would do bridges, the other would do necks. Martin got its reputation because they built *good ones*."

And it's not all about aging either. Gruhn pointed out that those eminently forgettable instruments of the 1970s were now as old as the prewar instruments were when Gruhn started in the 1960s.

"Even Stradivari and Guarneri, when they were alive, were competing against hundred-year-old violins," Gruhn argued. "And the average life expectancy back then was no more than thirty-five years. So I don't think people bought a violin thinking it was going to take fifty years to mature in sound. The originals don't sound good because they're old. They sound good because of what they are."

By this time we had arrived back at the store, and Gruhn had someone give me a tour of the upstairs while he checked his phone messages and e-mail. The repair shop was light, airy, and immaculate. There wasn't a speck of sawdust anywhere. Each repairman had his own tidy workspace, and the power tools and lacquer-spraying facilities were well off in the corner. Hanging on a rack above one of the workspaces awaiting attention was a bejeweled 1929 000-45, and the only Martin 000-30 ever built. It was a far cry from the convivial chaos on Tucker Road.

When I headed back down to Gruhn's office, he was happy to explain the shop's importance. "I've always had twice as much space devoted to repair as to sales," Gruhn explained. The repair shop has become increasingly important, because finding vintage instruments in mint condition gets harder all the time. Instruments that need work are far less scarce and can be bought at a much lower price—but it's only worthwhile buying them if you can put them back together. "It makes me in biological terms the equivalent of the animal that can graze on cactus in a period of drought, when the others who are adapted to feeding on grass are starving," Gruhn said, recalling the good old days when $200,000 sunburst Gibson Les Paul electric guitars could be bought for $100, and $40,000 Martin herringbones brought $250. "And I don't anticipate that the drought is going to improve much."

He cited the example of a Gibson SG that had recently commanded a shop-record price. "It didn't take long to buy it. It didn't take long to sell it—I put it up on the Web site and it was sold by the next morning," he said. "But we spent *weeks* on some restoration touch-up. But when we were done it looked perfect. Everything we worked on came out looking like we were never there."

And then Gruhn hit on the reason why so many of his repairmen went on to become great builders, and why he had so much trouble keeping good help. "The goal of the repairman is to be completely anonymous. When you do a great repair job on a guitar for someone, he'll thank you profusely and pay you well and never mention it to anyone again," Gruhn explained. "When Wayne or anyone else does custom building, if their work is distinctive, if they put their soul and personality in it, if you can look at it and say instantly that's a Henderson, that's a compliment. If they're doing repair work, and their work is as distinctive as a signature, that's a sign that they're a slob," said Gruhn.

"Building may not pay any better in terms of dollars per hour, but there's a certain psychological satisfaction that comes from getting recognition. The chairman of some billion-dollar-a-year corporation, outside of his industry, may be totally anonymous. But hundreds of years later a violin maker who may have made two hundred instruments in his lifetime—Stradavari, Guarneri, Galliano—is still remembered," Gruhn concluded, shaking his head. "Repairmen are not remembered."

CHAPTER EIGHTEEN

The Body Electric

T HE SUNDAY NIGHT before I met George, I went over to
the Exit/In to see Bill Frisell, who might be described as
the unassuming pioneer of modern jazz guitar. The magazine
writer Tom Junod once summed up Frisell far better in a *GQ*
piece aptly titled "The Guy Who Always Plays the Perfect Song":
"Indeed, when you watch him, he doesn't seem to play so much
as listen, and that's what gives his music its singular reverence
and beauty—it is wide-open, and it incorporates everything in a
single gesture, from the sweetest nostalgia to the harshest disso-
nance, from desert twang to urban squawk, from fairground
Americana to speed-metal, from the Beach Boys to Burt
Bacharach to Neil Young to Sonny Rollins to Charles Ives to
Henry Mancini to Aretha Franklin to Skeeter Davis to . . . well,
like I said, everything and everybody." And, yes, it occurred to
me that he and Wayne Henderson, who is another of music's
great listeners, could have a splendid time together some late
night in Rugby. Once they agreed on a common tempo—Frisell
plays at a funeral procession pace, while Wayne picks as though
he were heading to a fire—they'd sit and listen and jam, pulling
apart ancient tunes like "Wildwood Flower" and "Blackberry
Blossom," and then putting them back together in a thousand
novel ways. And that scene is not as improbable as it might
seem.

That night in Nashville, Frisell was playing with drummer Kenny Wolleson and bassist Viktor Kraus, who is Alison's brother. If we were playing the guitar geek's version of six degrees of separation, you can get from Wayne Henderson, who toured with Dobro virtuoso Jerry Douglas, who often plays with Kraus, who often plays with Frisell, in three easy moves.

But that night I was fixated not only on what Frisell played, but how. For most of the evening he stood stage left and riveted his attention on Wolleson. This had the effect of rotating the guitarist's husky body about 110 degrees, his back turned away from the audience like a gambler surreptitiously counting his bankroll, frustrating a roomful of fret freaks trying to observe his chord positions. It wasn't a pose though—at one point mid-set Frisell stepped to the mic, smiled timidly, thanked the audience profusely, and then apologized for not having anything else to say. Fellow musicians have suggested that the über-shy Frisell was "raised by deer."

But while his music was fraught with effort, it was mental effort. Frisell was playing a pale blond Fender Telecaster electric guitar, not a typical jazzbo tool, but the sort of axe played by Nashville studio cats. And with the Tele plugged into an amp, Frisell laid out a tapestry of sound, and in the process, he burned about as many calories as a channel surfer trying to find a rerun of Six Feet Under. Indeed, much of Frisell's physical effort, such as it was, was spent twiddling the dials on a slightly haphazard array of digital delays, samplers, and distortion pedals. Not that he would, but the gadgets at his fingertips could allow him to pluck a note or two, put his guitar down, and let the electronics continue the music entirely without his input. Watching Frisell do so much with so little got me thinking about the guitar as a device for making sound.

Despite their relatively large size, acoustic guitars are not all that loud, and the sound that they do emit must compete in a crowded part of the frequency spectrum. In a bluegrass band, for example, the violin is louder than a guitar. So is the mandolin.

Despite their small size these instruments play in a much higher register, to which the human ear is more sensitive. The Dobro, a guitar played horizontally with a metal slide, is louder because it has a metal resonator. The sound emanates from a mechanically driven loudspeaker—a metal version of what you'd find inside your home stereo—mounted inside an inert body. And the banjo is essentially a drumhead with a neck and strings, and played well or badly, it can drown out even the loudest guitar. This, in particular, has been a source of consternation to guitarists since, well, forever. In the post-PC world, banjo players have joined blondes as the last safe targets for cruel humor. And nothing gets a heartier laugh at the guitar shop on Tucker Road than a good banjo joke.

Q. What do you call a guy who hangs around with musicians?
A. A banjo player.

Or

Q: What's the difference between a harmonica and a banjo?
A: A harmonica only sucks on half the notes.

Or

Q: What's perfect pitch on a banjo?
A: When you throw it into a Dumpster and you hit an accordion.

And then there's this story about a particularly clever dog named Fletcher that Wayne once owned.

"Would you rather be a dead dog or a banjo picker?" he'd ask.

On cue, Wayne claimed, the dog would look back at him with his big brown eyes, and then fall over, legs outstretched, eyes closed, playing dead better than Shelley Winters in a disaster movie.

But it's not just about banjos, however, as all acoustic guitarists face the volume problem. Classical guitar virtuoso Andrés Segovia had to contend with it when he played in front of a symphony orchestra. Rhythm guitarist Freddie Green had to fight to be heard over the drummer and the horns in Count Basie's big band.

And indeed, the story of the guitar has in many ways centered on sound levels. At the Experience Music Project museum in Seattle, there's a compact exhibit on the history of the guitar called, appropriately, the Quest for Volume. Curated by Peter Blecha, with guitar historian Walter Carter, who chose the fifty instruments for their historical value, the exhibit is very well done. For example, you can hear many of them being played by virtuosos like Frisell and his sometime sidekick, slide guitar player Greg Leisz.

The Quest for Volume differs from the Dangerous Curves exhibit at the Museum of Fine Arts in Boston, which showcased some lovely instruments, but focused perhaps a bit too much on guitars that made bold design statements—from an inflatable guitar to a pedal steel made out of a hospital crutch for an on-the-mend Barbara Mandrell—but which weren't all that important as instruments. And it's a far cry from the Hard Rock Café approach where a guitar suddenly becomes a museum piece because it's been signed by three members of Whitesnake.*

But the Quest for Volume also has a point of view. This exhibit starts with one of the first modern guitars, a slightly odd-shaped instrument that dates from the turn of the nineteenth century. Next up is a tiny Martin Stauffer, circa 1834, followed by a nineteenth-century Gibson. The next flattop is a Martin 2-27. It's a fetching guitar with multicolored purfling and a delicate mother-of-pearl rosette. (I'm clearly not alone in this opinion: Eric Clapton sold a slightly bigger and newer style 27 Martin at the Crossroads auction for $30,000.)

And that's it as far as straightforward flattop acoustic guitars

---

* The very first guitar displayed in a Hard Rock Café belonged to Eric Clapton, who asked if he could hang it over his favorite bar stool in London. Two weeks later, a box arrived at the London bar containing a guitar and a note from The Who's guitarist, Pete Townsend, "Mine's as good as his, Love Pete." And thus a marketing gimmick was born.

go. The next guitar in the exhibit is a 1935 Gibson Super 400 archtop. Then comes a resonator—an acoustic guitar with a metal speaker cone attached, of the kind used by both delta bluesmen and Hawaiian slide guitar players. The exhibit quickly progresses to the amplified archtops of the kind played by jazz players like Charlie Christian.

And then it's on to solid-body electrics like Gibson's Les Paul model and Fender Strats, which have all the inherent resonance of a two-by-four, and only come alive when they're plugged into an amp.

If volume was the guitarist's holy grail, the easy answer was technology. Even the loudest acoustic guitar has its limits. That's why early jazz guitarists like Charlie Christian attached primitive pickups to their archtop guitars. This helped some, but the guitar's resonant nature caused howling feedback, so there was a distinct—and very moderate—limit to how loud they could play.

In 1941 guitarist Les Paul found the solution. He attached a neck and a pickup to a four-by-four railroad tie, and the result was the first viable solid body electric guitar, an instrument that allowed Paul to crank up the volume, unhampered by feedback. But the looks that he got from audiences and fellow musicians alike prompted Paul to cobble together a pair of entirely cosmetic "wings" that he attached to the sides of the instrument to make it resemble a conventional acoustic guitar.

It took the better part of a decade before Paul's invention made a real impact. Indeed, it was the commercial success of Fender's early Broadcaster and Telecaster models—simple, relatively cheap, and designed for mass production—that prompted Gibson to come out with their own mass market solid body, the Les Paul.

"When I introduce myself to people," the ninety-year-old Paul is fond of saying at his regular Monday night gig at New York's Iridium jazz club, "they are always surprised to learn that I'm not a guitar and I'm not dead." (Just as important in the history of popular music, if not to this particular discussion, was

Fender's invention of the electric bass, which allowed bands to carry an instrument that was only slightly larger than a guitar, rather than lugging around a mammoth upright bass.)

The story took another turn when guitarists discovered that amplified guitars could be coaxed into a wide variety of interesting, if unnatural, sounds. It started in 1951 with a single called "Rocket 88," written by Ike Turner, performed by the Delta Cats and sung by sax player Jackie Brenston. Its major claim to fame is that it's considered by many popular music scholars to be the first rock and roll song ever. It's also likely the first appearance of an intentionally distorted guitar sound. While driving from Mississippi to Memphis down Highway 61, Willie Kizart's guitar amplifier fell off the top of Turner's car. (Or so the legend goes—Turner claims it never happened.) Producer Sam Phillips, who would later produce Elvis Presley's seminal sessions, wadded up some paper and shoved it into the damaged speaker. He liked the distorted sound and used the battered amp anyway. Revolutionary though it might have been, the guitar sound is hardly a prominent feature in the song—through most of the track, the guitar blends in with Raymond Hill's sax. Even electrified, it was hard for a guitarist to be heard above the piano and the horn section. Kizart's moment of glory is a single slightly fuzzy chord stab as the rest of the band is winding down on the song's outro. But with that one bit of twang, a whole new means of six-string expression was opened up to guitarists.

By the mid-1960s guitarists had achieved a variety of new sounds by simply turning their amps all the way up until they distorted in ways that added an aggressive edge to the tone and allowed notes to be sustained almost indefinitely. Players like George Harrison of the Beatles, Keith Richards of the Rolling Stones, Pete Townsend of The Who, and Eric Clapton started on a game of more-is-better, using ever more powerful amps, stacking speaker cabinets one on top of the other, and using effects pedals to further modify the sound. Jimi Hendrix took things to the next level, intentionally coaxing his amps into full-blown feedback, then making the resulting howl part of the music. Volume and music had become one and the same. In the rock mockumentary *This Is Spinal Tap*, the incessant pursuit of decibels as an end in itself is taken to an extreme that's hilarious because it hits so close to home. Lead guitarist Nigel Tufnel, played by Christopher Guest, shows Rob Reiner his favorite amplifier.

"It's very special because all the numbers go to eleven," he crows.

"Most amps go up to ten. Does that mean it's louder?" Reiner asks.

"It's *one* louder, idn't it?"

This is the kind of scene that rock's detractors point to. The meta-message: It's cheating, technology compensating for a lack of musicianship. (For a real-life example of this, walk into any Guitar Center store on a Saturday afternoon, and absorb the cacophony for as long as you can stand it.) However, this view slights the very real—and different—artistry of plugged-in players from Chuck Berry to Bill Frisell.

But for Wayne Henderson, who doesn't even own an electric guitar, all of this is the road not taken. Which is not to say that volume is unimportant to him. It is one of the things that makes a Henderson guitar not only different, but better. In the world of bluegrass, a loud guitar is affectionately known as a cannon. It's not the most apt analogy—the *1812 Overture* notwithstanding, no one has ever touted the musical qualities of heavy artillery—but it drives the point home. In the world of the acoustic guitar, volume is an unalloyed good—so long as it's not achieved at the cost of delicacy of tone or structural stability.

And while talking about volume is all well and good, the best way to understand it is to play a truly loud guitar. Flip Breskin, one of the founders of Puget Sound Guitar Workshop, where Wayne often teaches, describes her tiny old guitar—a nineteenth-century Martin—in equestrian terms. "It has a soft mouth," she told me. And that's a good analogy. Playing one of Wayne's guitars is like having a powerful but oh-so tractable beast in your lap. You can have a civilized dialogue with the instrument, asking it rather than telling it.

The term that musicians use is dynamic range, the distance between the softest note and the loudest, and the term is particularly apt—the word dynamic is all about movement, and what is music if not movement? A loud guitar lets you impart a full range of emotion, from a pillow-talk whisper to a fire-in-a-crowded-theater shout. Pluck the string casually and the resulting note is surprisingly big and loud and full. Tickle the string, and you still get something that sounds like music. Pick it hard, and the sound will strip the paint off a Rambler.

But as technology has invaded the world of the acoustic guitar, this distinction has been lost. "So many modern builders don't really understand the difference between tone, volume, and projection," Gruhn had explained to me. "Volume is how loud a guitar sounds to the player. Projection is how loud a guitar sounds to the audience. The old instruments had to project. They didn't have to sound loud simply to the player. It was important what they sounded like with no amplification of any kind, not even a microphone, a hundred feet away.

"But if you're playing only in the studio, volume is irrelevant. You want it louder, just twiddle a dial. And what sounds rich and full to the human ear is not necessarily what records well when you're holding the instrument three inches from the mic and you have feedback and rumble and roar if you play it hard."

Gruhn notes that Nashville studio players want guitars that are easy to play, have accurate intonation, and good balance, with no string and no note, louder than another.

"The best way to achieve that is to have something that's acoustically miserable. It has poor volume, poor projection, it's uniformly lousy. But then you can twiddle the dials and tweak the tone."

An exception to that rule is another Gruhn customer, one

Eric Clapton, who has bought more than fifty guitars from the shop. He has the time, the money, and the clout to get just the sound he wants out of his guitars on his records.

"He actually has a very good ear for acoustic guitars," Gruhn explained. "He knows what a good Martin should sound like, and he likes guitars with good tone, volume, and projection." Guitars not unlike the ones built by a guy who used to work in the repair shop at Gruhn Guitars.

CHAPTER NINETEEN

A Place for Us

So I HEAR OLD ERIC'S finally getting a guitar."

It was Wednesday morning back at the guitar shop, and that can mean only one thing. Gabby. No sooner had the self-proclaimed Dumpster Diver pulled up in his white Nissan pickup truck than the banter began.

"Yeah, I guess so," said Wayne. "Pretty soon when someone asks me about Eric Clapton's guitar, I can say, 'It's gone, it's out the door.' And that'd be a load off of me."

Wearing his typical uniform of bib overalls, a feed cap, a white T-shirt, and a pair of white tennis shoes, Gabby put a bag full of Hardee's sausage biscuits down on the thickness planer, and sat down in his chair by Gerald's workbench. (In a typical bout of oversharing, he once told me he brought the chair from home because the shop's stools aggravated his hemorrhoids.)

"Ain't finding no old Martin herringbones in the trash or nothing?" Wayne asked.

"It's been pretty slow in the Dumpsters, today," Gabby bellowed in reply. "Must be all the Democrats got there first." It was only a few days after the 2004 presidential election, and this was Gabby's nod to topical humor.

Right behind Gabby bounded a tiny black blur of a dog. His previous canine companion, Bandit, had died of cancer this spring, so he brought along Bandit's successor, Oreo, a tiny black terrier puppy, hardly bigger than the bag of sausage biscuits Gabby was carrying.

Whereas Bandit would alternate his manic periods with long naps, Oreo was all energy. She'd grab a wood scrap and then do a couple of frantic laps around the bench, stopping now and again to pee on the floor. Finally, she grabbed a piece of cow bone from the corner that was bigger than she was.

"That's nuts and saddles that's Oreo's chewing on," said Wayne, not minding particularly. She began gnawing at the giant old thighbone, but only for a minute, before going back to running and peeing and running some more.

Shortly after Gabby made his entrance, Ralph Maxwell arrived, his arthritic knees slowing his gait as he made his way to an old oak office chair on the other side of the thickness sander, just in front of the jointer.

While Gabby relishes his rep as the shop's official lowlife, the man with a crude joke for any situation, Ralph takes the high road. He is Wayne's unofficial tour manager, and mostly that means letting Wayne drive his big old Lincoln sedan to gigs. Ralph is just past eighty, and long retired. He started paying visits to the shop when his wife, Harriet, was still alive and increased the frequency of his visits after she died. Like Gabby, Ralph was never much of a guitar player, even on his best days, and now he can barely grab even simple chords when his arthritis is acting up.

"I took lessons from Tim Lewis," he'll say with a laugh when you hand him a guitar. "He said he'd give me my money back if I didn't tell anyone."

One of the running jokes around the shop is Ralph's pen pal. His wife was a tournament-level Scrabble player and she started playing games by mail with a convict serving a sentence for a variety of drug-related crimes. When Harriet died, Ralph kept up the correspondence, if not the Scrabble games.

Although they have sat five feet apart for years, Ralph and Gabby rarely interact, talking to Wayne instead of each other.

But for reasons unknown even to Wayne, they show up every Wednesday. What they share is a sense of loneliness; Gabby's long been divorced—his front license plate reads "I Got a Gun For My Wife . . . It Was The Best Trade I Ever Made"—and Ralph clearly misses his late wife every day.

Wayne, for his part, maintains a certain benevolent indifference to the General Loafers. He doesn't treat them like company or like an audience, and he feels free to ignore them when he's got a phone call or a guitar making task that demands his undivided attention. Still, Wayne Henderson is happy to have someone around to gossip with and laugh at his jokes. When Ralph sat down, he launched into a good one whose shelf life was dwindling away.

"A guy in Texas walks into a bar, and heads over to the bartender and orders a shot and a beer. Drinks it right down. Then another one. And then another.

"And he stands up in the middle of the bar and says, 'George W. Bush is a horse's ass.'

"As soon as he says that the biggest cowboy in the bar comes over and punches him right in the nose.

"The guy gets up off the floor kinda slow, his nose is tore up pretty good. And he says to the cowboy, 'Hey, I'm sorry about what I said. I guess I was kinda drunk and I didn't realize you were such big Bush people around here.'

"And the cowboy replies, 'We're not *Bush* people. We're *horse* people.'"

Gabby laughed so hard that he practically fell off his chair.

Why do the loafers return here, week in and week out? I knew better than to ask Gabby. As for Ralph, he explained himself thusly.

"I've always enjoyed watching a man who knows what he's doing."

He recalled the time that a friend was having an addition built on his house. And while the friend was nowhere to be found as the construction was taking place, Ralph drove to the house every day and sat from morning to night watching this old man lay concrete block. "Wayne makes it so damn easy it's aggravating," Ralph added.

Today, Wayne Henderson was making it all look especially easy, but frankly, I was a little worried as I ambled over to the shop this morning. I wasn't quite sure what was going to happen after I got back from Nashville and Wayne got back from Washington. I was now fully invested in seeing these guitars get done. And the guitar shop, after all, is full of works in progress, glued-up backs, bent sides without tops or backs, bodies without necks. Wayne will throw himself literally and figuratively at the process of starting a new guitar. But getting him to finish one is a whole different matter. So it wasn't clear to me whether he'd dive right back into the Clapton guitars, or shift his attention to another project.

That said, I had a time-tested plan. In 1715, the king of Poland ordered twelve Stradivarius violins and sent J.D. Volumier, his director of court music, to Cremona to await completion of the instruments. There's no record of what exactly Volumier did while hanging around at Stradivari's shop—did he crack his knuckles? take off his shoes? snore?—but the king received all twelve instruments in only three months.

My plan? Watch the guitars being built and stay until they're done. If Wayne wanted me out of his shop, out of his guestroom, out of his life, at least temporarily, all he had to do was get these two guitars done.

But I needn't have worried. After a few days away, Wayne was channeling that old block layer. He was moving smoothly and efficiently from job to job. Then again, this was the golden moment in the process. The prep work was all done, and this was the day that a small pile of precision-cut pieces of wood would begin to come together quickly and easily. While it's not brainless, for the most part Wednesday's work was a straightforward assembly job, and, at least if you're Wayne Henderson, pretty tough to screw up.

The combination of being back at the shop with the prospect of an easy yet productive day put Wayne in a good mood. He was telling stories nonstop.

"I saw this guy down there the other day, sitting on the bench just a-jabbering away," said Wayne, telling of his trip to Washington. "I thought, man, that damn guy's lost his mind. He must be a banjo player." He paused for a long moment. "Then I see he's got one of these cell phones with this little thing that's stuck in his ear."

He segued into a long rambling tale about a Gibson Mastertone banjo he traded to a pistol-packing old-timer. "He was a rough old customer. The gun went off in his pocket one time, and the bullet went right through his bag. He was lucky to have anything left."

While he's doing his best Garrison Keillor, Wayne started gluing the braces to the back of one guitar, pressing it all taut on a clamping table that looks a lot like the Squeezer on steroids, another gadget that he had also designed and built with Don Wilson's help.

Wayne then moved to the sides of the other guitar, attaching the kerfing—those snakelike strips of finely notched mahogany that attach the top and back to the sides. He carefully squeezed out the right amount of glue onto the kerfing, spread it with his finger, and secured it to the rosewood sides with binder clips— the kind you'd buy at Staples to hold the pages of an annual report.

When it comes to guitar building, Wayne is old-school but he's not a purist. He's used Titebond to glue every joint on every guitar, the same run-of-the-mill wood glue that you can buy at Home Depot. And while guitar factories use a special glue roller, an educated digit suited Wayne fine.

"I guess I've used my index finger to spread the glue on every joint on every guitar," he explained.

Indeed, he wipes the glue residue on the same place, just under the back pocket on his Carhartt dungarees. When there's a big glob, he'll wipe it on the metal leg of one of the small work tables. The surface is now plastered with stalactites of dried Titebond.

Many guitar makers, like T. J. Thompson, will use nothing but hide glue on their guitars, because that's what they used back at the Martin guitar factory. But hide glue is also messy, needs to be heated before use, and has a short working time. And then there's the aroma.

"It smells like a dead horse," Wayne said.

Wayne also uses Super Glue aplenty. When he spied a tiny pinhole on one of the Brazilian rosewood backs, he made a tiny toothpick out of a scrap of Brazilian, put a dab of Super Glue over the hole, inserted the tiny plug, and snapped off the tiny dowel.

"A little drop of holy water, and you'll never know it was there," he announced proudly, as he grabbed the compressed air hose and squirted the sawdust off his dungarees in preparation for lunch.

"That's the only blow job you're gonna get today," Gabby said, trotting out one of his chestnuts.

By the time we ate the Hardee's burgers that Ralph had brought for lunch, Wayne had finished gluing the backs on both guitars, and had the braces glued and clamped to the first of the two guitar tops. Just like plywood day on a construction project, where a skeleton of two-by-fours can be transformed into something that looks and feels like a building in just a few hours, Wayne had transformed a pile of wood into something that was recognizable as a guitar in less than half a day.

On an easy sunlit morning like this, it was easy to understand why Gabby and Ralph chose this as the place to while away their hours. The workshop was a refuge. The biggest problem of the day was a messy repair or the fluctuating humidity. But matters of life and death were checked at the door, next to the Dr. Pepper machine. Drink some Cheerwine, breathe some sawdust, and you're living large again. Even the mess was a comfort, because the apparent chaos made the precision work that went on here seem all that much more remarkable. Both Gabby and Ralph had their share of health problems, and the guitar shop on Tucker Road was a place of creation and renewal, a spot where every day something new and good was built or something old got fixed as good as new. There was hope here, and you can't ask for much more than that.

But mostly this place was a reflection of Wayne himself. He had a rhythm if not a routine. Each guitar would be different, but Wayne's outlook was always the same. His half-full approach to his work—his approach to life—rarely varied. And even during those rare moments when he struggled, or fretted, or even seethed, he kept it to himself. But even at the guitar shop, real life sometimes intruded.

Just after lunch, on Wednesday, Wayne picked up the phone, figuring it would be a man about a guitar—one that needed to be fixed or one that needed to be built. It wasn't.

"Awww, heck," said Wayne. "That's terrible." This was one of those calls that dropped the other shoe. When Wayne got to Washington on Sunday, his buddy Robin Kessinger, who was also supposed to teach and play a show with Wayne, was nowhere to be found. He no doubt wondered if Robin had taken a wrong turn somewhere and was driving around the Lincoln Memorial somewhere. A little while later, someone gave Wayne the real scoop. While Robin was en route, his father had a stroke, so he turned around and headed back to West Virginia. This phone call relayed the sad news that Robin's dad had died. For the rest of the week, Wayne would wear the baseball cap Robin had given to him as a kind of silent tribute.

Later that afternoon, Wayne's sister called again, and again the news wasn't good. Her husband had been in the hospital with cancer. While the conversation focused on the news of the day— some new procedure is making him feel better, and the doctors might let him come home soon, but they won't be coming over for Thanksgiving—Wayne knew the prognosis wasn't good. Phone calls like these provided Wayne with another reason to deal with the things he can control, like turning pieces of wood into a guitar.

After lunch, Herb Key showed up at the guitar shop, as he did just about every Wednesday. Silver-haired and looking far younger than his 68 years, Herb is Wayne's bass player and his unofficial consigliere. A friend for close to thirty years, Herb shares Wayne's obsession with all things guitaristic, and with some patient tutelage from Wayne has become a skilled repairman in his own right. Wayne and Herb were scheduled to play Carnegie Hall in a few weeks, and while Wayne remained unfazed, Herb was itching to hear the young bluegrass phenoms they'd be playing with so he could practice the tunes a little. Typically, Wayne could find one CD but not the other.

"Either they didn't send it or it got bundled and trashed," Wayne replied as he squeezed the freshly kerfed sides back into the form in preparation for gluing back on. The thin Brazilian rosewood let out a loud distressed creak like the floor of a haunted house. "Sometimes they're really hard to get in," he explained, sensing my concern. "They'll do an awful lot of popping and cracking, when they get in this shape."

Herb used to work as an executive in a furniture company—indeed he and Wayne hooked up because he offered to mill some of Wayne's tonewood on the factory's thickness sander—but he's hardly taking it easy in retirement. When he's not playing music or fixing guitars, he's making honey—or at least harvesting it from the hives he keeps at his house.

"Have you ever gotten stung?" I asked him

"Oh, hundreds of times," he said. "It don't bother me none."

While the hyper-speed bluegrass from those hot young pickers blazed in the background—"They're full-blast," said Wayne—Herb brought a small black guitar case to the bench. Inside was a small ancient Martin guitar inside. This wasn't an instrument, it was an icon. This 1929 00-28, it turns out, had belonged to A. P. Carter, one-third of the legendary Carter Family.

While A.P. wasn't much of a guitar player—Maybelle was the picker in the family—he was responsible for helping to imprint timeless songs like "Wildwood Flower" and "Keep on the Sunny Side" on the American consciousness.

"He held it more than he played it," Wayne explained. A.P. was actually more of a fiddler but he refused to play it on records out of respect for his mother who considered the fiddle the devil's instrument.

Indeed, he grew up only a few miles from Rugby, and even to this day members of the extended Carter Family are practically neighbors. The Carter Fold, the family's performance venue, lies just over the other side of White Top Mountain, and Wayne plays there a couple of times a year. A.P.'s daughter Janette is the Fold's grande dame, and while she's frail, she still knows what she wants. To her, old-time music is dance music, and she judges a band's success by the number of people on the dance floor in front of the stage. If no one is dancing, she'll tug on the band-leader's pants leg and suggest, "Play 'Liberty'—you're losin' 'em." Needless to say, she rarely had to tug on Wayne Hender-son's Carhartts.

This guitar that was now sitting on the cluttered workbench had gone missing for decades. "No one knew what happened to it," Wayne explained. "They figured it got stolen or something. It was only last year, after Johnny Cash died, they were settling his estate, digging up stuff, and they found that guitar stashed under a bed in a bedroom he had in a recording studio. It'd been there that whole time, stuck there for twenty-five years or more." Indeed, this guitar not only outlived old A.P., it outlived his niece, June Carter Cash, and her husband, the Man in Black. The Carter family asked Wayne to repair it. As if all this history wasn't enough, this guitar is also a dead ringer for Ella. It's the same year, the same model, two of only fifty-one 00-28s made in the last year of the Roaring Twenties, the year of the stock mar-ket crash.

"I think me and Oreo are going to hit the road," said Gabby

as he hauled himself up out of his chair. Perhaps thinking about Bandit, he'd been in a rather subdued mood all day.

"You're leaving?" asked Herb. "How the hell we gonna keep things straight without you?"

Wayne and Herb pored over the petite guitar like a couple of surgeons consulting on a particularly touchy case. At first glance, the outside looked pretty clean. But the pickguard wasn't original, the tuners had been replaced, as had the bridge, all with period-incorrect models. "There's a little hole where the pickguard had been," said Herb. "And right there looks like some overspray."

"The word is that nobody's ever worked on this guitar except the Martin factory," Wayne added. However, this less-than-restoration-quality work was done probably fifty years ago, when this was nothing more than just an old guitar.

Then Herb got out the lighted inspection mirror and that told another story.

"There's a big crack, Wayne," he exclaimed. "There's a damn piece of cloth around the side." Probing further revealed even more unpleasant surprises. There was a giant bridge plate that's sitting atop the tiny original one. "Look at that big sucker," Herb exclaimed.

Herb explored further still. "Is that a cracked brace?" Herb asked.

"Oh, yeah," Wayne agreed.

After a brief tête-à-tête, Wayne and Herb agreed that the best course of action was to simply stabilize the patient. They would fix the cracks, remove the neck and reset it to lower the action, and restore this piece of Americana to some respectable level of playability.

"We should probably save these strings," Herb reminded Wayne. "Johnny Cash was probably the last one to play them."

When the two doctors were done with their consultation, I picked up old A.P.'s guitar. I thought about the guitar's former owner. A little weird and fidgety, but a true American original, all the same. I couldn't help but think that old A.P. would have fit right in at the guitar shop, pacing the floor frantically in front of Ralph and Gabby, occasionally stepping on Oreo's tail. And as I held the gossamer-light guitar in my lap, I thought of Ella. I picked a riff or two and then stopped. That all-too-familiar sound made me a little sad and homesick, like a phone call from home that only reminds you what you're missing.

I gave A.P.'s guitar the once-over instead, spying the straight-grained Brazilian and the delicate herringbone purfling. As I took a peek inside the soundhole, I stole a good long sniff. Like an oenophile judging a venerable pinot, I savored the smoky bouquet of the wood, the sweat, and the smoke that guitar picked up over three-quarters of a century. But my reverie lasted only a second—the guitar shop is not a place for excessive introspection.

"I hear that old A.P. used to fart in that guitar," Herb said. Too bad Gabby wasn't still around to hear.

CHAPTER TWENTY

1948

"HE DON'T NEED A GUITAR that sounds this good," said Wayne Henderson.

The "he" that Wayne was referring to was me, and the guitar in question was my old '47 D-18. His words were cruel. But true. But cruel. And they set in motion a chain of events that would ultimately tip the balance of our relationship.

It all began the previous afternoon. When Herb came to work on A.P. Carter's guitar, he also brought in a 1947 D-18 that he had saved from self-destruction. A half-century of string tension had taken its toll on the guitar. Its neck was pulling up, the top had bellied up like a pregnant hound dog, and the bridge had pried loose. Worst of all, someone had once tried to refinish the instrument and thinned the top too much. To compensate, someone else put a big, nasty bridge plate on the guitar that stifled any sound that tried to come from the top. "This old guitar has been through a lot," said Herb with uncharacteristic understatement.

Thirty years ago, when old instruments weren't appreciated the way they are today, this guitar would have been a candidate for last rites. But using a technique that he and Wayne had devised, Herb undid those clumsy old repairs, laminated a paper-thin veneer of spruce under the top to restore its previous strength, and then proceeded with the more conventional repairs. New bridge plate. New bridge. Fresh neck set. After a month or so in the shop, this guitar was now ready for another fifty years, sounding better, no doubt, than it had in decades.

"We gave this guitar a hysterectomy," Herb said, laughing.

The price tag for this major surgery?

"A hundred and fifty dollars?" Wayne suggested.

"I think we could charge a hundred seventy-five," Herb countered.

That bit of business settled, Wayne pulled up a stool and fetched his fingerpicks out of the right-hand pocket of his britches. He's had the same set of fingerpicks—custom-forged by a friend of his—for more than thirty years. The picks are in that pocket 24/7 and he never, ever puts anything else in that pocket. Indeed, if you look closely at the tips of his index and middle fingers, you'll notice that they're just slightly pinched on the sides from the fingerpicks, the way a wedding band will leave a mark on a ring finger. He slipped his fingerpicks on, propped the newly repaired old Martin on his knee, and began to play. He ripped through a tarted-up version of the old fiddle tune "Sally Ann," and then followed that with a little Doc Watson medley, "Deep River Blues" into "Blackberry Rag."

There are few more singular pleasures than simply handing Wayne Henderson a guitar and watching him play. Wayne has a unique and distinctive style of playing. Unlike most bluegrass players who use a flatpick, he uses metal fingerpicks and a plastic thumbpick. As a youngster he kept dropping his flatpick into the soundhole of the guitar. His mentor, E.C. Ball counseled, "If you want to be a guitar player, son, you'd best get yourself some fingerpicks." But Wayne used those fingerpicks to play fast fiddle tunes in a flatpicking style, the way Doc Watson did. He often practiced out in the woodshed, out of earshot of his father, Walt, an orthodox fiddler who believed that guitarists ought to strum and not much else.

"When I'd get to playing too fancy, he'd shake the fiddle bow at me," Wayne recalled.

Today, when Wayne performs with a band, he does what any

bluegrass flatpicker does: he plays the lead clean, fast, and fancy, albeit with a distinctive drive and bounce that's the result of his picking style. But when he's playing solo, he opens up his box of influences wide. Using those two extra fingers to great advantage, he'll fill out the sound with syncopated strums in the style first played by Maybelle Carter of the Carter Family and updated by Norman Blake. He'll throw in some of the banjo-style rolls that Merle Travis applied to the guitar and now and then tart things up with some twangy rockabilly-style riffs that sound like an outtake from *The Sun Sessions*. He'll try his hand at some hillbilly jazz—a standard like "Don't Get Around Much Anymore"—or an aficionado's tune like Django Reinhardt's "Minor Swing." Or he'll play some straight fingerpicking like Sam McGee's "Buckdancer's Choice" or Elizabeth Cotten's "Freight Train." It's a whirlwind tour of American guitar styles, but it never sounds like Wayne's showing off, because he's not.

As I watched him, I noticed that Wayne plays differently than I do. Better, of course, but different too. When I'm playing, a part of me is always at arm's length, listening, judging. Thinking and perhaps thinking too much. Wayne's not doing that. He's totally in the moment, riding the wave of notes, one after the other. It's the same Zen-like see-wood, carve-wood approach that informs his guitar building.

When he was done picking, he nodded. He liked the old D-18, liking it especially because it's the same age as him. He put it down for a minute, and picked up the cherry chicken coop guitar. It was loud and ringy, but it had a brighter, happier sound than the others—it was, after all, still just a puppy. But its true potential was shown when Wayne played chords up the neck. Most guitars sound like a tinkly toy piano when you play the high strings near the twelfth fret. This one rang like a glockenspiel. Blindfolded, you'd be hard pressed to tell this freshly made guitar from its sixty-year-old elder. "It's powerful up the neck," said the man who built it, a little surprised, it seemed, at the quality of his own work. "Put a bone saddle on that and it'll be killing chickens out in the front yard." Then Herb handed Wayne my old '47. Since I'd first brought it to the shop in the spring, I had waved it under his nose a bit, first at the Puget Sound Guitar Workshop during the summer, then at the Old–Time Music Camp North up in Boston, but he hadn't really sat down and played it at any great length.

Herb had just gotten done poking around inside the guitar with the inspection mirror. Unlike on the other old '47, the work on this one had been done right, up to and including replacing the previously removed Popsicle brace that spans the crack-prone area under the fretboard.

"That's a right nice guitar," Herb said, with more than a touch of covetousness in his voice. "Where'd you get it?"

I told him the story about how it was my grandfather's guitar, and he had taken it to Europe when he served in World War II, and dragged it up the beach at Normandy on D-Day, and played "Bill Bailey" on the beachhead. That crack on the side? That's where he bopped a Nazi on the head with it . . . Herb was buying it, right up until the Nazi bopping. In any case, it made a better story than buying it from the classifieds of an Internet guitar bulletin board six months before.

Wayne started playing my '47, and he riffed through "Sally Ann" again, then "Blackberry Blossom," then "Windy and Warm" and "Leather Britches." Wayne's reluctance to give the guitar back made it clear that my '47 was the close but decisive winner of the bakeoff.

"That's a right good-sounding guitar," said Herb.

Then Wayne dropped the bomb: "He don't need a guitar that sounds this good." En garde.

"You're right," I countered. "I'm thinking of trading it for a D-35," evoking his ill-fated three-for-one trade. Touché.

Wayne gave me a long look, wondering if he had crossed the line and truly hit a nerve. But I have always followed the creed of that great contemporary philosopher Clint Eastwood: "A man's got to know his limitations." And I do. The truth is that I try hard and I practice a lot, but I can't play like Wayne, and I never will. And it doesn't matter. But Wayne had it backwards—I need all the help I can get. And while I can't make an old plywood Harmony sing like a great old prewar Martin, what I bring to the party is an appreciation for great instruments old and new. To paraphrase George Gruhn, this old Martin is my backstage pass. But I didn't say any of that. We just let it drop.

The next morning the guy who owns the '47 Martin that Herb had repaired, Edward Pfeiffer, but known to his friends as Ebo, came to the shop.

"That guitar came out pretty good," said Wayne. Ebo played it a bit, timidly at first, a little embarrassed to be picking in front of a musical legend. From the smile on his face, you could see that the repair exceeded even his expectations.

"I don't suppose you want to sell it?" Wayne asked. Ebo demurred. He's had the guitar for years, paid $150 for it along with an old Gibson J-45. He'd given first dibs to the previous owner.

"I've got a guitar that's even more beat-up than that one," Wayne explained. He went into the guitar vault and fished out a battered case with most of the vinyl covering stripped off the bare plywood. He flipped open the latches. Inside was an old Martin D-18. The spruce top was so dark it was now the color of an overripe pumpkin. The top had darkened from being out in the sun, from being sweated on, from having the odd beer spilled on it. It was worn but in a beautiful rode-hard-and-put-away-wet kind of way. There was no Plastic Wood or anything really funky or disrespectful, just good honest wear and plenty of it. It was, after all, the guitar world's equivalent of a mechanic's car. Nothing broken, just broken in.

"What year is it?" I asked Wayne.

"1948 as near as I can tell," he replied. "It looks like it had been shot right through the middle of the serial number." He pointed out a tiny hole in the side on the lower bout that could have been made by a BB. "I think that's your entrance wound," he guessed. A rather strange place to shoot a guitar, but forensics is forensics.

Even the case was a walk down memory lane. It wore a Skylab sticker, and some stickers from the bicentennial of Thailand. The coolest thing? A UPS label from Peter Rowan, a legendary picker and Henderson guitar owner, to Wayne's old address in Sugar Grove. Folded up in the corner of the case was a newspaper clipping from 1991.

Wayne played that old '48 a bit, then passed it around. I put the '48 down in my lap. And with one strum, I knew my guitar had been dethroned. There was a new sheriff in town, a new winner in the bakeoff. Even with strings that had been on the guitar for a decade or more, Wayne's old guitar had a voice that was resounding and a tone that was simply easy. This guitar had mojo, soul. It had *it*. As I picked, Wayne told me that while this '48 hadn't been played for ages, for a long time it was his main guitar, before he built old 52, his everyday guitar.

Wayne had bought this boomtime Martin in 1976 in a music store in North Carolina. "It looked terrible," he said. "It wasn't strung up because it was missing a tuner." Then as now it had been played to within an inch of its life. "I had never seen a guitar that had been used *that much*," he explained, emphasizing the last syllables to let you know that was a positive. It wasn't the condition, but the $400 price tag, that gave him pause.

"I had to think about it quite a bit," he recalled. "I didn't just snap it up. They thought it was kinda crazy buying a beat-up guitar that didn't even work."

He found a tuner that had been affixed to a fiddle his wife had bought, and he had his new horse. "I used that guitar just about all the time."

Later on, after Ebo claimed his guitar, said his thank-yous, forked over a small wad of cash, took a few pictures, and said his goodbyes, I posed a question to Wayne.

"How much do you want a '47 D-18?"

"Its something I sure would like to have."

"Would you be willing to trade your '48 for it?"

"I reckon I might," he said. "I guess I could turn loose of a guitar I've had for probably thirty-five years."

Indeed, he seemed less worried about parting with the guitar than about me getting the short end of the stick. My guitar is prettier and less worn. And he worried about the case—mine has a rare original case, while his is almost ready for the trash. Mine's more valuable on the open market, but this one has a history.

"Herb'd have a fit if I traded that guitar off. He's been trying to get it out of me forever," he said.

I gave him a look indicating that as much as I wanted the guitar, I didn't want to get in the middle of a forty-year friendship.

"Herb's like me," Wayne assured me. "He wants all of them." He looked over at the old '48. "I used to play that thing a lot," he said. "It's a great playing guitar."

While I respected my 1947 D-18, I hadn't bonded with it. We had developed a casual friendship, not an outright love affair. And our interactions haven't always been the most pleasant. I found that when I played the guitar on muggy summer days the lacquer on the upper bout would develop a white hazy fog. There's something in my sweat that doesn't agree with the finish on that old Martin. It's all chemistry, I guess.

Once the deal was done—I considered the '48 officially mine when I changed the strings—I told Wayne about my real motivation for the trade. "I'm going to scrape off all the fretboard mung, take it to a lab where they can separate out the DNA, and have you cloned," I said with mock seriousness.

"Just be careful," he warned, "or you'll end up with some hillbilly blues player who don't know how to play anything but a D chord."

And now that he pointed it out, I noticed the groove on the bass side of the neck, made by a previous owner who'd hung on to that one chord like a life rope, singing as if his very existence depended on it.

"I'll be sure to take the DNA from the upper frets."

Which reminded Wayne of a joke. "Did you hear that they were going to do *CSI West Virginia?*" Wayne deadpanned. "But they ran into a problem. All the DNA was the same. And there weren't any dental records." Bada boom.

This was the proverbial trade that helped both teams. Wayne got the birth-year guitar he had long coveted, and I got Sally Ann, as I quickly nicknamed this '48 D-18, after my wife and one of Wayne's favorite fiddle tunes. But I don't think this is a trade that Wayne would have made with just anyone. I don't think that Ebo would have gone home with this slice of the Henderson legend. This was a deal between friends.

Wayne felt good that this guitar, which hadn't been out of the case but a couple times in at least ten years, was going to a good home where he would have visitation rights. This great '48 won't get played the way Wayne Henderson once did, but it will get played, every day.

So, no, I don't need a guitar that sounds as good as that '47 D-18. I've got one that sounds better.

CHAPTER TWENTY-ONE

Clean on the Inside

WAYNE HENDERSON SEEMS most at home when he's whittling on the bracing of a guitar top. He always sits in the same chair for whittling—Gabby's chair near Gerald's workbench. When I pointed this habit out to him he claimed never to have noticed.

"Maybe it's the light," he said. And indeed, this morning, with the mid-morning sunlight pouring through windows that almost touch the ceiling, Wayne could be posing for an Andrew Wyeth portrait, an indoor version of *Lawn Chair*. Although the light is delicate and playful in that corner on a sunny day, I've also seen Wayne gravitate toward the same spot in the wee hours of the morning, when the only illumination is provided by the greenish glow of a couple of fluorescent tubes. I almost think it's about the sound, the shavings falling on the hard concrete floor with the faint whisper of a snowfall in a February forest.

Wayne sat with the pure white spruce top of Clapton's guitar in his lap, one edge braced against his chest, almost as if he were playing a washboard in a zydeco band. As he folded himself over the piece of wood, I couldn't help but think that he was some-how taking its measure.

"What does it need?" he asked silently.

While Wayne is far from fussy when it comes to the building process—he could no doubt glue up braces with a wild boar running through the shop—whittling is something he saves for just the right time, the way a kid might save the chocolate-covered cherry from a box of Valentine candy. This was, to borrow a phrase from photographer Henri Cartier-Bresson, the decisive moment in the building of Clapton's guitars, and it seemed only fitting that it had a little drama. And Wayne Henderson is enough of a performer that he knows how to set the stage.

Wayne can hold a conversation while he's whittling, but he'd really rather not, and you'd best be quiet too. This morning, the assembly of the guitar had become much more intimate. The placid deliberate pace made me want to draw closer, but also stay still, so as not to intrude. The sounds of guitar making had changed on Tucker Road, and for the better. Gone was the whine of the band saw, the growl of the belt sander, the rafter-rattling rumble of the Shopsmith. Now the sounds had become more human in scale. The scraping of a knife against the edge of a brace, the scratching of a small piece of sandpaper on a spruce top. And there was a rhythm to it too. Whereas the machines howl until they're turned off, the sound of Wayne doing hand-work had a pulse—*scrape-a, scrape-a, scrape-a*—just like the person doing it. It was ancient, a beat that harkened back to a caveman sitting in the corner of his cave scraping a soft stick with a sharp rock while contemplating the world and his place in it.

Wayne's instrument this day was a Boker penknife, between three and four inches long, that Gabby had acquired at a flea market. It's a vintage knife, probably about forty or fifty years old, German-made, with the company's venerable Tree Brand mark on both the brown bone handle and the blade. It's a good tool but not a particularly rare one. Wayne has a supply of knives around, and he will wear out a knife in a year or two, sharpening it past the point where the blade's tempering will hold a fine edge. Before he sat down Wayne got out his Lansky knife sharpener—a jig-shaped contraption that holds the blade at a precise angle. It's unusual that Rugby's own Mr. Eyeball would use such a thing—

one would guess that he'd be slapping away at a soapstone. But when it comes to tools, he's all about results. "It does such a good job," he enthused.

And as if to demonstrate, he turned the freshly honed blade and casually sliced a few of the curly black hairs off the back of his hand as cleanly as a barber with a straight razor. This blade was clearly just right.

Wayne ran the knife along one edge of each brace smoothly and carefully, and then the next, rendering the profile just a little leaner, a little sleeker with each pass. With each stroke, delicate little curlicues of spruce spiraled down onto a small pile around his ankles.

Whittling is the endpoint of a process called voicing the top. This is the thing that Wayne Henderson does that no one can teach. Every guitar has its own voice, an individual timbre that's as distinctive as a human voice—there's no doubt that some techie could program voice recognition software to respond to the idiosyncratic strum of a particular guitar. Where does this voice come from? In a way, it comes from God or Mother Nature or whatever name you choose to apply to those things we can't quite fathom and can't quite control. Wood is—or was—a living thing, and the roulette wheel of genetics coupled with the X-factor of the environment renders each tree, and each slice of each tree, unique.

But the sea of variables doesn't end there, it merely begins. A guitar doesn't have a voice until it's played. The voice of the guitar and the voice inside the player's head somehow merge and meld and become one, something that's greater than the sum of its parts. Wayne's task is straightforward but daunting—to render these guitars willing and able to do Eric Clapton's musical bidding.

And as he whittled on the top, Wayne played out the great balancing act of guitar building. Leave a few grams too much on the braces and the guitar will sound dull and lifeless. Too little, and it'll be boomy and tubby. Take just a little more off and the guitar is an implosion waiting to happen. Wayne doesn't dwell on any of this much. It's a swift and efficient triage: Those bits of wood that aren't quite guitar-worthy are summarily dispatched to the floor.

Wayne stopped every now and then and held the piece of spruce up to his ear, using just the thumb and forefinger of his right hand. He tapped a little on the top with the index of his left, listening as this piece of spruce spoke for itself. It was not the initial attack, not the sharp sound of the tap itself that interested him, but the overtones afterward that made the difference. He invited me to listen. I put my ears just below the soundhole. Like a wave on a big-surf day, the sound swelled quickly and with attitude after the initial attack, and then died slowly. It hummed.

"That's about as much ring as I've ever heard," Wayne said. He's not bragging on himself—far from it. Most of the credit for that ring goes to a giant old spruce tree that was planted four centuries ago. But Wayne's role was to squeeze every ounce of tone out of this amazing piece of wood. From the look on his face, he seemed convinced that he'd done that. He tapped again, just for fun. "That's as long as a guitar string." He did it once more, and I attempted to quantify it—one Mississippi, two Mississippi, three Mississippi, four Mississippi, five Mississippi, six Mississippi. I reached seven Mississippi before the sound fell below my threshold of hearing.

"This is what it's normally like," Wayne explained. He tapped the top again and then lightly damped it after a short three count.

This multistep process started with roughing out the shape of the braces on the band saw and the belt sander and gluing them down to the top. Then Wayne scalloped the braces. The braces start out as a long taper, and by the time the scalloping is done, they look like a giant stylized M with a shallow trough in the middle and ends that taper flush with the edge of the top.

At the Martin factory, the workers on the assembly line will scallop a brace with one quick chisel stroke in each direction, ripping through a guitar in something like a minute. "It looks like she's using a shovel," Wayne recalled. Wayne was much more careful, if not self-consciously precise. He started at the peak of the M, took aim, and took a short, even slice off the top edge of the brace. Then he made another short stroke, and then another, the soft spruce forming tight curls ahead of the chisel's finely honed leading edge. When he was done, the guitar top looked like a little diorama, and the braces themselves a miniature landscape of hills like white elephants.

Wayne made it look easy; it's not. He glued up a piece of brace stock onto a scrap of spruce and let me try it. The leeward slope of the bracing wasn't too bad. Then I looked and realized that my chisel blade had shifted just a little to the left, and its sharp corner dug into the soft spruce, leaving an unsightly scar.

"You'll see many an old Martin with those marks," Wayne consoled.

When trying to make the trough, I blew it completely, driving the chisel just a bit too hard and basically splitting the brace in half.

"I think that one might sound a little tubby," the master guitar builder said with a laugh.

After the whittling came the sanding. When he's happy with the sound of the top, Wayne gets out a piece of 800 grit sandpaper that's barely more abrasive than a morning newspaper, and rubs the inside of the guitar until it's silky-smooth. This was the inside of the guitar, where no one but a repairman would ever see the precision of the work, or feel the satin texture of the freshly polished braces. But Wayne pressed on.

Partly it's genetic. "My dad used to sand on my guitars, and if you let him, he'd keep sanding until there wasn't anything left," he explained.

Partly it's scientific. "I think it makes them sound better. The notes just have a smoother trip coming out of the guitar."

But it's mostly about doing things right. "It's just showing pride in your craftsmanship, I guess. That's what my guitars are known for, being clean on the inside."

Wayne lavished an amazing amount of attention on the hidden details of this and every guitar. Indeed, Wayne devoted more time and obvious care to fine-finishing the braces than he did to, say, putting the inlays on the fingerboard. It was a ready-made riff on that old Mies van der Rohe warhorse: "God is in the details." But it was more than that. Every Henderson guitar is a self-portrait of its maker. And it's a measure of the man's character that he does this level of work knowing that no one will ever see it.

Sometimes, in fact, Wayne takes this to extremes. After he finished gluing the backs on these guitars, he spent half an hour filling in the tiniest gaps—maybe the width of a piece of writing paper—where the kerfing had to be cut to fit around the back braces. He used the most diminutive slivers of mahogany, secured by the most minuscule dabs of glue. These will be buried deep inside the guitar, invisible even with a light and an inspection mirror. By contrast, on many, even most, modern guitars, even high-end ones, the kerfing doesn't even extend all the way to the end block simply because no guitar buyer is likely to see it.

It says something about my disposition that watching Wayne work often made me nervous. My adventures in the physical world required a certain amount of attention on my part, or the results were likely to be disastrous. I was happy to have survived seventh-grade shop class with all my fingers and toes intact. Wayne's approach seemed so casual—too casual. So I fretted for him.

When he stood a guitar body up on end, still teetering as he walked away, I would imagine gravity yanking it toward the center of the earth—bam!—1,000 Brazilian rosewood toothpicks. But it never seemed to fall. He'd eyeball dimensions, measuring with nothing more than his calloused fingers, and it always seemed to fit. When I was tempted to second-guess Wayne Henderson, I remembered the appendix brace. On the very first guitar I ever watched him build—Scott Fore's contest guitar—I watched with rapt attention. He had finished fussing with the human-hair tolerances on the kerfing, but the back stripe was a good eighth-inch short of the heel block. This was a flaw that would take more than a sliver of wood to correct. I cringed but I didn't dare say a word.

And sure enough, Wayne walked over calmly, found a tiny piece of maple, about half the size of a business card. He test-fitted it on the surface of the end block, and lo and behold, it filled the gap perfectly.

"You'll see these braces on nice old guitars," Wayne said. "But they tend to fall off."

There isn't a name for this piece, so I dubbed it the appendix brace. The only piece of maple, besides the bridge plate, on the whole guitar, it raised more questions than it answered. If it's purely structural, why not use a scrap of more stable, more accessible mahogany? If it's largely decorative, why not use a piece of spruce that would continue the line of the back stripe? Whatever the answer, Wayne dutifully installed the appendix brace deep inside the guitar in a place that Eric Clapton—or anyone else—will likely never see it.

These details are why Wayne has an affinity for the Martin guitars of bygone days. Cheap guitars like Harmonys and Silverstones don't even pay lip service to craftsmanship—their braces look like they were shaped by a beaver looking for a snack. Even vintage Gibsons aren't much better. "Some of the best J-35s and Advanced Jumbos I ever played, wonderful-sounding guitars, are a mess inside," Wayne told me. Martins, on the other hand, are tidy—Germanic, almost, the tight ensemble playing of a fine symphony orchestra rather than the loose groove of a Dixieland marching band that you'll find in a Gibson guitar. Wayne takes Martin's tidiness to the next level. It's ironic that the cleanest guitars on the planet come from the messiest shop anywhere.

As he finished the sanding, Wayne tapped the guitar again just to hear it reverberate. He recalled his pet turkey, and the days he was still building his guitars in a shed on the farm. "Old Smedley used to gobble four times whenever I would tap on a guitar top," he announced. Would Clapton's guitars have passed the Smedley test?

Not exactly. At first Wayne thought all that gobbling was a good omen. Then he began to realize that old Smedley wasn't all that discriminating. He was a turkey, and turkeys sometimes drown in rainstorms because they can't remember to close their mouths. No, old Smedley would gobble at pretty much any instrument, good, bad, or indifferent. So there would be no turkey test for Clapton's guitar. Just a more intimate examination, the crucial, lazy hour spent in the master's lap that makes a guitar a Henderson.

CHAPTER TWENTY-TWO

Maker's Mark

WALK INTO THE Frank Gehry–designed Experience
Music Project in Seattle's Denny Regrade district, and
you're immediately confronted by an installation called Roots
and Branches. Like a Thanksgiving Day table, a museum needs a
centerpiece, and like *La Grande Jatte* at Chicago's Art Institute,
or the giant blue whales suspended from the ceiling at New
York's American Museum of Natural History, this three-story-
high cone-shaped collage of guitars is designed to stick in the
memory while traveling exhibitions come and go.

But what exactly is it? A giant ice cream cone? The bell of
Miles Davis's trumpet aimed heavenward? A Guitar Center
caught in a tornado? As I moved closer one thing became clear:
It's a totem to the primacy of the guitar, both acoustic and electric. It contains six hundred stringed instruments, almost all
guitars, with a few odd dulcimers and a fiddle or two for good
measure.

I thought about this exhibit as Wayne was about to seal up
the bodies of the two Clapton guitars on Friday afternoon. These
instruments are numbers 326 and 327 of an unbroken line that
began with guitar number one, which is sitting in his guest bedroom.

Wayne got out a set of little metal dies he got from Brook-
stone more years ago than he cares to remember. He picked up

the fretting hammer that Max made for him, and a razor-sharp pencil. With twelve sharp taps—two three-digit serial numbers, on each guitar, one in the conventional place in the neck block and another, hidden number in the heel block to thwart potential thieves—these guitars earned their place in a body of work.

Wayne numbers his guitars as an homage to the C.F. Martin company's penchant for order. They began numbering their instruments in 1898, and even today, if you call the company with the serial number of any of its guitars, a staffer can tell you the exact date work was done on it. But there's still a bit of Hendersonian wiggle room in Wayne's system. For example, guitar number 300, Carmine Rocci's D-45, was still sitting around when the Clapton guitars were in progress, stuffed in a black Hefty bag to keep it from drying out and cracking. That guitar didn't get done until three months after the Clapton guitars. Unlike the Martin factory, which chronicles its output in musty log books, Wayne Henderson keeps a tangible record of each guitar he builds. The disc of spruce punched out of the sound hole of each guitar is preserved, in sequential order, laced onto an old guitar string, and stored under the big bench.

Three twenty-six and 327. Those numbers prompted me to do the math. Wayne had built roughly three hundred guitars to date. If he can keep up his annual post-retirement output of about twenty guitars a year for fifteen more years—or until he's seventy-three—that will equal roughly six hundred—or the number of instruments in Roots and Branches.

But beyond that numerical similarity, Roots and Branches is the utter and absolute antithesis of Wayne Henderson's work. It's a triumph of quantity over quality. All of the six hundred instruments—cheap factory-built Yamahas, Ibanezes, and Fenders—are thoroughly generic, mass-produced, anonymous. While most Henderson instruments are among their owners' most prized possessions—right at the top of the Things to Save in Case of Fire list—the Roots and Branches guitars are hung out of reach, destined never to be touched, save by the museum's maintenance staff. There's hardly an owner of a Henderson guitar who won't eagerly hand you his instrument just to share his good fortune.

And while most of the instruments don't even have strings, Roots and Branches does make music, of a sort. A series of microprocessors control small motors that activate cantilevered arms that pluck the strings of the few functioning instruments. The music is perfect—in a way, too perfect: slow, haunting, and sterile, exactly the opposite of the animated, blazing bluegrass that Wayne Henderson and his friends pick. Impressive and puzzling at the same time, Roots and Branches begs—and answers— the question: Do androids dream of electric guitars?

Here's yet another way to think about Wayne Henderson's oeuvre. W. Henry Hill, Arthur F. Hill, and Alfred E. Hill, who wrote the definitive biography of Stradivari, estimate that the master violin maker made 1,116 instruments—including two guitars—during a career that spanned seven decades, for an average of a couple of violins or one cello per month. That means that a Henderson guitar is more than twice as rare as a Stradivarius violin. Then again, Stradivari never had to run a mail route.

To Wayne though, these numbers had less lofty significance. "My brother Max used to have a 327 Chevy that would run like a scalded cat," he said as he embossed that number on the warm, tan mahogany. Indeed, as the days rolled on, these two all-but-identical guitars began to take on personalities of their own. Number 326 was the more old-school of the two. Its Brazilian rosewood back had slightly straighter grain and a more subtle variation in hue, its top had a finer texture and fewer of the gradations in color that are typical of Adirondack tops.

Its sibling, 327, was a little flashier, a little racier. The rosewood back had a little more contrast from dark to light, including a pair of distinctive black pinstripes. The sides had a pair of little swirls in the grain on the bottom bout. And the top destined for 327 had a light caramel-color streak—a racing stripe, perhaps?—that ran along either side of the fingerboard. But these are the subtlest of differences, the tiny birthmarks that parents of identical twins use to tell their offspring apart, in lieu of writing their names on their butts in permanent marker. Indeed, early on in the construction process, Wayne, who is used to building one guitar at a time, took to writing numbers on the fingerboards, the necks, and the bridges in pencil just to keep them all straight.

"Which one's Clapton going to pick?" I wondered.

"I'll let you know after I play 'em," Wayne replied without hesitation.

YESTERDAY, WAYNE BRANDED the guitars. For years, he used to mark his guitars with nothing more than a pencil. But then one morning, Wayne went to his mailbox and found a package containing a small branding iron, a gift from a customer in England. The act of branding was quite the production, and it clearly appealed to the show-off in Wayne Henderson. He heated the business end of the iron with the blue flame of an acetylene torch, and when the brand was hot beyond hot, he practiced a couple of times on a piece of scrap wood. Then he moved over to the guitars, and stared for a second at the spot on the back where they'd be marked. When he touched the hot metal to the soft spruce it sizzled and smoked slightly, just like in a 1950s western. No mistaking these guitars for ones from another herd. When he finished, Wayne hung the branding iron gingerly up on two nails above Gerald's bench. If he'd put the red-hot iron down haphazardly the way he does most of his other tools, he could easily have burned the place down.

With the serial numbers stamped and the backs branded, it was time to sign these works of art. And in this way, Wayne took a step away from the Martin tradition. Most of the company's guitars are neither signed nor dated simply because they don't trace their existence back to one single craftsman. A very few instruments were initialed, usually by whichever of the Martins was running the company at the moment or by the foreman, John Deichman. Wayne told me that the presence of initials and a date under the top are clues that a guitar might be a prototype or an instrument of some special distinction.

"Lloyd Loar signed and dated guitars, though," Wayne reminded me.

During his brief but important tenure with the Gibson company in the mid-1920s, Lloyd Loar, the acoustic engineer for Gibson, signed the paper labels inside a few select top-of-the-line mandolins and archtop guitars, although there's no evidence that he actually built any of them. Nonetheless, Loar-signed instruments, especially mandolins, have become tremendously valuable, fetching the kind of money commanded by Stradivari violins not long ago.

Wayne found a pencil and made his mark.

"What's today's date?" he asked.

"November 18th."

He looked at the clock then looked at me. This means that the other top—for 327—which won't be finished until tomorrow morning, will have the same date.

On some guitars, this would be the extent of Wayne's inscription. Other guitars have more personal greetings. Take Joe Wilson's rosewood triple-ought. Executive director of the National Council for the Traditional Arts, Wilson is a great friend of Wayne's, and a benefactor as well, the guy who hooked him up on the Masters of the Steel String Guitar tour, and any number of gigs since. Wilson wanted a guitar. He asked Wayne politely and not so politely for years. Seven of them, by Wilson's count.

Then he started putting it in writing. He mailed a postcard a day for almost three months, eighty-nine of them in total. These postcards went well beyond "Wish you were here." A postcard picturing a native from New Guinea addressed to Dead Meat Henderson, Mouth of Wilson, Virginia, read: "I've got this headhunter working for me. He'll eat anybody—Sinners. Banjo pickers. Even Republicans. But he's balking about eating you. Says he doesn't think he can clean you. Finish that guitar!" Many are even worse, and Wayne has kept every one of them.

So Wayne built a guitar that was perfectly suited to such a good friend—and such a grand pain in the ass. He dug around in the woodshed and pulled out some of his best Brazilian rosewood. These pieces had a history—they were once the countertops in Truman Capote's yacht, and when the boat was refitted, these priceless pieces of old-growth lumber were replaced with Corian or some other modern synthetic atrocity. Fortunately, a few of the pieces were picked out of a Dumpster by one of Wayne's friends. Wayne stashed the wood, waiting for just the right guitar, Joe Wilson's guitar.

"I often think about the conversations that must have taken place over that table," Wilson told me.

But after that magnificent guitar body was completed, branded, numbered, signed, and dated, Wayne decided to personalize it. Inside Wilson's magnificent guitar, on the back side of one of the tone bars, so far inside the belly of the guitar that you'd need a laparoscope to see it, is a private dedication.

"I wrote, 'Joe Wilson Eats Shit and Likes It,'" Wayne confessed, further admitting that this wasn't the only time he's tagged a guitar body that way.*

Do either or both of these guitars—326 or 327—bear a similarly personal message to Eric Clapton? Wayne Henderson's not telling, and neither am I.

---

* Wayne is not the first luthier to send a client a private message under a guitar top. A repairman working on Joan Baez's vintage Martin 0-45 penciled, "Too bad you are a Communist." The message wasn't discovered until years later, by another repairman, and Baez was so taken by the gesture, if not the sentiment, that when Martin produced a limited-edition reissue of her guitar, she requested that each of them bear that same inscription under the top.

CHAPTER TWENTY-THREE

La Vraie Chose

A<small>W, HECK,"</small> <small>SAID</small> W<small>AYNE</small> into the receiver. "Bring him over."

When the bright red cordless phone rings at the guitar shop, you're never quite sure what surprises the caller may have in store. Late Friday afternoon as the Clapton guitars began to take shape, Scott Fore, the guitarist who won the Tournament of Champions guitar contest at the festival, called. He had a houseguest he'd like to bring over to visit the shop. The houseguest was David Doucet, the guitarist for the Cajun crossover band BeauSoleil.

Doucet isn't a celebrity exactly—people don't stop him for autographs when he goes out to buy a quart of milk—but something better. A player. A pro. A guy who knows his way around the instrument and the music world well enough to make a good living at it. The kind of guy who's always welcome at the guitar shop.

So Wayne made preparations. Did he pick up the wood scraps and vacuum up the sawdust? Did he buy cookies and soft drinks? Beer and pretzels? Did he put on a clean pair of jeans? No. He had me write out a note—Went to Ona's. Be Back Soon.—and post it prominently on the messy workbench when we went to meet Wayne's girlfriend, Helen, for dinner. Wayne doesn't have to tidy up or cater to his guitar-playing guests any more than a toy store has to give away candy.

And sure enough when we get back from dinner, Fore is sitting there playing my $100 Japanese-made Washburn mandolin, tearing through a version of "Black Mountain Rag" while Doucet is playing rhythm on the Collings guitar he brought. Doucet is a big amiable man with a close-trimmed white beard and wire-rimmed glasses. He's the kind of rugged, yet easygoing guy you could almost see at the helm of a 12-meter yacht.

We exchanged pleasantries, then got down to business.

Wayne got out the chicken coop guitar. Doucet, the guest of honor, got first dibs. He picked out a few bouncy choruses of the Merle Travis tune "Bye Bye Bluebell."

"Sweeeeet," said Doucet, elongating the single syllable for emphasis. Fore's grin suggested that he agreed. Then we trotted out the two old D-18s—the 1947 and the 1948. Fore launched into a version of the old fiddle tune "Whiskey Before Breakfast," with a distinctive Celtic lilt.

"It's got a loose sound," he said of Wayne's, I mean, my Martin D-18. "The sound just kind of flows out of this one."

"This is a '48?" asked Doucet.

When Wayne said that the '47 is his first birth-year guitar, David Doucet casually mentioned that he's never played an instrument built the year he was born. Wayne dived into the guitar vault and came out with a 1957 D-21, and proceeded to tell him about the time that he had a 1957 D-21 with the very next serial number in the shop for repairs. It looked worse, but sounded better. Doucet played the '57 for a few minutes. I took the '57 and handed him my '48.

He beamed. "That one's got the shit too." This was a good thing.

Wayne needed this kind of excuse to fish these great old guitars out, the same way a New Yorker needs an out-of-town guest to prompt a trip to the top of the Empire State Building. Doucet just sat on Gabby's chair and smiled the slightly overwhelmed smile of a hound dog who's just swiped a three-pound porterhouse from the kitchen counter. He wasn't evaluating the guitars in any serious way. He was just playing.

And Wayne, for his part, seemed to get even more of a kick out of watching his friends play his guitars—wide-eyed and all-but-drooling—than he did from playing them himself.

We fondled A. P. Carter's 00-28, and then a '29 0-21. Wayne then fished out a severely battered '46 000-28 with a top that's almost black from grime, an instrument that's lived an even rougher life than the '48 D-18. It's beautiful in an ugly sort of way, or maybe vice versa.

As this one was passed around, the conversation turned to tales of guitar abuse. Wayne told of the time that a friend of his was doing some construction work on a house, only to see two young kids dragging an old guitar around the yard. "It was an old herringbone and the kids were riding it like a stick horse," he recalled with a laugh. When Wayne's friend approached the mother and asked if she wanted to sell it, she replied, "We can't sell that one because the kids are playing with it, but we've got this nice one in the house that we might could sell." This smacked of rural legend, except for the fact that Wayne saw both of the instruments in question, the dirt-encrusted herringbone, and the minty pearl-bound '29 00-42 that had been sitting under a bed for a couple of decades.

And speaking of rural legends, the conversation—which floated atop a carpet of Doucet's very hot guitar playing—turned to the Mongoose Story. In Wayne's old shop around the corner, he played a practical joke that still resonates a decade after its last run.

In the doorway of the shop stood a large metal cage with a hand-scrawled sign: *Rare African Mongoose. Beware! Extremely Quick and Dangerous!* Inside the cage were wood shavings, a couple of half-empty bowls, and a big bushy tail sticking out from a little burrow in the back.

"Everyone who walked in wanted to see the mongoose," Fore recalled. "You could see its tail. And Wayne would be over there sawing on something, saying, "Don't mess with that thing. It'll take your finger off.""

But invariably the quarry pressed on, and Wayne would reluctantly hand over a piece of fret wire or something similar.

"Stick it back through the screen and into that little hole back there," he'd instruct. "It'll piss him off but at least it'll get him out where you can see him."

"And about the time they're concentrating real good," Wayne explained taking over the story from Fore. "I'd hit the lever and the top would fly open and the tail would come up and hit them in the face." There was screaming, cussing, and perhaps even a pair of soiled Carthartts. More than one palpitating victim ran clear out of the shop.

"I'm surprised that someone didn't get tipped off that it was coming and then drop to the floor and pretend to drop dead with a heart attack," said Wayne longingly. "That would have fixed me good." Wayne reluctantly retired the mongoose before someone really did buy the farm. Wayne now made due with the remote-controlled fart machine he'd often sneak under one of the shop's chairs.

Then it was time to go over to Wayne's house for the truly good stuff. First Wayne got out a 1937 D-28 herringbone. With a sunburst top that was amber in the center and darkened to a deep sienna near the edges, it was simply the most fetching guitar I've ever seen.

And when Fore picked it up and began to play into it, it sounded like the gates of heaven had opened. The tone was demonstrative, but it was controlled, balanced. Its voice was stately, regal, Olivier playing King Lear. But you didn't have to be a world-class flatpicker to appreciate this magnificent instrument. I strummed a simple E chord and in an instant I was enveloped in a blanket of harmony, each note blended yet still distinct. And the wave went forever—thirty-five, forty seconds later I could still hear faint overtones dying away. Playing this guitar, or hearing it played the way Fore, Doucet, and, yes, Wayne can play it was a sensory explosion, a great Bordeaux, a stolen kiss.

"Damn," said Doucet when it was his turn. "I'm in awe, here."

"I always think that's just about the best one I ever played," said Wayne matter-of-factly.

Then came the moment of truth. Scott opened his case and brought out his Henderson, the Brazilian rosewood dread that he won in the contest. With its old-school Martin specs, Wayne had clearly modeled it after the old sunburst 'bone. But it was also just a whipper-snapper in guitar terms, not yet a year old, and still on its first set of strings. By any logical measure, this was not a fair fight. It was David Spade against Mike Tyson.

Doucet picked up the Hendo and launched into "Sail Away Ladies."

"Play that same song again on this one," said Fore, taking back his instrument, and handing back the 'bone.

"We're making it tough on you," I said.

"I'm working," Doucet said with a laugh, as he obliged with a repeat performance.

Wayne and Scott and I sat back and listened. We looked at each other, then we looked back at Scott's guitar. The family resemblance was striking, and even a little spooky. This guitar was a time machine, a six-month-old instrument that sounded like it should have its own AARP card.

"It sounds old," Doucet concluded about Fore's almost new Henderson.

"It's definitely got the lows and the highs," said Scott. "The middle's not there yet." Like a young wine, the Hendo didn't have quite the mid-range sophistication of the best damn sixty-five-year-old guitar on the planet. Those middles are really the voice of the guitar, the last degree of refinement. That can't be rushed. But like the bud of a rare tea rose still on the vine, the sound of this guitar is magnificent, but it also whispers: "The best is yet to come."

"If we play your festival do we get to stay at your house?" Doucet joked.

But these guitars aren't toys to Wayne. They're tools. They are his reference library. If he wants to know what a shaded-top dreadnought should look like, he picks up the '37 sunburst. If he wants to feel the curve of a vintage 30's neck, he can check out the triple-ought. If he needs to see how a particular set of abalone compares to the stuff from the good old days, he just needs to trot out his D-45. Pickguard shapes, binding widths, inlay patterns, it's all there for the asking.

But most important is the tone. All these magnificent vintage guitars have robust, mature voices. They're not shy. They speak their minds with little provocation from the player. As Scott and David swapped guitars, picking and grinning, Wayne's current mission came into clearer focus. What should these Clapton guitars be? How about a guitar that plays as easy as that squeaky clean triple-ought? Looks as pretty as the D-45? And will someday sound like the D-28? Not an easy task. But it's a challenge that Wayne welcomes.

This jam session could have gone on all night, but reality intruded. It was getting late and Fore and Doucet had a long drive back and a gig the next night. Before he grabbed his coat, David picked up the herringbone one last time and sped through a quick version of "Windy and Warm."

"C'est la vraie chose," he said as he put the old guitar down on the worn leather loveseat. The real thing indeed.

CHAPTER TWENTY-FOUR

So Finite, It's Untrue

T HAT'S CLASSIC BELT BUCKLE rash on that one," said Wayne Henderson in the middle of Saturday afternoon, while I was on the phone ordering the pizza from Osborne's General Store. "And that one there has been played sitting down." Wayne was flipping through the Christie's catalogue for the Crossroads auction, and in a moment he nailed the difference between Lot 19 and Lot 20, the *Unplugged* guitar and its doppelgänger. The first guitar, Lot 20, bore a circle of wear right in the center of the rosewood back, where the guitar had been rubbed against a belt buckle. That guitar spent its life being played standing up hanging off a strap, the way bluegrass and old-time players usually do. And according to Christie's VP Kerry Keane, who put the auction together, this guitar had the bright, twangy sound that ensemble players favor.

The one with wear marks clustered near the top of the guitar was, indeed, the *Unplugged* guitar. It had been played sitting down, resting more on the player's chest than on his stomach. And many, if not most, of those marks were made by the buttons on Eric Clapton's Armani shirts or Versace jackets.

Indeed, every guitar is a miniature ergonomics project. A great-sounding guitar that doesn't feel right is no bargain. And while that comfortable-as-a-loafer feel may be hard to quantify, it really means everything. And that was what the final days of the

Clapton guitar project were all about: the intersection between instrument and individual. And that synergy was most apparent at the neck of a guitar, where hand meets wood, and in Wayne's World, at least, it's the last piece of the instrument to be finished.

Over the preceding days, Wayne and I had been trying to channel Eric Clapton in absentia to figure out what a guy neither of us had ever met would want in a guitar. The question of what body size to build was an easy one. Most of Clapton's favorite guitars had been midsize fourteen-fret Martins.

But what should the scale length be? Martin made that body size with two different neck lengths. The first fourteen-fret guitars, designed in 1929, were made in the 25.4-inch OM scale length. And five years later, for reasons that have been largely lost to history, the company switched all its smaller body guitars to a shorter 24.9 scale length.

Each design had its advantages and adherents. The short, triple-ought scale had the frets placed closer together, which made fingering some tricky chords easier. The longer, OM scale put more tension on the strings, which resulted in a different sound, louder, punchier, with a little more string-to-string separation.

Lots 19 and 20 were both short-scale ooos, as were Martin's Eric Clapton signature models. So the obvious thing to do would have been to make Clapton's guitar a ooo. But a brief interview of Clapton conducted by Kerry Keane in the Crossroads auction catalogue suggested that Clapton's preferences might have changed.

EC: I bought this sight unseen from Gruhn's. I have three guitars of that ilk and I decided to sell these two [Lots 19 and 20] and to keep the OM.

KK: Are OMs better for you tonally?

EC: No, I think it's in the playing. The tone is different on all of them but I think it's the playability. It's so finite, it's untrue. Nobody else but me would probably care, but I'm picky because I'm lazy. The guitar has to do quite a lot of the work for me.

But the biggest piece in the puzzle came from Clapton himself. "Just like this one," he said while playing Tim Duffy's Henderson guitar those many years ago. And Duffy's guitar was an OM.

That was really the target. Wayne's pretty good with names, and not bad with figures, but he never forgets a guitar. An OM like Tim Duffy's? No problem. And once that decision was made, everything else fell into place.

A guitar neck is made of mahogany because it's the most stable of woods. It is strong and steadfast, straight of grain and resistant to cracking and bending. The pieces that Wayne used looked like lumber, simple four-by-fours two feet long. As he sawed the neck blanks, Wayne got out a square for the first time in the whole guitar making process to make sure each one was completely flat and perpendicular. While the guitar body is all about complex curves, the neck is all about straight lines, pure Euclidian geometry. The neck is attached to the body with the most elaborate—and the most crucial—piece of joinery in the guitar, the dovetail neck joint that Martin has been using since the nineteenth century. It's a remarkable compound joint that tapers from a perfect equilateral triangle in the front to a perfect point on the back. How precise is a good dovetail joint? You can press fit the neck without a drop of glue, and it can be strung up and it'll play fine. Other guitar makers have found easier ways to attach a neck—just bolt the neck on and hide the screws—but none better than a dovetail joint.

Wayne fashioned the joint on the table saw, using two little wedges of mahogany that looked like so much of the scrap wood that sits on the floor. The only thing to distinguish them from something that belongs in the trash was a couple of small drill holes and two tiny tacks on the side. Wayne has been using these same templates for thirty-five years or more. But he doesn't put them away except in the most general manner, stuffing them on the overcrowded shelf above the table saw. And a couple of years ago they came dangerously close to a permanent home in a landfill. One of the General Loafers, Don Wilson, took the great notion of cleaning up. A few days later the dovetail templates turned up missing. One plus one equals two, and sifting through the still unemptied shop vac, Wayne rescued these two precious pieces of mahogany.

This was typical of the glorious mess that is the guitar shop. Wayne recalled a set of bridge pins from an old herringbone that he was planning on putting on his '37. They were packed carefully in an old film canister. Now they're missing in action. Wayne hasn't completely given up hope, but he's realistic enough to assume that, likely as not, he's seen the last of them.

Fitting the joint is a bit of a finicky job, and often there's a fair bit of shimming and trimming and tweaking and retweaking to get the angle of the neck just right. Not this Saturday. These pieces of wood, like most of the wood in this project, were unusually cooperative. They seemed to actually *want* to become a guitar. The only gap in the joint—a small eighth-inch opening on the bottom—was completely intentional. It was a nod to the future. Even in a well-built guitar, over the span of decades, the inexorable pull of the steel strings will tug on the spruce top and the neck millimeter by millimeter so that they start—as Kerry Keane said—to meet in the center. And when that begins to happen, the strings sit too high above the fretboard for comfortable playing and the neck needs to be removed and its angle adjusted, as T.J. Thompson did for Ella. Wayne puts that little gap in so some guitar repairman—thirty, forty, sixty years down the line—can steam off the neck the way Wayne does on an old Martin. Wayne pulls out the fifteenth fret with a pair of pliers, drills a tiny hole in the fret slot, and proceeds to steam out the glued-in neck. He once used a pressure cooker with a hose, and a needle from a basketball pump, but he's more recently graduated to an espresso machine likely spirited from the kitchen of one of the guitar shop widows. In the dark ages of guitar repair, some luthiers would simply lop a neck off with a hacksaw. Now, Wayne can remove a neck and reset it in less time than it would take a mere mortal to replace a set of strings.

When it came time to shape the neck, Wayne adhered to his "carve away everything that doesn't look like a guitar" doctrine. He'll rough some of the pieces on the band saw, carefully saving the mahogany scraps to make kerfing with. At this early stage, the neck remained squared off and chunky.

Then he took the neck to the belt sander and began to use the machine as a kind of AC-powered whittling knife. He rounded off the edges on one side. Then the other. He smoothed off each side in turn while the mahogany not destined to become a guitar rose toward the ceiling in a miniature dust storm. With each pass this piece of lumber became more accommodating to the human hand as the guitar neck within revealed itself. In five minutes, a lowly chunk of wood was transformed into something that just begged you to touch it, hold it, caress it.

And that was only the beginning. Wayne then sat down in his chair and again pulled out that Boker Tree Brand knife. He pared away the honey-colored wood, forming the graceful curve where the neck proper meets the neck heel, which attaches the guitar to the body. He scraped steadily, and all around his feet lay a perfect pile of mahogany curls, all fuzzy and conical.

"How's that feel?" he asked as he handed me the guitar.

Like something you want to hang on to for the rest of your life, I wanted to say. But I knew that wasn't the kind of feedback Wayne wanted.

"Good. Real good. Maybe just a little bit more of a V-shape," I suggested.

Wayne's secret is a neck shape that's just lightly asymmetrical, like the natural nook between the left index finger and the left thumb on the guitarist's fretting hand. Near the headstock, the point of the soft V is shifted ever so slightly toward the bass side of the guitar, all the better to fit the fretting hand. Closer to the guitar body, that apex is shifted just a tiny bit toward the center, because on these high frets, players tend to grab the neck with their thumb rather than their whole palm. This slight bit of asymmetry is all but invisible to the naked eye, but grab a Henderson guitar neck and you'll notice right away how well it cradles your hand.

After we were both satisfied, he handed me a piece of 400 grit sandpaper, and asked me to sand the neck of Eric Clapton's guitar. Then he walked over to the band saw and did it all over again with the second neck blank. The truly amazing part? This second neck was the same as the first. In most guitar factories necks are made by CNC machines, computer-controlled routers that are able to replicate complex shapes with perfect precision. On this project, Wayne proved that his full name including initials should be Wayne C.N.C. Henderson.

Just as Wayne finished with the second neck, a young woman bounced in. She was wearing black jeans and a black T-shirt, her long dark hair tied back in a ponytail, her infectious smile preceding her.

"Wayne, you got a capo?" she drawled.

Her name was Lisa Robertson, a local fiddler. She and her husband, Will, were playing at the Rugby Rescue Squad pre-Thanksgiving potluck dinner just around the corner.

Her arrival startled me simply because it highlighted what I had been missing. Lisa was the first unaccompanied young woman—besides Wayne's daughter, Elizabeth—that I can recall entering the shop in all the hours I'd been there. While there isn't a NO GIRLS ALLOWED sign on the door, the guitar shop is a de facto boys club, a place where guys go to tell scatological jokes and engage in the simple joys of male bonding.

Wayne handed her my capo—it's an accessory that clamps on the fretboard and raises the pitch of each string, so that the guitarist can play in the same key as the fiddler or the singer—and she smiled and bounced out as quickly as she came in. Maybe it was just the sawdust.

Our stomachs rumbling, Wayne and I headed over to the Rescue Squad ourselves. The turkey was gone by the time we got there, but there was ham, potatoes, slaw, beans, corn, and a wide variety of other country victuals.

After dinner, Will Robertson, a burly, bearded guy with a quick wit that belied his rugged appearance, auctioned off a variety of desserts—German chocolate cake, pumpkin bread, Bundt cake ("Doesn't that have something to do with baseball?" Will wondered).

The prize of the night was a genuine, authentic, homemade pecan pie. The bidding got hot and heavy and Wayne bid six, then eight, then ten dollars, and it was sold to the man in the baseball cap for ten dollars.

"Did I just pay ten dollars for a pecan pie?" he said with mock amazement. "I hope it's good."

"That's how someone ended up paying $790,000 for an old Martin guitar," I retorted.

Will and Lisa invited Wayne up to play "Alabama Jubilee" with the band—it was a particular favorite of the band's pedal steel player. And that was Wayne Henderson in a nutshell. In two weeks he would be playing at Carnegie Hall, but he was still perfectly happy picking for free at the Rugby Rescue Squad. As the hall began to empty out, Will Robertson played "Rose Connolly," a classic murder ballad about a man who's hanged for killing his sweetheart, and then introduced his wife for one last instrumental. Near the stage was a sign that boldly and unequivocally pronounced NO DANCING. I thought this was some kind of curious insurance regulation—sure, you can fall while you're dancing, but where better to do it than the Rescue Squad? It was, instead, a nod to the strict beliefs of the local minister.

"The Baptists around here won't have sex standing up because it's likely to lead to dancing," Wayne told me. I'd find out later that the prudish minister was actually a relative of Wayne's. Still, Wayne himself wasn't much for churchgoing. "I'm a buzzard Baptist," he admitted. "I only go to church when somebody dies."

UP UNTIL NOW, the two matching Clapton guitars could be mistaken—except upon close and expert inspection—for an OM made by any number of makers, including the Martin company itself. But with a few swipes of the band saw after we returned from dinner, Wayne fixed all that. He grabbed a green Plexiglas template, traced a quick outline, and with just a couple of quick cuts, that square blob of wood at the end of the neck known as the peghead took on a unique and sensuous curve.

Wayne seems to take a particular pride in his pegheads, the prominent area at the top of the neck where the tuners are attached. Most luthiers and guitar companies who build Martin-influenced models put squared-off pegheads on their guitars. Not Wayne. The peghead shape is Wayne's trademark, his calling card. The curvaceous and gently pointed shape is actually derived from an obscure, long–forgotten Martin mandolin model. And from a distance, it's easy to see that this is a Wayne Henderson guitar. The pegheads for the Clapton guitars were overlaid with a piece of wildly figured slab-cut Brazilian rosewood, far more eye-catching than the old-school wood used to make the body. The peghead veneer was inlaid with silvery mother-of-pearl, rather than the more colorful abalone that would adorn the rest of the body, all the better to read the name from a distance.

When it came time to do the finer finishing work, Wayne headed over to his newest shop toy. It's an oscillating drum sander with a cylindrical drum about nine inches long and an inch in diameter that bobs up and down rhythmically. One doesn't have to be a trained Freudian—or even Gabby—to see the possibility for lewd jokes here. Wayne hadn't yet found something to prop it up on, so he got down on his knees to finish off the peghead, holding the edge of the curve gently against the oscillating appendage.

The whole question of peghead pride was one of the many paradoxes of the Wayne C. Henderson Guitar Company. Wayne wants his guitars to look distinctive and be easily recognizable—and the peghead is a big part of that. On the other hand, he totally eschews marketing in every other way.

Unlike most instrument builders, Wayne Henderson doesn't advertise his craft. He's never taken out an ad.

He doesn't have a Web site.

He doesn't have a brochure.

He doesn't have business cards.

He doesn't have a sign on the shop door.

Why? Simply because he has more orders than he can fill and it's been that way from the first moment he picked up a whitting knife. Wayne's marketing is organic—people see one of his guitars, play one of his guitars, and want one just like it. That's how it worked with Eric Clapton, and that's how it worked for me. It's more like oral tradition than modern commerce.

But it's also the reason Wayne Henderson has remained the biggest fish in a very small pond. Even knowledgeable guitar junkies outside of southwest Virginia have never heard of Wayne or his guitars, unless they bumped into him at a festival, or had a chance encounter with one of the members of the Henderson owners club. The members of the wannabe Henderson owners club tend to keep things quiet because it's very possible that an order taken this month will get done before your guitar, which you ordered two years ago. There's no sense increasing the competition for Wayne's time and attention.

Indeed, Wayne quietly engages in a subtle, but active, counter-marketing campaign. The most widely seen Henderson guitar is also the homeliest by far. It's number 52, his very own guitar. It's a plain-Jane D-18 copy, made by Wayne twenty-five years ago. The pickguard is an ugly plastic that hasn't aged well. The top has darkened to a yellowish hue, but any vestige of gloss has been gone for decades. The back and sides, made of the most pedestrian mahogany, were finished with a dark shoe-polish-brown stain that has taken on a sickly greenish hue. The peghead of old 52 features the Henderson name inlaid in almost institutional-looking block letters that don't match the sinuous lines of the headstock.

This is the guitar Wayne plays every single day and it's the only playable Henderson guitar that he owns. It would be romantic to tell the tale of how Wayne developed a magical bond with the guitar from the start, the one instrument he loved so much he couldn't bear to give it away, but that's not the case. Wayne didn't keep number 52 because it had unmatched sound or feel. His reasons for keeping that guitar were, like so many parts of his legend, simple and practical. After building his first fifty guitars with a plain square Martin-style peghead, he had devised that trademark peghead shape.

"I needed something to show people," he explained.

Of course, playing this homely guitar is a different matter altogether. All the finish has been worn off the neck, and the wood itself was now talc-smooth. It has that perfectly worn-in feel of a five-year-old pair of Levi's 501s, an object transformed slowly and subtly by use. The action was set so low that the guitar practically played itself. The sound? It was round and full and open, as smooth as a shot of sippin' whiskey.

Not that Wayne is particularly protective of his main instrument. Unless he's taking it on an airplane, he carries old number 52 in a green nylon gig bag. While it provides some measure of protection against knocks and scrapes, a full-fledged drop—or something dropped on it—would likely inflict some serious damage. Indeed, one night after a gig, he loaded the guitar in the back of the truck, and whacked old number 52 on the bumper.

When he picked it up to play in the shop the next day, someone said, "Wayne, what happened to your guitar?"

The top was split away from the sides. For most guitar players, this would be a disaster. It didn't bother Wayne much. A couple clamps, a little glue, and number 52 was good as new.

He leaves the guitar around the shop and invites anyone and everyone to play it. After that VFW gig, I saw him hand the guitar to a slightly starstruck twelve-year-old fan named Asa, who picked the guitar tentatively for a good twenty minutes, seeming more than a little overwhelmed by the whole experience.

But it makes sense. Number 52 is Wayne Henderson's litmus test. Like all those fairytale princes disguised as frogs, this guitar's beauty is real but not readily apparent. If you can see past the worn and funky exterior and really listen to its powerful and mature voice, then maybe, just maybe, one day you'll have a Henderson guitar to call your own. One that will be prettier, but not any more beautiful.

ON MONDAY EVENING, Wayne started finishing the guitars. Appropriately enough, the last step was installing that tricky piece of pearl inlay around the edge of the fretboard, which was the first thing I had ever seen him do on a guitar, on Gabby's more than two years before. But this time, with no dog yapping, Wayne made this final step, so fraught with the potential for disaster, look so damn easy.

And when he had completed eight perfect little miter joints, Wayne walked over to the guitar necks, checked the numbers, matched 326 with 326 and 327 with 327, tapped the dovetails gently with the heel of his hand, and joined completed neck to completed body for the first time. And with that simple gesture, at 5:23 P.M. on Monday, November 22, 2004, almost twelve days to the minute from when he made the first cut on the first piece of wood, the two Clapton guitars were essentially done. Wayne picked up each of the guitars, held them for a moment in the playing position. He then gave each of the bodies a firm tap on the back, the way you might burp a colicky baby, and as the hum faded out, he nodded his head.

In celebration, or what passed for it at chez Henderson, we headed over to the house for a late dinner of smoked turkey sandwiches. Wayne uncorked a bottle of Old Fart Chardonnay, and I proposed a toast to the work just done.

"To Brazilian rosewood, Adirondack spruce, and remote controlled fart machines."

Clink.

We sipped and chewed and did what we always did: talk about guitars. After dinner, we walked back to the shop and

Wayne headed over to the tiny vise on Gerald's workbench, with a jeweler's saw in hand. I assumed that he was cutting another piece of abalone inlay. He wasn't.

"I'm making something for your wife," he said when I asked. "But you're going to have to get the chain for it."

He made a quick stop at the buffing wheel, and then handed me an exquisite little cameo cut from a Liberty Head Dime, the rim of the coin forming a perfect little halo around the figure's head. The back side was almost prettier than the front side.

"That dime's the same year as my D-45, 1942."

I was moved, almost speechless.

"You think she'll like it?" he asked.

I nodded.

"Maybe you can get a whole bunch of these things from the flea market in New Jersey?" he asked.

Hardly. Genius doesn't come cheap anywhere.

The last thing that needed to be completed on the guitars before they were lacquered—a long, messy process that Wayne sometimes farms out to a friend with a bigger, better spray booth— is the pearl border around the top, but we were still waiting for the pieces of greenheart abalone, the multicolored shell material that was used on the best vintage Martins, to arrive in the mail. So on Tuesday, while Wayne went into Galax for a meeting to discuss building a permanent stage for the festival, I hung out at the shop. While I was alone, I dug through a pile of wood buried beneath the big workbench, searching for a set of fiddleback Brazilian that had had my name on it for more than two years now. Eureka. I found the silver pencil and wrote my name in large bold letters and casually dropped the pieces of wood on top of the mess on the bench where they'd be impossible to miss, for a few days at least.

That mission complete, I spent a fair amount of time that afternoon mooning over the Clapton guitars. "These things are going to be around for years, maybe hundreds of years," Gerald said. "When our friend Lloyd, the barber, gets to bragging, we tell him that his best work is going to be grown out in two weeks."

"To perpetuity," I replied with a mock toast, hoisting my can of Cheerwine.

When Wayne returned late in the afternoon, he debriefed Gerald on the meeting. There were still headaches about who'll build the stage, how, and with whose money, but Wayne, who can usually find the silver lining in anything, was happy. He got a new baseball cap out of the deal. The hat was an attractive shade of maroon, but it's a Gibson cap, they of the less-than-pristine workmanship, and it's got an electric Les Paul embroidered on the crown.

"I'd like it a lot better if it was an F-5 mandolin," Wayne said, but it didn't bother him much. In fact he wore the hat onstage at Carnegie Hall two weeks later.

"Did the pearl come?" Wayne asked me.

No such luck. The raw pieces of abalone that would provide the last bit of panache on these elegant guitars were still sitting in a UPS depot somewhere. Wayne never did get to show me one of the great secrets of guitar building. This seemingly elaborate inlay that adorns the most valuable guitars ever made can be done at lightning speed and requires no particular skill. We could complete two guitars inside an hour and still have time for a couple of stories. Since I wouldn't get the chance to complete the inlay on Clapton's guitar, his daughter, Elizabeth, did it a few days later when she came home for Thanksgiving. Within minutes, I'm told, she was snapping, fitting, and gluing the pearl strips like a pro.

With Thanksgiving coming up fast and the guitars all but done, I loaded my new/old '48 D-18 in the back seat of the car. It was foggy and drizzling and I was hoping to get in a few hours of driving before evening turned to night.

"Come back again sometime when you can't stay so long," Wayne said and then gave me a long look to make sure that I was laughing too.

I waved, flicked on the headlights, and turned northward, toward home.

CHAPTER TWENTY-FIVE

The State of Mind

I AM NOT EASILY SURPRISED. Trick endings to movies don't take me aback. The evening news often disgusts me, but rarely shocks me. But as I headed back to Rugby in early December to find out what these guitars had become, my thoughts kept turning back to something T.J. Thompson said to me at lunch one midsummer afternoon before this whole Clapton guitar adventure had even started. I was shocked by what he said, and shocked at the fact that I was shocked.

We had just left T.J.'s shop in that funky industrial building in West Concord, Massachusetts. And while his shop isn't large or fancy—in square footage it's barely a third of Wayne's space—it's supremely organized, with a place for everything and everything in its place. He and Ken Fallon, the luthier he works with, each have an organized little work desk, maybe three-by-two, covered with carpet remnants that are replaced when they get too encrusted with glue. T.J. has task lighting and an ergonomic chair—"I paid a fortune for this thing and it's falling apart," he said as he showed me an arm that had come unbolted yet again.

All morning, I peppered T.J. with stupid questions about guitar building, and he answered each one patiently and carefully.

Thompson, I discovered, is the thinking man's guitar builder. He lives for the variables and the way they interact. He looks at the guitar he's building the way Gary Kasparov looks at a chessboard. Before he does anything to an instrument, he thinks about all the steps that came before, and the impact that his next move will have on every subsequent move. "Everything affects everything else," he said.

We headed to lunch at a nice Italian place in a nearby shopping center, the walls of the restaurant painted in a tasteful homage to Van Gogh's *Starry Night*. Over pasta, the subject turned to memorable guitars, great guitars, the best guitars, and finally, the one you can't quite forget.

"It's a C-2 that I converted," T.J. explained without hesitation. The C-2 archtop was one of Martin's many failed experiments. While Gibson was successful at making many things in addition to flattop guitars—banjos, mandolins, archtop guitars, electric guitars—Martin was not. From the mandolins they started making at the turn of the century to the electric guitars they made in the 1960s and 1970s, virtually all of the company's efforts to expand the brand failed. Their archtop guitars of the 1930s and 1940s were no exception. But in the 1970s, after the company stopped making Brazilian rosewood models, a few enterprising players and builders—namely picker extraordinaire David Bromberg and his friend, guitar shop owner Matt Umanov—discovered that once retopped, these mediocre and still inexpensive archtops could be made into very fine flattop guitars.

An L.A. lawyer named Dean Herman bought a beat-up old C-2 archtop, and after the Martin company declined to do a flattop conversion, he was referred to Thompson, who retopped it with an old piece of Adirondack spruce.

Did he ever.

"It's a mind-blowing guitar," Thompson enthused. "This guitar just has everything. That was thirteen years ago and whenever I see it I've never heard anything like it. Everybody who plays it offers Dean any amount of money for it and he just won't sell it. Dean has forty or fifty guitars, but he'll never sell this one."

But what made this particular guitar so special?

"It just worked," he replied. "It's a freak thing."

I steered the conversation toward the Big Question. What is it that separates a magical guitar from a merely great one? What is the nature of that freak thing? I pressed on, figuring that I would get one of two answers: a) It's about choosing the right wood for the top and the right bracing configuration, or b) It's like Louis Armstrong said about jazz, "If you have to ask, you'll never know."

"I think . . ." said T.J., and then he stopped. He paused for eighteen full seconds before he uttered another syllable. "It's a combination of, I guess, about six hundred things. And it's hard to say what's more important than the other. It's the amalgam."

"Do you want any coffee?" the waitress interrupted. We argued about the check briefly—I insisted on picking up the tab—and T.J. refocused on The Question.

"What would be number 1 and what would be 597?" I prodded.

"I can probably answer that. Number 1 is . . ." T.J. paused for eleven more seconds. "Number 1 is the state of mind of the person building the guitar."

I was stunned.

In a single sentence, he had articulated the hypothesis I had been gradually creeping toward. An instrument is the sum total of not only the builder's experience, but his *experiences*. You need to be a good man to build a good guitar.

"Actually, this could be 1 through 20," T.J. continued. "When people ask me how to build a better guitar, I always think and sometimes say, 'Be a better person.' You can't keep your personality out of the work. It's impossible."

I leaned in, as T.J. pressed on with his philosophy lesson.

"If you're rigid or you're distorting reality it goes into the guitar. And when you play it, it comes back out. It's disturbing," he continued. "I used to believe that but I never had any proof of it. But I've played enough handmade guitars and then later met the maker. Sure enough, it's inseparable."

T.J. grasped for a metaphor. "It's like looking at a beautiful person who's had cosmetic surgery. You can see in their aura that something's twisted, or something doesn't fit, doesn't flow, the energy lines have been broken, the meridian lines have been cut."

I let it sink in for a moment while T.J. reached for his glass of water. He knew that he was treading on thin ice.

"I've never heard anybody say it," Thompson continued. "Most of the people in our business want variables that are quantifiable, variables that they can manipulate and control. When you start talking about personality, you're in trouble." You want an Engelmann spruce top? Sure, no problem. A fatter neck? You got it. More empathy? Um, well, I'll see what I can do.

"But I put it at the top," T.J. said as we got up to leave.

I TESTED THIS THEORY against my own experience. Does it hold? Oh, yes. Wayne and T.J. are members of a small club, the group of guitar builders who build instruments that are directly comparable to the greatest guitars ever built. Who else is in this club? I'd argue for John Greven of Portland, Oregon, Kim Walker of North Stonington, Connecticut, Lynn Dudenbostel of Knoxville, Tennessee and maybe a few others. But unless you're an easy grader, you're going to run out of guitar builders before you run out of fingers.

T.J. and Wayne build guitars that are a lot alike. They're loud, they have a big sound, but they respond to a delicate touch. They're responsive. They're rich and full, but the overtones never swamp the primacy of that initial note. In a word, they sound a lot like really great old Martins.

And once you scratch the surface, you realize the guys who build these guitars have a lot in common too. Wayne and T.J. are both men of integrity. They work hard. They don't take shortcuts. They know and care about the people they're building guitars for. And they're both humble—restoring magnificent prewar 000-45s will do that for you.

They also build guitars for the right reasons. Neither Thompson nor Henderson is motivated by money. They don't use dollars and cents as a way to keep score. They could build many more guitars each year if they turned away some of their repair work, or farmed out some of the grunt work to assistants. And they could charge far more for their instruments. Neither of them has ever solicited a sale. Indeed, Thompson goes out of his way to actively dissuade new guitar customers, insisting that they go out and try the instruments made by other companies and other builders before he'll consider putting them on his list.

"I only want to take the order if I'm the last guy on the planet who can do it," Thompson admitted to me.

Wayne is less blunt about it, but he tells his customers right up front that there'll be a wait, and most likely a pretty long one. His metamessage: If you want instant gratification, go to Guitar Center.

And they're both unafraid to tackle a daunting challenge head-on. Take the best guitars ever built, and try to build new ones that may one day sound just as good. Is it an ego thing? What artist—or craftsman—doesn't have a sense of his own place in the pecking order? But really, it's a community service project. Why build a guitar that sounds like an old Martin? Because there aren't enough great old Martins to go around anymore. Even a relatively humble old guitar—like a prewar D-18—now has a price tag that looks like the sticker price of a nicely loaded Japanese car, and pearl-bound Brazilian rosewood guitars are priced like real estate, with most players needing a home-equity loan to afford one. A Henderson or a Thompson is as close as a select few guitar players will ever get to owning a prewar Martin.

And while the common ground that Wayne and T.J. share comes through in each guitar, so do their stylistic differences. A Thompson's tone is a little more precise, a little more delicate. His guitars are meant to be played solo in a quiet parlor. A Henderson guitar, on the other hand, is a little looser, and it responds better to a heavier touch. It's a guitar that sounds best in a small jam session with a couple of close friends.

It's not a matter of better or worse, just different. Different men revealing different sides of themselves through their work. T.J.'s clean aesthetic might nod toward Hemingway, while Wayne's more romantic vibe leans a little more toward Fitzgerald. But make no mistake about it, both clearly belong in the pantheon, the embodiment of Thompson's riddle about how to build a better guitar.

CHAPTER TWENTY-SIX

In Death I Sing

As I approached Rugby down Route 16 from Marion, it was beginning to look a little like Christmas. There was just the slightest dusting of snow, enough to stick to some of the dirt and turn it white. It seemed strange that I had to drive almost six hundred miles south to see the season's first snow a week and a day before Christmas, but I had begun to expect the unexpected when I headed to Grayson County.

It was the second biggest day of the year in Rugby, the day of Wayne Henderson's annual Christmas party, so when I arrived in mid-afternoon, Wayne was on a mission. He was in the garage frying the turkeys. Yes, frying.

This holiday ritual involves plunging a fourteen-pound Butterball into five gallons of peanut oil, heated by an open flame. The real trick is getting the bird into the giant stainless steel pot without knocking over the cooker or having the hot oil overflow onto the flame.

"Do you want to pull the Thunderbird out?" I asked before he did the honors, knowing that his stash of Brazilian rosewood and Adirondack spruce and curly maple would become nothing more than kindling if something went awry.

"I was thinking about that," Wayne replied. "But when I tried to start her up, she wouldn't budge. The battery was as dead as a doornail. Do you want to come in for the excitement?"

Actually, I was thinking about staying outside where I could call the Rugby Rescue Squad. I peeked in through the door as the bird was readied for its splashdown. Wayne held the turkey suspended over the oil for a long moment, guesstimating how much the still wet and partially frozen bird would stir up the cauldron of oil. The smoky smell and the roiling foam weren't nearly as disturbing as the sound that emanated from the pot as bird met oil. It wasn't the chirpy snap, crackle, pop you might hear from a french-fry basket. Far from it. The bird emitted a deep growl, the kind of guttural bowels-of-the earth groan that might precede a volcanic eruption.

As he slapped the metal cover on the pot and backed away, Wayne Henderson did something I'd never seen him do before—he looked at his watch. "It's two forty-seven," he announced. "At three minutes a pound, it should be done at three thirty-one." These turkeys would get the precise timing that, say, guitar sides didn't need.

Two days earlier Herb Key had come over to the shop, working as usual, and putting his new acquisitions, a nice old D-28 and D-18, on the bench. Wayne went out for a bit to buy the three turkeys, and when he came back Herb was nowhere to be found, although his car—and the guitars—were still there. Herb was back at the house, lying on the coach moaning, greener than the hills around Rugby in springtime. Wayne offered to drive him the fifty miles to his home in North Carolina.

"He was throwing up his toenails," Wayne recounted. "He couldn't hardly breathe. When we got near Jefferson, I thought we should stop at the emergency room, and he didn't even argue. That's when I knew he was in bad shape."

After he dropped Herb off, Wayne was charged with the practical issue of driving Herb's car back home, picking up his wife, Mary, and dropping off the instruments.

"There were all those nice old guitars in that beat-up old car," he said. "I didn't think it was going to make it."

By the time they got back to the hospital the doctors were

wondering the same about Herb. "He's in serious condition," the doctors warned. They had already transferred him to a bigger hospital in Winston-Salem. And that's the last that Wayne heard of it for two days. "I called the hospital and they wouldn't tell me nothing. I said, 'I've known him for thirty years, and he's like a brother to me.'"

But the switchboard operator wouldn't budge, and Herb didn't have a phone in his room. "Herb's just about my oldest and dearest friend," Wayne added, with a concern I'd rarely heard in his voice. He headed back to the garage and took the first bird, slightly overdone, to the kitchen table.

"Wayne Henderson. Master guitar builder and turkey fryer," I announced. "Not necessarily in that order."

Maybe it's memories of his dear departed pet Smedley, but I finally found something that Wayne isn't much good at: turkey carving. First he struggled with assembling the electric knife, unable to get the blades to lock in correctly. I pondered the irony of someone dancing around a table saw for years, then losing a finger cutting up a hunk of poultry. And Wayne's actual carving technique left plenty to be desired. The uneven slabs of breast meat looked like the work of a hyena in a hurry. And when it came time to work on the drumsticks, Wayne was equally clueless, trying to force the knife through the thickest, gnarliest section of the joint.

"I think that's cartilage," said Wayne's daughter, Elizabeth, as she spat out a piece of inedible tissue, while the rest of us picked at the crisp skin on the charred carcass. Wearing a yellow North Face shell over a pink T-shirt she had silkscreened herself, Elizabeth had arrived just in time to decorate the still barren Christmas tree. She had brought Piper, her mother's tiny black terrier, who had been to the groomer this morning. His misshapen doggie-do was downright comical; if this kind of work had been done by a doctor it would have been grounds for a malpractice suit.

"My mom said to make sure we don't make fun of his beard," Elizabeth explained dutifully. "He doesn't know how he looks."

"You want to see those guitars?" Wayne asked casually as he went out to check on the second turkey.

I thought he'd never ask. I walked out the back door and headed over to the shop with a mixture of anxiety and anticipation, while Wayne stayed behind, ostensibly to monitor the poultry frying. I found the first of the two guitars—number 327—across from the pop machine, sitting in a cheap chipboard case that most players wouldn't use to protect a $100 Yamaha. Its twin sister rattled around in an oversized case meant for a much larger dreadnought.

I laid 327's case on the broom-clean concrete floor and cracked it open. (Wayne's elves had come and done some measure of pre-party cleaning.) Seven coats of lacquer had turned the paper-white Appalachian spruce tops the soft warm color of sweet butter. The iridescent abalone trim glistened in the late afternoon sun, as did the flamey headstock overlay juxtaposed against the cool glow of the nickel-plated tuner buttons. This guitar was stunning, and, as Yogi Berra might have said, the more you looked the more you saw. The miter joints around the fretboard were Shaker-perfect, and even the ivory-colored bridge pins kept the theme, each adorned with a tiny, perfectly round dot of abalone. I just let the guitar lie in the case for a long minute, soaking up its understated beauty. Before I even dared to pick it up, I laid my index finger on the top. The finish was smooth and cool, but also properly paper-thin so that you could almost feel the grain of the spruce through the lacquer. I turned it over gingerly. The Brazilian rosewood backs offered similar subtle pleasures, espresso turned dark in the center, mellowing to a cappucino tan near the edges.

Now for the moment of truth. I picked up the guitar. And as Wayne always did, I fretted a big old E chord, every guitar's supposed favorite. I stroked the guitar with a deep, slow strum. I stopped for a second and let the guitar vibrate in my lap and the sound wash around me, taken aback by the sheer richness of its voice, the way the chord swelled in a rush and took its own sweet time fading to silence. For a moment, words failed me.

"Writing about music is like dancing about architecture," wrote eighteenth-century pianist and composer Clara Schumann, although the quote has been since misattributed to Elvis Costello, Frank Zappa, and Laurie Anderson, among others. That, of course, has never stopped anyone from doing so. And if writing about music is difficult, applying the right words to an instrument that is merely one part of the musical equation is doubly so. An Internet acquaintance of mine, Todd Stuart Phillips, has earned a small reputation writing guitar porn. Not literally, of course. But on the Unofficial Martin Guitar Forum, and a few other Web sites, he described guitars and their tone in lengthy, languid, almost lurid detail, fashioning metaphor-laden meditations hundreds, sometime thousands of words long. His essays often exceed the bandwidth limit of the sites.

"Toasted wheat underpinnings." That was the quality that TSP attributed to a certain special D-18. Indeed, Todd's cult of personality was such that when he fell in love with a very expensive new Brazilian rosewood Martin that he couldn't afford, the other members of the group offered to take up a collection to buy the guitar for him. (He declined the donations, but ultimately bought the guitar anyway.)

I thought about toasted wheat underpinnings. Then I thought the better of it. But as my thoughts about this guitar began to crystallize, I ran smack into a paradox. Was this guitar a reflection of the personality of its builder? Yes. Oh, yes. But wasn't every Henderson guitar? Aye, there's the rub. If each Henderson instrument is a little slice of its maker, each is also a different slice. Some guitars, like that cherry dreadnought, are bubbly and cheerful, quick with a joke, like Wayne up onstage. Some guitars, like old 52, are as warm and welcoming as a pot of homemade soup. Some guitars like Fore's contest guitar, have the gravitas of a judge's gavel.

So I'll forge ahead and describe 327, which is one of those guitars that draws a fuller portrait of its maker, in all his seeming

contradictions. This guitar is loud and responsive, purring at just
the slightest touch. But there's more. The most dominant tonal
color is that rich ringing quality of the Brazilian rosewood, giving
the guitar a voice that can be as resonant as the choir at midnight
mass. But push it just a bit harder and there's just a hint of a
growl that can be as spanky and bawdy as a roadhouse on Saturday night. Three twenty-seven is like Grace Kelly in *Rear Window*. When she comes to visit the invalid Jimmy Stewart in his
apartment she's the picture of elegance in a floor-length couture
gown. But when she brushes her cheek suggestively against his,
it's a hint that she's wearing something from Frederick's of Hol-
lywood underneath.

And it was perfectly appropriate, this delightfully bawdy elegance. That's the essence of Wayne Henderson, maker of heirloom instruments and operator of a remote-controlled fart
machine. And for that matter, it also captures the spirit of Eric
Clapton, the man who sings the blues wearing an Armani suit.
Wayne had nailed it.

And as great as this three-day-old guitar was, it offered a mere
hint of what it was likely to become, a great Burgundy straight
from the vineyard. I was reminded of the time I saw LeBron
James in a high school game. Part of the excitement was the air-
borne tomahawks he laid on a bunch of future poli-sci majors.
And part of it was the drool-on-your-Nikes anticipation of what
the future held. This guitar too was potential incarnate.

"Aw heck," I said out loud, shaking my head and grinning at
the same time.

And perhaps that's what holds Wayne Henderson's attention
after forty years of building guitars, the enchanting mystery of
not knowing exactly how each one's going to turn out. Each guitar will possess a little bit of him, but which qualities and in
what proportions? Wayne Henderson is the Gepetto of the guitar
shop, but while the things that he creates are indisputably alive,
they've also got a life of their own.

And remarkably, when I picked up 326, it sounded, well . . . the same. Whatever minuscule difference existed between them could be chalked up to the fact that, for the moment, 326 wore a set of light-gauge strings, while the 327 had the slightly thicker mediums. Don't believe in cloning? You've never played 327 and 326 back to back.

It seemed that the cosmos, or at least the package delivery authorities, were on the side of these guitars. While I was playing the 327, the UPS man arrived with a giant box full of guitar cases—one for each of the Clapton guitars, and one for my not-yet-started instrument—along with a box of smoked turkey, a Christmas present from a grateful guitar owner. In the mailbox was a batch of custom-made pickguards—which came from Wayne's old friend and co-worker John Greven, who had gotten sick of the cheesy silk-screened pickguards on modern Martins, and decided to make his own old-school repros. Greven's little package had arrived with the mail only a few minutes before I did, and a good thing too. With the Christmas party just minutes away, it wouldn't be safe to hand these guitars to a bunch of flatpickers with their tops unprotected. "Good thing they got here," said Wayne, who'd fried the last of the turkeys.

Wayne turned his attention to the pickguards. We sorted through the selection that Greven had sent and settled on a golden brown one that mimicked the lovely marbled guards on lots 19 and 21. By the time Wayne found a precut pickguard to use as a template, a crowd of early arriving partygoers had gathered. They stood quietly spread out in a semicircle on the far side of the bench, physicians in an operating theater trying not to disturb the master at work. Wayne, who's used to working with yapping dogs, blaring banjos, and bawdy jokes in the background, was visibly disconcerted.

"This is a tough-ass little job," he muttered under his breath.

As the party proper began and people dropped their potluck dishes and opened up their instrument cases and began to jam, I took on a new role: the curator of the Clapton guitars. When any-one asked—and there was a lot of asking—they would get referred to me. I'd open the cases, hand the guitar over carefully, answer questions, maybe snap a picture.

"Are the Clapton guitars here?" wondered Bunny Dannelly, one of the festival's tireless volunteers.

I opened the new case and handed her 326. Not much of a guitar player, she held the instrument tentatively, but she smiled broadly while I snapped her picture.

Holding Eric Clapton's guitar. Priceless.

"It's kind of sad, though," she said as she handed the guitar back to me. "It's been so much of a story around here, building these guitars for Eric Clapton. We're going to have to get another one."

And as Bunny said that, I realized that the ball was now squarely in my court. Wayne had held up his end of the bargain by building the guitars, and now it would become my job to deliver them. I mulled that prospect for a moment, until it was time for the next showing.

Don Wilson, inventor of the Squeezer came over to inspect the guitars. For him, it was all about the details.

"Look at that miter joint," he said. "That's perfect. Wayne's craftsmanship is always high-level. But this goes above and beyond." He attributed this even better than usual result not to the famous recipient, but to the steady work schedule. "He didn't pick it up and put it down for a month. He worked on them steadily day after day and it shows."

Don marveled at the family resemblance between the guitars, because he owns the only other matched pairs of Henderson gui-tars—two simple mahogany dreadnoughts.

"Forget about building me that one fancy guitar," he announced to Wayne one day. "Build me a matched pair of D-18s for me and my son."

And over the course of six months that's what Wayne did, crafting two guitars from the same materials. Did these two identical guitars sound the same? Hardly. "If I handed you the first guitar, you'd say 'That's a really nice instrument.' But when I handed you the second one, you'd go 'Wow.'

"Why is one guitar 20 percent louder and stronger?" he asked rhetorically. "It's the voodoo of how pieces of wood go together." He looked admiringly at 327. "And more voodoo happens here than anywhere else."

WHEN? WHERE? AND HOW? After an evening spent answering questions about the Clapton guitars, including doing an interview with a reporter from the *Galax Gazette*, I spotted a man who could answer some of my questions. It was John Arnold, the man who had cut the fine Appalachian red spruce top for 326. John not only built fine guitars, he also knew as much about tonewood as anyone alive.

"In '95, Hurricane Opal came through, or the remnants of Hurricane Opal," Arnold explained. "It dropped these four-hundred-year-old trees in the Smokies. Now normally everything dead is protected in a National Forest but they came down right on Highway 441, and they had to hire an outside contractor to clear up the mess. And once the trees crossed the boundary of the National Forest, the trees no longer belonged to the government, they belonged to the contractor."

How big were they?

"The biggest red spruce I ever cut. The biggest was thirty-five and a half inches in diameter. Over a hundred feet tall. Over four hundred years old.

"I saw it in the newspaper," Arnold recalled. "There was a picture in the paper of them clearing the road. And even in a low-quality newspaper photo I could tell that those were red spruce. I first contacted the Park Service and they said, 'Talk to the contractor.' They were going to cut it into two-by-fours and build a house with it.

"I said, 'I think it's worth more to me than it is to you,'" he recalled. "Between me and my partner Ted Davis we cut over a thousand tops out of those trees. Probably never happen again," he said with the look of a man who sometimes finds himself wishing for hurricanes.

The top of 327 doesn't have quite the same intrigue, but Arnold could tell its story too.

"I know this tree," he said. "It came from West Virginia. I know the guy who cut it. We cut two trees in this area."

What else can you tell?

"This business here"—he pointed to a couple of tiny pin knots in the center of the top that Wayne had considered slicing off—"is only found on the old-growth trees. It's damage to the outer bark of the tree from ozone. It's only happened in the last thirty or forty years." It turns out that the oldest trees are especially susceptible to pollution. Arnold suggested that it wasn't easy being a big spruce in an increasingly harsh world. He noted that many old red spruces—including the one sitting in Wayne's garage—were being attacked by the southern pine beetle. This insect normally doesn't attack red spruce, but it's not above picking on the weakest examples of this species.

Arnold pointed at a different kind of irregularity in the top, well inboard of those first marks. At first glance, it looked like just a particularly wide gap between grain lines, which is pretty typical of red spruce. Upon closer inspection, it turned out to be seven or eight almost infinitesimally tight rings masquerading as one.

"That's from a spruce bud worm that attacked in that area in the 1880s and again in the 1930s," Arnold explained. "It eats the bark off the twigs and the needles fall off. It doesn't necessarily kill the tree." It does however slow its growth to a virtual standstill, hence the super-tight rings.

What about the marks on either side of the fretboard?

"The old-timers call that red horse. That's where a limb has died, and those are mineral deposits that collect on the bottom side," he explained. But unlike the bud worm, which affects the whole tree, these mineral streaks are birthmarks of a particular piece of wood, prominent in one slice, and virtually gone in the next.

As Arnold continued with the life story of a couple of trees that were planted while the United States was just a set of British colonies, I thought about something Wayne had once inscribed on the peghead of a guitar. It was, he thinks, the English translation of the Latin words carved in the top of Vassar Clements's fiddle: "In life I am silent. In death now I sing."

AFTER A DOZEN OR SO showings of the Clapton guitars, the party had evolved into an after-party. Steve Kilby sat at one end of the shop, his large frame cramped a little by the jointer. Kilby had 327, Wayne grabbed 326. They started to pick, with the familiar ease of a couple of major league outfielders tossing the ball around on the green grass on an August afternoon. "Leather Britches" ran into "Down Yonder" ran into "Billy in the Lowground " ran into "Steel Guitar Rag."

What did Wayne think of the guitars now that he'd had a chance to test-drive them? Which one was better? "The one I played last," he replied. He was speaking like a proud papa asked to choose between his children, but at the same time he was also speaking the God's honest truth. I picked the guitars up, to put them back in their cases, and I stole a few licks myself, and the difference was striking. Not the difference between them. The difference from three hours ago. Like a thoroughbred after a morning trot, these guitars responded to the exercise, the tone a little sweeter, a little crisper, a little fuller, a little more responsive. There was a little more *there* there. But between the two of them, it was a dead heat.

Steve Lewis and Brandon Davis walked into the shop. Both are former champions of the festival's guitar contest. Lewis is a tobacco-chewing construction worker with a ZZ Top beard, a hyperaggressive picking style, and a gift for on-the-fly improvisation. But before you jump to conclusions, his guitar is the one that bears that translated Vassar Clements quote.

Davis, on the other hand, is a fresh-faced computer programmer, almost thirty, and but for his trim little mustache, he looks like he could be going on fifteen. When he was eleven, his dad issued a dare—learn to play "Blackberry Blossom" and I'll buy you a guitar. Brandon did and, boy, did Dad make good: under the Christmas tree was a brand-spanking-new Henderson guitar. It didn't look brand-new by the time Brandon used it to win the festival's guitar contest, and his second Henderson guitar.

Davis, who had clearly watched a few hours of MTV in his day, picked up 327 and riffed the first few bars of "Tears in Heaven." There was no spark of recognition in anyone besides me as he segued into the acoustic version of "Layla."

"Do you think Clapton can play 'Blackberry Blossom'?" Davis wondered.

"He could do 'Whiskey Before Breakfast,' but then he'd have to check back into rehab," Lewis joked. And with that, Lewis picked up 326 and they launched into a rollicking version of that perfectly quirky fiddle tune, rattling the strings, vibrating the top, and helping Eric Clapton break in his new guitar.

CHAPTER TWENTY-SEVEN

Good Enough for Who It's For

WITH THE CLAPTON GUITARS completed and the Christmas party over, Wayne had earned some time off. He didn't take it, at least if you discount watching the tail end of a documentary about Hawaii on the Travel Channel—"Aw, heck," he said as the molten lava flowed into the sea—and one quarter of a frigid cold football game from the frozen tundra of Green Bay. "I have a friend in Green Bay and he has season tickets," he said. "And he said he'd take me to a game. But I don't want to go when it's that cold."

He headed back out to the shop. The reality is that Wayne is never at a loss for something to do. The List is his motivation to get out of bed in the morning—but it's also his foreman, the reason he's sanding backs or bending sides at an hour when most people are long asleep. And this particular afternoon, his conscience was bothering him. A guy named Jerry Smith, the father of one of his good friends, fell off a building about a year ago, and the doctors told his family it was touch-and-go. Wayne went to visit him in the hospital. "He looked as dead as anybody could be and still be alive," Wayne recalled. "And I said to him, 'If you come out of this mess I'll work on your guitar.'"

Whether it was an acute case of guitar lust, or just an ordinary will to live, Jerry pulled through, not that much the worse for wear. And as soon as he came out of his coma, his family told him about Wayne's promise.

"I don't know if I can do it, but I'd like to get his guitar built before Christmas," he said, as he looked for the pieces of Jerry's guitar. "They'll do anything to get a guitar," he added with a wink.

That jibe notwithstanding, Wayne was subdued. The weather was nasty cold—below zero temperatures and blowing snow made Rugby seem like Green Bay—and Elizabeth was going back to her mom's house near Roanoke to celebrate her twentieth birthday. Wayne and I had planned on going to Gerald Little's house, bringing the Clapton guitars to a jam session with Doc Watson. But the weather was too nasty even for a veteran mailman with a four-wheel-drive pickup. The only good news of the day came from Herb, who was still in the hospital but on the mend.

Wayne turned his attention to the Clapton guitars for the last time. He played 326. Then 327. Then the 326 again. He was dialing in the final setup. I had brought along some bluegrass gauge strings—medium on the low strings and light on the high strings—which would give Clapton thumpy bass and silky bendable trebles and Wayne installed them. And even in something as simple as that, something every guitarist does week in and week out, Wayne's got a trick. "You got to tug at them, push them down, press 'em over here, press 'em over there," he explained, as he forced the strings down on either side of the nut and saddle. The string tension would eventually do the same naturally, but it would take days and maybe even weeks until the strings stayed in tune the way you'd like them to.

As Wayne played 326, I held the 327. As soon as he hit that first note, the other guitar came alive, vibrating in harmony, virtually humming in my lap, without me so much as touching the strings. I could swear that these two guitars were trying to communicate telepathically, the way that twins do.

Wayne wasn't pleased with the saddle on 327. The action was just a tiny bit too low and it buzzed a little when he played it hard. "I think I took a hair too much off of that one," he admitted. I had spent so much time in the shop that he had anticipated my question and attempted to quantify the problem. "A thirty-second of an inch." While most luthiers would put a tiny shim under the saddle and declare themselves done, that's not Wayne Henderson's way. He grabbed another piece of ivory salvaged from a piece of antique jewelry—kept well out of Oreo's reach—and headed to the band saw and the belt sander to begin shaping a new saddle.

But the truth was that he was futzing, tweaking, stalling, like a mother finding one more thing to stuff into the luggage of a college-bound child. Wayne has no trouble starting guitars, but it's well-documented that he has trouble finishing them. The world was different eight years ago when he started these guitars—the World Trade Center was still standing, and Elizabeth, who was today celebrating her last day as a teenager, was still playing with Barbies—and now they were soon going out the door. If it was a reason to be happy, it was perhaps more of a reason to be sad.

When he was done with the guitars, he sat down and played them in turn for a good long time.

"Good enough for who it's for," he said with a laugh.

I picked up 326 and said, "How 'bout a quick turnaround on 'Buckdancer's Choice'?"

Wayne led off, not too fast for once, and I played some tentative rhythm until it came time for me to pick the lead.

"How about this one?" he said, and he played a bit of "Done Gone," a tune that he had taught me beneath the towering pines at Puget Sound that summer.

"Why not?" I replied. He started playing the rhythm, and I picked the lead until I got to a series of sliding double-stops, where the combination of my sweaty hands and the freshly lacquered neck ground the tune to a halt.

"That was pretty good," Wayne lied.

As I returned the guitars to their cases, he gazed at a couple of nice pieces of red spruce that he had bought from John Arnold at the Christmas party.

"Maybe I'll save one of those pieces of wood for my own guitar."

"Your own guitar?"

"After playing these two, I want to build myself an OM-45," he replied.

"Really?"

"Yeah," Wayne admitted. "But maybe it'll pass."

FOR WAYNE, AT LEAST, this frigid Sunday was all about endings. While Wayne Henderson loves building guitars, sometimes it seems that he hates having built them, or at least sending them out the door. So on this cold, quiet Sunday he did what he knows best: he went back to work.

I once asked Wayne how he decided what he's going to work on at any given moment of any given day? "Well, I think about what's going to get rid of my biggest headache."

And for the moment, that headache was Gabby, who would be coming tomorrow, expecting that his guitar would be done and complaining if it wasn't. The serious luthier tasks were dispatched quickly. Gluing the bridge onto the bare spot on the freshly lacquered top took Wayne only a couple of minutes—it took him longer to find the clamps than to actually fit the bridge. Drilling out the string holes took only a couple of moments more, although the sight of a giant corded drill in close proximity to a delicate finished guitar body is not for the faint of heart.

What takes time is the finish work, the tiny aesthetic details that separate a Henderson guitar from a factory built instrument. Take the bridge pins. Wayne went to the drill press and cut out a period-size circle of abalone. He picked up one bridge pin from a little plastic bin on the bench and walked it over to the lathe on the Shopsmith.

He bored a tiny hole in the face. He walked counterclockwise to the bench where the bottle of Super Glue sits. He applied a dab, and continued to the area in front of the guitar, where he picked up an abalone dot, set it in the hole, and pressed it down hard. He put the now-completed pin down on the bench, picked up another pin and headed over to the Shopsmith for another lap.

You don't need to be an efficiency expert to realize that there's a quicker way to do this. Indeed, even world-class luthiers who work alone, at least the most productive ones like John Greven and Steven Gilcrest, have adopted a one-man production line mentality, building instruments in batches, gluing up backs one day, bending sides the next, gathering up the economies of scale that accrue with not having to set up the work area again and again. Gilcrest, the Australian master mandolin builder who visited the shop once, told Wayne that he finishes a whole batch of instruments at once, cranking the heat and stripping down buck naked to apply the temperamental varnish.

But Wayne Henderson has always eschewed even a hint of the production line. This was really a perpetual motion machine. That tiny jolt of instant gratification that comes from completing one inlaid bridge pin seems to provide just enough momentum to send him along to the next step.

Wayne works in this almost comically inefficient way because he wants to, and it doesn't affect his efforts to keep costs down. "I charge my friends wholesale," he said. "I don't want to charge them two, three thousand dollars. I wonder if Steven Gilcrest even knows the people he's building instruments for?" Wayne wondered, more curious than judgmental.

"Good enough for who it's for," he pronounced again, as he finished the last little lick of work on Gabby's guitar.

Of course, it was a joke. He paid no less attention to Gabby's guitar than he did to Clapton's. If anything, he may have paid more, realizing that he's far more likely to see Gabby's instrument somewhere down the road than Eric's.

Monday morning dawned frigid and nasty—"colder than wiz" in Waynespeak. Overnight, it had hit nine below on the outside thermometer, and Wayne hustled out to Sandy's doghouse expecting the worst. "I hope she's not froze to death," he fretted. The old dog was made of hardy stock, hardly even shivering, but a guilt-ridden Wayne let her into the shop to warm up. Once inside, Sandy seemed more disturbed by the unfamiliar noises of the machinery than she was bothered by the subzero cold outside.

"Hey," said Gabby, "if I've got to see a Yankee today, I'm glad it's you." We shook hands as he took his seat. I tried to pet Oreo as she buzzed around the shop, adding to poor old Sandy's confusion.

I asked Gabby if he had any words of wisdom for the recipient of the week's other newly completed Henderson guitar, and for once the Dumpster Diver was at a loss for words.

Wayne came to his rescue. "Gabby's just about the *crudest* person and Eric Clapton don't even want to know what Gabby has to say."

This guitar of Gabby's is lovely, a twelve-fret double-ought, the same size as Ella. The back is made of pieces of what would have been scrap Brazilian once upon a time, which Wayne had glued together in an attractive multipiece slab. Wayne sat down with the guitar for a long while, on the opposite end of the shop near the heavy machinery. Ostensibly, he was giving the guitar a once-over, but the quality control was taking longer than it needed to. The big bench almost obscured the guitar—and the guitar player—from Gabby's view. He played one song and then another, picking and picking and picking and picking, playing for as long as I've seen him at one time outside of a jam session or a concert. Dangling the guitar just out of reach, he was teasing Gabby a bit, but the General Loafer didn't mind, or even notice. Wayne seemed reluctant to give the guitar up.

When Wayne did finally hand it over, he did so without much fanfare. Gabby strummed a loud G chord, then picked a bass run so aggressively I half-expected the bridge to pop off and come flying across the room.

"That's a beauty," Gabby pronounced, as he started flipping the small guitar around, giving it the once-over the way you might inspect a used car.

Wayne had nailed Gabby's reaction to a T. He loved the guitar, and his effusive praise was a given. But, as Wayne predicted, he had zeroed in on the two tiny corners that Wayne had cut: the plastic strap button and the end pin. They're commercially made products—he's got a small bin of them. They were pretty ugly—oversized and molded out of a stark white plastic that's out of character with the warm tones of the rest of the guitar. Indeed, Wayne declined to install one on the Clapton guitars, speculating that Clapton would probably install a pickup anyway, which requires a larger-diameter end pin. The truth of the matter was that he didn't want to mar a near-perfect guitar with a clunky strap button. But Gabby would insist, so Wayne had tried to dress these cheap ones up. He had turned the plastic strap button on the lathe, until it took on a more delicate shape. He'd spent even more time on the end pin, inlaying a dot of abalone in the end, and using first some shellac and then some wood stain in an unsuccessful attempt at mellowing the color of the largely impervious plastic. Gabby got some additional negotiating leverage when he noticed that Wayne had cracked the plastic strap button just a bit as he installed it.

"That's the only thing I don't like about it," he declared. "The other ones have bone or ivory," said Gabby, citing precedent. Wayne was noncommittal, pretending not to hear Gabby's mild protestations, but both he and Gabby knew that, eventually and more likely sooner than later, he'd make another set of buttons from scratch for the tiny guitar.

But it wasn't merely Gabby's complaining that put Wayne off this morning. He'd been a little distant since he got up, quieter than usual, not quite making contact with those baby blue eyes of his. For the guy who's getting it, a freshly built guitar is like a baby that's still pink and wet and full of wonder, a perfect little bundle of potential. But imperfect though the analogy may be, Wayne is more like the obstetrician than the father. He doesn't get to watch his babies grow up.

"I think I want an ought next," said Gabby, referring to the single-o-size parlor guitars that were popular at the turn of the last century, played in the drawing rooms by ladies of leisure.

"I don't have a mold for a single-ought," replied Wayne, truthfully, and without hesitation.

I was leaving this morning too. And when I started making noises about hitting the road, Wayne conjured up an errand—a trip to the post office—that just couldn't wait another hour. It's a McGuffin, a reason not to be around when I put the guitars in the back of the Acura and pointed it north. The truth of the matter is he didn't want to be here when the guitars left. I was ready to assume my role as foster parent, with temporary custody until the day one of these instruments finds a permanent home with Eric Clapton, and the other with some guitar lover yet to be determined. But Wayne Henderson's job was now done.

So he picked up some CDs and strings that had been sitting on the bench for as long as I could remember, addressed a box, and decided at that moment that the recipient absolutely, positively needed them before Christmas. I walked him to the car.

"You be careful driving," he said. "And you call me when you get home so I know you got there okay."

"Yes, Dad," I said under my breath.

"Thanks," I said out loud as he hurried to the car. "For everything."

And with that, Wayne Henderson slipped out the door, the world's greatest guitar builder finding a way to avoid saying goodbye to the most notable, and perhaps even the best, instruments he's ever made.

When Wayne was fully out of earshot, Gabby changed his tune a bit. "Maybe I'll have him build me a Nick Lucas," he said. "Out of cherry. It shouldn't be hard to find a piece of cherry." Gabby doesn't much need another guitar. What he does need is an excuse to keep coming by the shop twice a week, bringing Oreo, and Hardee's sausage biscuits.

"Tell Eric Clapton if he doesn't like the guitar, not to throw it out," Gabby said with a chuckle, as I picked up the case containing 326 and walked it toward the door. "If he don't like it, *I'll* come up there," he added by way of mock threat.

"So, Gabby, what do you have to do to get Wayne Henderson to build you a guitar?" I knew that Gabby's angle is a collection of vintage L.C. Smith shotguns that Wayne prizes as much as Martin guitars, but I just wanted to hear what he has to say.

"It's those pictures of Wayne and the sheep," he announced proudly. I picked up the next guitar case, careful not to trip on Oreo or let Sandy out.

"You know what hip boots are for?" Gabby asked no one in particular. "You put the sheep's back legs down in there," he exclaimed with a belly laugh.

"Gabby, I think you've spent a little too much time thinking about this," said Gerald, forcing a smile. I headed out to the car with 327 and my computer bag.

I shook Gerald's hand. "See you later, buddy," he said. "Safe trip."

I bid farewell to Gabby. "If Eric Clapton wants another guitar, tell him I'll send him a sheep," he bellowed. "Wayne's favorite." That was my cue to hit the road.

With the guitars nestled safely in the back seat, I had 600 miles to watch the odometer roll over and to reflect on these amazing instruments and the man who built them.

Over the past month, I had been afforded one of life's singular pleasures: the opportunity to observe a master at work, a man who does something as well as it can be done.

Watching Wayne Henderson work was a joy, but it was also a tease. To the untrained eye, it may have seemed that these guitars were built fast and easy, almost as an aside to the banter and the joke telling. But don't be fooled. They were also built right, balanced defiantly on the razor's edge between being as responsive as bamboo-fly-rod and ready to implode like an old Las Vegas hotel. Breezy talk and radical work. I'm sure that's what it was like in a little violin shop in Cremona in the seventeenth century.

And as for these borrowed guitars, they, too, tantalized in a different way. I made my overnight stop at a Marriott Inn outside of Hershey, Pennsylvania. With both guitars sprawled out on the king-size bed, and the muted television tuned to some reality show, I played 326 and 327 in turn, amazed by their power.

These were time machines. Their story, which began with a chance meeting, a pile of good wood and a sharp whittling knife, would stretch into the future a century or more. If one of man's central yearnings is to be remembered, there are few better ways to achieve it than by crafting an heirloom instrument. These twin guitars will be part of a world that's very different from the one Wayne Henderson knows. War and peace, obstacles and inventions, songs old and new, what would 326 and 327 encounter that their maker would not? But as long as these guitars and their less celebrated brethren survive, one thing is certain: Wayne Henderson, a skilled and principled craftsman who works in a messy shop in a tiny town with a baseball cap on his head and genius on his shoulders, will be a part of that world. Eric Clapton may be first to own one of these guitars, but he won't be the last.

And as promised, I called Wayne as soon as I got home, before I even unloaded the guitars..

"How was the drive?" he asked. "Any slick spots?"

"The drive was good. The roads were fine."

"I feel bad that I didn't get you anything for Christmas," said Wayne Henderson. I started to tell him about all he had already given me, but he cut me off.

Then Wayne said the words that were music to my ears, and just maybe to his too. "I started your guitar today."

Epilogue

FOR SIX MONTHS, four feet to the right of the old desk my
wife's grandfather built, sat two guitar cases. Inside them
were two magnificent instruments, guitars that spoke to me
even when I wasn't playing them. But they weren't mine.

I was merely the courier of Wayne Henderson numbers 326
and 327. I had promised Wayne that if he built the guitars, I
would figure out a way to get one of them to Eric Clapton. He
held up his end of the bargain. Now I had to hold up mine. Of
course, approaching Clapton is easier said than done.

Soon after my return to Montclair from Rugby, I tracked
down Lee Dickson, Clapton's long-time guitar tech. We traded e-
mails, and when I got him on the phone in late January at a
recording studio in London, we had a conversation that could
have been an out-take from a Woody Allen movie. He told me at
great length how he didn't have the time to talk to me. Clapton
was in the middle of recording an album, and Dickson had a
thousand things to do.

"It's easier when we're on the road," Dickson explained in
his Scottish accent. "There, we've got a tour manager, and I just
have to take care of the guitars." In the studio, when Clapton's
kids visit and they need lunch, or when the dry cleaning needs to
be picked up, those jobs often fall to Dickson, who has been

Clapton's aide de camp for almost thirty years. After a ten-year wait, even a Wayne Henderson guitar wasn't a top priority at a time this hectic. We agreed to talk later.

A recording session would soon be interrupted by Clapton's wife, Melia McEnery, giving birth to the couple's third child. This happy event was then followed by more recording sessions; a Tsunami-victims benefit concert; more recording sessions; the annual Rock and Roll Hall of Fame bash in which Clapton inducted blues guitarist Buddy Guy; more recording sessions; and rehearsals for a reunion concert of Cream, his band from the 1960s. Even with more than forty albums under his belt, Clapton hardly had a moment to himself.

A month passed. Then another. More e-mails bounced back and forth across the Atlantic. I tried to strike a balance between being persistent and becoming a pest. In May, Wayne had a quick tour of France planned, set up by one of his European fans. I sent an e-mail to Lee wondering if Wayne might make a side trip to England to drop the guitar off on his way home. The day Wayne was scheduled to leave Paris for Rugby, I got a sorry-I-missed him reply from Lee, with an address of where to ship the guitar.

I considered sending the guitar by overnight courier, but then I thought about the possibility of this decade-long odyssey ending with a crushed shipping box or a lost-in-transit claim form. No, I would hand-deliver the guitar myself. After more intercontinental telephone tag, I got Lee's cell phone number and a commitment that he would be in London on a Tuesday in mid-June.

Before I left, I took both guitars with me and went to see Kerry Keane at Christie's auction house in New York. The plan for the second guitar was simple. Auction it off in the service of raising money for Junior Appalachian Musicians and other worthy grassroots music charities. When I had spoken to Keane almost a year earlier, he spoke wistfully about Lot 19 and Lot 20, the *Unplugged* guitar and its doppelganger, guitars that clearly captured his imagination.

"They were both phenomenal. But both very different in how they responded and how they played," he recalled. "One very dark. One very bright.

Which is the mystery of musical instruments," he continued. "How does that happen with trees from the same forest, made months apart from each other by the same craftsman, and yet they are so different? Is it the craftsmanship? Is it the materials? Or is it the life it's lived?" He paused. "It would have helped solve that question to have been there in 1939 when those two guitars were finished."

This would be the next best thing: the chance to play the twin Hendersons, identical instruments both built in the spirit of those sixty-year-old guitars, but still only months old. Looking retro-cool in a seersucker suit, Keane examined the guitars, spying the subtle details that only a maker would catch. "Look at the edge of that bridge," he said, pointing to the delicate taper of the ebony toward the spruce.

Since Keane had only a few precious days in the office before a two-week road trip, I expected a fifteen-minute meeting with him. We talked for more than two hours. As he played each guitar in turn, Keane enjoyed three perspectives. The first was as the appraiser—Keane appears frequently on *The Antiques Roadshow*—assessing the value of a precious object. The second was as a classically trained luthier admiring the work of a master. The third was as a guitar junkie yearning for one just like it. He played the instruments slowly, savoring their quality.

"Really lovely," he said after he played John Fahey's arrangement of "In Christ There is No East or West," the old Methodist hymn. "Just gorgeous. It's not what they do in Nazareth today," he said, referring to the modern Martin guitar factory in Pennsylvania.

After a few more tunes, Keane shifted to the long view, divining not only what these guitars were, but what they would become.

"They both have this amazing..." Keane said, searching for

just the right words. *"Openness in tone.* You can feel the wood resonating. They've got great response."

He paused again. "There's all this quality in there just waiting to get out. Just by playing them." And with that, he strummed another rich major chord.

I asked him which one he thought Clapton would like better. He swapped back and forth several more times. A close call.

"This one," he said finally, with 326 in his lap. I concurred.

With that, it was off to London. I smiled sweetly at the gate attendants, and managed to stuff the decidedly oversize case in to the overhead bin of a 747-400. When I arrived in London I called Lee Dickson from my room at the Chesterfield Mayfair Hotel.

"I've caught this bug, man. I'm really sick," he said, coughing. "Maybe Tuesday or Wednesday. Call me Tuesday morning."

And just before he hung up, he remembered his manners. "Welcome to London."

When Tuesday morning came and went with nothing but Lee Dickson's voice mail, I felt the stirrings of panic. Would I have to camp out in London until this guitar was delivered, squatting in Hyde Park busking for beer money after my sold-out hotel evicted me? Finally, in the early afternoon, I got Lee on the phone and the meeting was set. My hotel. Eightish.

With a well-groomed beard, slightly graying hair, and a wiry build, Dickson could have been a retired race-car driver. He was wearing a butter-soft black leather jacket with the Fender guitar company logo on it. He opened the case.

He gave the 326 a quick once over. "Very nice," he said with British understatement as he strummed a couple of quick chords.

I picked up my camera. "I'd really rather that you didn't," he said. I put down the Nikon.

"This is Eric's guitar," Dickson explained. "It's Eric's girlfriend. I wouldn't stand next to his girlfriend and pose for a picture."

"I understand," I said.

"I'm a little funny about that," he said apologetically, as he returned the guitar to its case. "Maybe that's why I've had this job for so long." It was a point of pride for Dickson that he didn't play Eric's guitars, except in the line of duty.

We left the hotel and walked through the narrow streets of Mayfair toward his car. We talked about guitars and English beer and toy shopping, and a gig that Eric had played not long ago at a tiny pub in this fashionable neighborhood. I laid the guitar down carefully in the back of the silver Mercedes-Benz station wagon. Lee thanked me, and I him, and he handed me a guitar pick. It was a Fender medium with E.C. WAS HERE printed in gold letters.

I stuffed the pick in my wallet as I watched Lee drive away into the waning daylight. I breathed a sigh of relief and allowed myself a broad smile at the irony of my errand. Never had anyone been quite this happy to let go of a Wayne Henderson guitar.

GLOSSARY OF TERMS USED IN THIS BOOK

oo See *double-ought.*

ooo See *triple-ought.*

18 style In Martin guitar company nomenclature, a mahogany guitar with relatively simple appointments, including tortoise-grained binding and a simple rosette.

28 style In Martin nomenclature, a rosewood guitar with Ivoroid bindings and sometimes herringbone purfling around the edges. This style is further distinguished by the lack of abalone trim.

42 style A rosewood Martin guitar with abalone trim around the top edge, the rosette, and the fretboard extension.

45 style A rosewood Martin guitar with pearl trim around every edge of the back and sides and the rosette.

abalone a shell used for the decorative inlay on fine guitars.

action The height of the strings above the fretboard. Typically measured as the height of the first and sixth strings at the twelfth fret. A lower action is easier to play but can be prone to buzzing if played aggressively.

Adirondack spruce See *Appalachian spruce.*

Appalachian spruce A now uncommon tonewood that's used for guitar tops. Also called Adirondack spruce and red spruce.

archtop A guitar with an arched top and back, often with violin-style f-holes, usually favored by jazz players.

back stripe The decorative stripe to which the two pieces of a guitar back are attached.

binding The decorative plastic or wooden trim around the edge of the guitar body that serves to protect the instrument.

'bone See *herringbone.*

bout The wider areas of a guitar body. The upper bout is above the guitar's waist, the lower bout is below.

braces The internal struts, usually made of spruce, that reinforce a guitar top or back.

Brazilian rosewood The endangered wood used for the back and sides of pre-1968 Martin guitars, and a select few modern guitars.

bridge A wooden plate, usually ebony or rosewood, glued to the guitar top, to which the guitar strings are anchored.

bridge plate A thin piece of hardwood, usually maple, glued to the inside of the guitar under the bridge to prevent the ball end of the strings from digging into the soft wood.

cannon A slang expression for an especially loud guitar.

classical guitar A nylon string guitar used for playing classical music.

double-ought or oo A Martin guitar that's the next size smaller than a triple-ought or OM model.

dreadnought A large guitar often used by bluegrass players. Also referred to as a D, in Martin guitar nomenclature, as in D-18, D-28, D-45.

fiddleback Wood that's distinguished by the presence of figure running perpendicular to the grain, as often seen on the maple back of a violin.

figure The grain pattern in a piece of wood.

fingerboard See fretboard.

flattop A steel string acoustic guitar with a nonarched top and a hollow body.

fretboard The piece of wood, usually ebony or rosewood, attached to the neck, into which the frets are set.

frets The metal bars on a guitar's neck that raise the pitch of a note when the player presses the string against them.

headstock The top of the guitar neck, to which the tuners are attached.

heel cap The decorative triangular trim piece that covers the back side of the neck heel.

herringbone A pre-1946 Martin Brazilian rosewood guitar, distinguished by its herringbone purfling around the edges of the top. Sometimes shortened to 'bone.

inlay Decorative trim, usually abalone or mother of pearl, that is glued into a slot in a guitar's fretboard or headstock.

Ivoroid Synthetic imitation ivory used for guitar binding and trim.

kerfing The flexible, partially slotted wooden strips, usually made of mahogany or cedar, that attach the top of a guitar to its sides.

koa A highly figured Hawaiian wood that's sometimes used in guitar building.

Loar A now valuable F-5 mandolin built by the Gibson company during the brief tenure of acoustic engineer Lloyd Loar.

luthier An instrument builder who specializes in building or repairing guitars or other stringed instruments.

mahogany A tropical tonewood used for guitar backs and necks.

marquetry Decorative wood trim on a guitar body. See *herringbone, back stripe.*

C.F. Martin & Co. The world's leading builder of quality steel string guitars. The Nazareth, Pennsylvania–based company has been building guitars since 1833.

neck block The piece of wood, usually mahogany, to which the sides are glued at the top of the guitar body and the neck is attached. On Martin and Henderson guitars a serial number is stamped on the neck block.

neck heel The section of the neck where it curves to meet the guitar body.

nut A slotted piece of bone, ivory, or synthetic material located between the headstock and the fretboard, which keeps the strings in alignment.

OM Short for orchestra model. An OM has the same body dimensions as a triple-ought, but it has a longer scale length.

peghead See headstock.

pickguard A thin plate, usually made of tortoise-grained plastic, that's glued to the treble side of a guitar top to protect the wood from abrasion by a flatpick.

pickwear Damage to a guitar's finish caused by rubbing a pick against the top wood while playing.

purfling Decorative trim on a guitar top adjacent to the binding.

red spruce See *Applalachian spruce.*

resonator A guitar with an inert body that holds a mechanical speaker system that amplifies the vibration of the strings.

rim Another word for a guitar side.

rosette The decorative trim that surrounds the soundhole of a guitar.

saddle A piece of bone, ivory, or synthetic material that fits into a slot in the bridge over which the strings pass.

scale length The distance between the nut and the saddle, along the path of the strings. Longer scale length yields tighter strings but can sometimes be harder to play. Martin's OM and dreadnoughts are 25.4 inches, while 000 and smaller guitars have a shorter, 24.9-inch scale.

scalloped bracing A bracing configuration in which some of the braces are thinned in the middle, allowing the top to vibrate more without compromising strength. The Martin company stopped using scalloped bracing in late 1944.

Shopsmith A multiuse floor-standing power tool.

slothead A guitar with tuning pegs that run perpendicular to the face of the peghead, and the strings wrap around posts inserted in two long slots in the peghead, in the style of a classical guitar.

soundhole The large central hole in a guitar top from which the sound escapes.

spoke shave A manual plane for wood shaping that is operated by pulling rather than pushing.

tail block A square piece of wood, usually mahogany, at the bottom of the guitar body to which the sides are glued.

tone bar Additional braces glued to the underside of the top south of the X-brace, which help control a guitar's tonal qualities.

tonewood Wood noted for its acoustical properties, used to build musical instruments.

triple-ought or ooo Martin's nomenclature for a midsize guitar that's smaller than a dreadnought. Identical to an OM but built with a shorter, 24.9 scale.

truss rod A metal rod, often adjustable, inserted into a guitar neck, to help keep the neck straight.

tuner The mechanical device on the headstock of a guitar that adjusts the pitch of a string. Sometimes called tuning peg.

waist The narrowest part of a guitar body.

X-bracing The bracing pattern on most modern flattop guitars, in which two large braces cross in the area between the soundhole and the bridge.

DISCOGRAPHY

MUSIC BY WAYNE HENDERSON

Les Pik: Hey Holler 1357
Wayne C. Henderson and Friends: Hey Holler 107
Guitar Extravaganza (with Steve Kilby, Steve Lewis, and Randy Greer): Independent release
Not Much Work for Saturday (with Steve Kaufman): Hey Holler 109
Rugby Guitar: Flying Fish 542
Contest Favorites (with Robin Kessinger): FC-010
Masters of the Steel String Guitar (with Eddie Pennington, John Cephas, Johnny Bellar): Arhoolie 485

BY WAYNE'S FRIENDS

Gerald Anderson and Spencer Strickland: *Headin' South:* Independent release
Helen White: *No One Smiles Like Me:* Independent release

WAYNE HENDERSON'S FAVORITES

These ten discs just scratch the surface of the deep, rich genre of old-time and bluegrass music.

E. C. Ball with Orna Ball and the Friendly Gospel Singers: Rounder 11577
Bluegrass: Can't You Hear Me Calling: 80 Years of American Music: Sony Legacy
The Camp Creek Boys: County 2719
The Carter Family: *Wildwood Flower:* ASV Living Era 5323
J. D. Crowe and the New South: Cracker Barrel Heritage Music Series
Sam McGee Complete Recorded Works: Document 8036
Ricky Skaggs and Tony Rice: *Skaggs and Rice: The Essential Old-Time Duet Recordings,* Sugar Hill Records

Ralph Stanley: Sony 86625
Doc Watson: *Southbound:* Vanguard 79213
Doc Watson and David Holt: Legacy, High Windy Audio

MY TOP GUITAR DISCS

To compile a truly comprehensive discography of great guitar music would take a book in itself. Here's a baker's dozen of guitar-heavy discs that always seem to float to the top of the pile in front of my CD player.

Anthology of American Folk Music (Various artists, edited by Harry Smith): Smithsonian Folkways, S/F 40090
Paul Asbell: *Steel String Americana* (www.paulasbell.com)
Etta Baker: *Railroad Bill:* Music Maker EB100
Norman Blake: *Way Down on a Georgia Farm:* Shanachie 6045
Eric Clapton and Friends: *Crossroads Guitar Festival:* WEA B0002 Y4T92 (DVD)
Pat Donahue: *American Guitar:* Blue Sky Records 927
Howard Emerson: *Crossing Crystal Lake* (www.howardemerson.com)
Bill Frisell: *Ghost Town:* Nonesuch 79583
O Brother, Where Art Thou: (Various artists, soundtrack): Lost Highway 170069
Eddie Pennington and Cary Black: *Just My Style* BEENEPHI-CD2000
Tony Rice/David Grisman: *Tone Poems:* Acoustic Disc 10
Robert Shafer and Johnny Staats: *Pickin' Up Steam* www.johnnystaats.com
Gillian Welch: *Revival:* Alamo 80006

RESOURCES

A portion of the author's proceeds of this book will go to two causes:

The Music Maker Relief Foundation, which helps meet the day-to-day needs of pioneering blues artists (www.musicmaker.org).

The Wayne C. Henderson Scholarship Fund, which provides educational and social support to young traditional musicians in the southwest Virginia region, including the Junior Appalachian Musicians Program. (www.waynehenderson.org).

WEB SITES

www.allenstjohn.com: Learn more about the making of these guitars, including avaliable clips of Wayne Henderson playing 327, and information about the auction of that guitar.

The 13th Fret: www.13thfret.com: A discussion board for general acoustic guitar topics, including guitar building.

Unofficial Martin Guitar Forum: www.umgf.com: A discussion board devoted to the guitars of the C.F. Martin company.

www.frets.com: Frank Ford's site provides detailed, illustrated explanations of guitar repair and maintenance.

www.grevenguitars.com: The Web site of master luthier John Greven.

www.walkerguitars.com: The Web site of master luthier Kim Walker

www.countysales.com: A source for traditional music CDs, including many in the discography.

PERIODICALS

Acoustic Guitar: www.acousticguitar.com
Flatpicking Guitar: www.flatpick.com
Guitar Player: www.guitarplayer.com

The Old-Time Herald: www.oldtimeherald.org

Vintage Guitar: www.vintageguitar.com

VINTAGE GUITAR SHOPS

If you want to really understand what separates a great guitar from a merely good one, there's no substitute for firsthand experience. These top shops can help educate you about the best instruments of the past, whether you play or not.

Elderly Instruments: 1100 North Washington, Lansing, Michigan (517) 372-7890, www.elderly.com

Gruhn Guitars, 400 Broadway, Nashville, Tennessee (615) 256-2033, www.gruhn.com

Intermountain Guitar and Banjo: 712 East 100 South, Salt Lake City, Utah (801) 322-4682, www.guitarandbanjo.com

Jet City Guitars: Seattle, Washington (206) 361-1365, www.jetcity-guitars.com

Lark Street Music, 479 Cedar Lane, Teaneck, New Jersey (201) 287-1959, www.larkstreetmusic.com

Mandolin Brothers, 629 Forest Avenue, Staten Island, New York (718) 981-8585, www.mandoweb.com

Schoenberg Guitars: 106 Main Street, Tiburon, California (415) 789-0846, www.om28.com

The Twelfth Fret: 2132 Danforth Avenue, Toronto, Ontario (416) 423-2132, www.12fret.com

Vintage Instruments, 1609 Pine Street, Philadelphia, Pennsylvania (215) 545-1000, www.vintage-instruments.com

Matt Umanov: 273 Bleecker Street, New York, New York (212) 675-2157, www.umanovguitars.com

ACKNOWLEDGMENTS

Michelangelo is reported to have said "Genius is eternal patience."
He wasn't referring to having a writer scrutinizing your every move
every day from morning 'till night, armed with a tape recorder, a
camera, and an endless supply of stupid questions. Wayne Henderson endured all that and more with grace and humor, affording me
that rarest of opportunities: a chance to watch someone do something as well as it can be done. I'm honored to call him my friend.

I want to thank the denizens of the guitar shop—Gerald Anderson, Herb Key, Dave Neal, and Don Wilson, who were trying to
work while I watched, and all the General Loafers, especially
Ralph Maxwell and Gabby Bumgarner—who helped me understand why they keep coming back to Tucker Road.

Guitar building Wayne Henderson–style is a family affair. Elizabeth Henderson, Max and Pat Henderson, and the amazing Sylvie
Henderson made me feel like an honorary member of the clan. For
that I can't thank them enough. Special thanks to Helen White, who
helped me understand how music can change lives.

Before I started on this book, I knew just enough about guitars to
be dangerous. My deepest gratitude to all those who helped to fill in
the gaps in my knowledge, including the late Michael Katz, Eric
Schoenberg, John Greven, George Gruhn, Stan Jay, Kim Walker, John
Arnold, and especially T.J. Thompson, who truly understands what
makes a great guitar tick. The same goes for traditional music, and
my heartfelt thanks goes out to Tony Rice, John Lohman, Kinney
Rorrer, Nick Spitzer, Roy Curry, Scott Fore, Brandon Davis, Robert
Shafer, and Adam Wright. And a shout to all my Internet guitar bud-
dies including Todd Stuart Phillips, Mark Durso, Michael Collins,
Tim Porter, Dean Herman, Mac Carter, Steve Stallings, Dave
Skowron, and Chester Prudhomme who helped point me toward
Rugby.

If not for a hundred moments of happy serendipity, this book wouldn't have happened. I'd like to thank Joe Wilson for bringing Wayne to New York when he did and Tim Duffy for having the foresight to bring his Henderson guitar the day Eric Clapton was there. Kerry Keane is a good enough guy to have become a great guitar builder. I have nothing but admiration for the incomparable Lee Dickson, who is the very embodiment of grace under pressure. And my deepest gratitude to Eric Clapton, who not only makes great art, but recognizes it too, and has helped to call attention to the world's greatest guitars, both past and present.

Thanks to my friends at the World Guitar Congress, the Penland School of Crafts, Mike Holmes at Old-Time Music Camp North, Mark Burford and Dan Pelligrini at Carnegie Hall, and everyone at the Puget Sound Guitar Workshop, especially Flip Breskin, Janet Peterson, and my teachers Cindy Kallet, Eddie Pennington, and Pat Donahue, all of whom made the research for this book full-fledged fun. And thanks to Heather Flock and everyone else at Major League Baseball for providing the tickets for the night of a lifetime.

Those were the people who helped make the story. These are the people who helped make it a book. Thanks to my agent, Mark Reiter, for listening to my guitar story and recognizing in an instant that there was a book there. Thanks to my editor, the inimitable Martin Beiser, who, along with Dominick Anfuso, gave this book a home at Free Press. I quickly discovered that Marty is every bit as skilled with a pencil as Wayne Henderson is with a penknife. I gave him a manuscript and he deftly cut away everything that wasn't a book. What writer can ask for more than that? And a big shout out to Pam Redmond Satran, matchmaker—or should that be *bookmaker?*—extraordinaire. Thanks to Kit Frick for a thousand things little and big in making this manuscript into a book. Thanks to Eric Fuentecilla who made this into a book any author would be happy to have judged by its cover, and to copyeditor Fred Chase who made these pages as clean as a Henderson guitar. Thanks also to John Hartman, Al Mercuro, and Jerry Beilinson for reading this manuscript as a work in progress, and Nick Paumgarten for some crucial research help. And thanks to Nicole Esposito, for borrowing my guitar and starting this whole adventure.

And thanks to all my editors past and present, but especially: Jim Kaminsky, who has been my friend longer than he's been my editor, Michael Anderson, who makes me think even when I don't want to; the visionary Paul Steiger and the rest of my colleagues at *The Wall Street Journal:* Joanne Lipman, Amy Stevens, Tom Weber, Jeff Grocott, and Steve Barnes. And a long overdue thanks to a couple of friends who've gone to bat for me more times than I can remember: Allen Barra and Dana White.

Finally, I don't have words to express my gratitude to my family, Sally, Ethan, and Emma, who listened to my guitar stories, waited for me while I was gone on research trips, and lived this book along with me every step of the way. I love you all more than I can say.

INDEX

ABOUT THE AUTHOR

ALLEN ST. JOHN is the co-author of *The New York Times* best-selling *The Mad Dog 100: The Greatest Sports Arguments of All Time*, with radio personality Christopher "Mad Dog" Russo, published in 2003. St. John is a columnist for *The Wall Street Journal*'s Weekend section. He has written for a wide variety of national publications including *The New York Times Magazine*, *Rolling Stone*, *The Village Voice*, *Playboy*, *Salon*, *Popular Mechanics*, *Men's Journal*, and *Maxim*. His work as a reviewer appears frequently in *The New York Times Book Review* and *The Washington Post Book World*. He has won a variety of awards, including top honors from the North Jersey Press Club, the North American Ski Journalists Association, and the United States Tennis Writers Association. His story "Fall Classics" earned an honorable mention in *The Best American Sports Writing 2002*. He has written or contributed to a dozen book-length projects including the award-winning *Skiing for Dummies* (IDG) and the hardcover and CD-ROM of *The Way Baseball Works* (Simon & Schuster). He lives in Upper Montclair, New Jersey, with his wife and two children.